PROLOGUE.

Why did I decide to write my Autobiography? There are so many things in my life that I took for granted and accepted as normal but when I now look back in hindsight my life was far from normal. I am of mixed race / Coloured background born from a white Father and black Mother. For many in today's world, this word Coloured is an offensive racist terminology but to me and to my fellow Zimbabweans including South Africans, it is a Culture. A mixed bag of cultures, a little bit of white, a little of black and a little of Indian descent all mixed together, even our language was a mixed bag many of us spoke at least two languages, one being Afrikaans or one of the indigenous vernacular languages (Ndebele or Shona) or chilapalapa (a form of patois - a combination of English and the vernacular) 'a language that is not a language' as described by some plus of course English. Our spoken English was also a mix bag of mainly British English and American English. Most of us young coloureds, in fact all, spoke slang too, derived from a mixture of some Afrikaans words and some English.

By way of this biography I intend to provide a detailed account of my life's journey through a mainly racially divided society in Southern Rhodesia and Rhodesia and will endeavour to answer the following questions that the young generation of my fellow Zimbabweans may have pondered over including my children, grandchildren and all those interested in our experience, questions such as these: What was life like in Southern Rhodesia and Apartheid Rhodesia? What was life like when you were growing up, when you went to school? The challenges you faced and how did you overcome them?

I was born in 1953 in a little village called Farvic just outside a Cement Mining settlement of Colleen Bawn in Southern Rhodesia as the country was then known then. I lived through the political and cultural changes from Southern Rhodesia-which was part of the Northern Rhodesia (Zambia) and Nyasaland (Malawi) Federation (1953 to 1964) thereafter through to the unilateral declaration of independence by the Rhodesian Front Government under Ian Douglas Smith in 1965 followed by Zimbabwe-Rhodesia in 1979 a coalition government of Bishop Abel Muzorewa and finally to independent Zimbabwe in 1980 under Robert Mugabe's Zanu Patriotic Front party. The term Rhodesia was first coined by White British settlers in the 1890's who formerly named their new home Rhodesia after Cecil John Rhodes. This was achieved via the prospecting company named British South African Company under the leadership of its managing director Cecil John Rhodes which governed it until the 1920's. It became a self-governing colony of the United

Conquering Apartheid, Prejudice And Adversity My Reflections: From Rhodesia To Zimbabwe And Beyond

Francis Cohen

Kingdom in 1923 and thereafter referred to itself as Southern Rhodesia during the Federation in order to differentiate itself from the northern part named Northern Rhodesia. I am not qualified to write about politics nor do I wish to do so but I will write about my experience of those years including the forced military conscription during that difficult period of the Guerilla war of 1965 to 1980. The Independence of Zimbabwe in 1980 brought peace and prosperity including opportunities we were never exposed to during the previous apartheid government. It was certainly a time of positive and exciting changes. The following years proved rather unsettled as I left Zimbabwe for a time and moved my family to Gaborone the capital city of Botswana working for an expatriate engineering establishment from 1991 to 1994 following that we spent a short three months in Pretoria South Africa and finally moved back to my beloved home in Zimbabwe in early 1995.

In 1997 my wife expressed her desire for us to immigrate to England in search of her father and father's family. Her father had been deported by the Rhodesian government for meddling in politics in around 1964 when she was only a 5-year-old toddler. Her mother had sadly passed away in 1995 prompting my wife's prolonged sadness. I very reluctantly obliged to be honest. I loved the country of my birth, I had created a comfortable life for my family, had a secure well remunerated Job in a senior position with benefits in a well-established engineering business, and the environment in the country was safe and secure at the time but my dear wife was unhappy. I thought the matter through for some time and decided to set aside my own personal feelings and accept my wife's concerns for the benefit of my family as a whole. I had absolutely no idea what awaited us, but I concluded that if my wife was unhappy her sadness would be detrimental to the whole family. We eventually immigrated to England together with our four children of varying ages from two to sixteen. Life in England was not 'a walk in the park' it was the most challenging time in my life, an introduction we never anticipated. My wife and I had to find employment almost immediately, to start off with, to support our growing family. I took on a number of different jobs in a number of cities to do so and during that time I met many work colleagues and acquaintances with whom I had the opportunity to listen to and share life's journeys; being of different backgrounds, persuasions and nationalities. Eventually I got the job of my dreams in January 2002 in the city of Bristol, a beautiful picturesque city, in the South west of England. I was employed as a Manufacturing Engineer, a role that I loved and carried out with great passion. My new employment was continuous until my retirement in November 2018.

During that employment my job role included visits to different engineering facilities throughout England, Scotland, Spain and New England in the United States. I was part of a small group of Engineers with differing professional backgrounds. It was during one of these trips, probably around 2005 that I shared my brief life story with a work colleague by the name of David Melksham, an experienced Welding Engineer. David was the first friend who encouraged me to write my book after listening attentively to my story which he felt was rather unique. I accepted, with much appreciation, his unsolicited comment but kind of parked the idea until the middle of 2022 when someone else close to me, my nephew Aidan Cohen made the same suggestion during my visit to my very ill brother George in Botswana in December of 2022. Sadly, my brother succumbed to his illness, a severe case of prostate cancer which had lodged in his lower spine paralysing him from his waist down to his legs, and passed away that month. This was another tragedy in my life. He was the youngest of us Cohen boys and very close to me. I spent an agonising three weeks with him and his young family providing emotional, spiritual, and material support until his death on 30 December 2022.

In March 2022, by sheer chance, I made contact with my old friend John Woodend of whom we had shared our childhood, from Primary School, through Secondary and thereafter until we parted ways when he immigrated to Canada in 1978. "John my friend, thank you for having also encouraged me to write my story". A special thanks too to my nephew Aidan Cohen, whom I had an opportunity to spend time with during my brother's terminal illness with cancer in the month of December 2022, who encouraged me to write my story after hearing it for the first time in his 42 years of life. A special thanks too to my cousin Lionel Klein who furnished me the missing details of our fathers history, their journey from their place of origin, Lithuania in the late 1800's, to Southern Rhodesia in 1930's.

Thanks to Kudzai "Shumbanation" Sibanda, a young man I briefly met during the arrangements for my late brother's memorial service in Bulawayo in January 2023. "Kudzai, thank you for your encouragement to write my story, a story you said and were convinced would inspire many young Zimbabweans of colour to appreciate the struggles of their fathers, mothers and grandparents during the apartheid years of Southern Rhodesia and Rhodesia. A story you felt would also inspire other peoples of colour around the globe who have contended with or currently struggle with racial or other forms of discrimination and adversity".

I would like, finally, to say a profound and special thanks to my close friend Tommy Canessius whom I have known for some 39 years and who has witnessed some of my experiences. Thankyou Tommy for assisting me in gathering my thoughts during this writing, last but not least, to my beautiful wife who has always been at my side throughout our journey through life's trials, failures, and successes. Her guidance throughout my life has been profound. Thank you for your support in writing my story because, for one, I was never a reader, nor did I ever contemplate being able to write this story.

It is my intent that my life's journey will encourage and inspire all young and old alike to never give up on life, to be determined to be themselves not allowing the worlds prejudices no matter in what form they come, to put them in a 'box', with the intent to prevent them from achieving their goals in life nor to bow down to adversity when it comes but to face it head-on as a challenge to be defeated for victory belongs to those that prevail.

Francis Cohen

CHAPTERS

1. Origins.

2. Early years.

3. Primary school years.

4. Secondary school years.

5. Segregation and Apartheid.

6. Military conscription – Guerilla War 1967 to 1980

7. Doors of opportunity.

8.Conversion

9. My family

10.Migrating to England

11.New beginnings.

12.Navigating through new challenges.

13.Retirement.

14.Reminiscing – Life's successes and regret

15.Conclusion – Contentment.

ORIGINS

I was born on September 21 1953 in a small village called Farvic just a few kilometres from Colleen Bawn, a little cement mining settlement some 184 kilometres from Bulawayo, Southern Rhodesia (now known as Zimbabwe). My mother is a Black indigenous Ndebele woman, still alive and well as of this writing, of strong character, principles and great intelligence despite her very limited education. My mother was born Elina Ncube on 6 June 1936 in the Tuli Emafubu District some distance outside Gwanda a small town 86 kilometres from Bulawayo. She was always well groomed, smart, a beautiful looking woman with a dark brown complexion, tall in stature. My father on the other hand, was a white man, rather short in build at this point in his life, a little stout with a freckled bald crown with white side locks, and a typical curved Jewish nose and blue eyes that seemed to change colour to a light grey depending on the sunlight. He was rather tall and slim built in his younger years judging from the photographs we have of him. He was of unclear background originally from Lithuania in Europe. All we know of his identity is what is stated on his British Naturalisation Certificate, of Southern Rhodesia, dated 26 May1937 which reads: Beniamin Leibe Kaganovicu commonly known as Benne Leve Cohen born 25 January 1888. Father was a Yiddish speaking Jew as far as we know and was probably of Russian descent residing in Lithuania. He originally lived in and around Johannesburg, South Africa and at some point also settled in Harrismith, a town in the Free State province of South Africa. He married his first wife, a Jewess, in Rhodesia and raised his first family which included two daughters Janet and Isabella and a son Issy. The marriage somewhat ended at some point. His two daughters settled in Bulawayo whilst his son Issy moved to Johannesburg South Africa. Isabella, later known as Bella, eventually relocated and settled in Salisbury / Harare. Their whereabouts at this point in writing is unknown. I can only assume that, if alive, that they would be in their late 80's or early 90's.

My father became a successful Storekeeper and established a number of Stores including an Abattoir in Masase, Filibuzi and finally settled in Farvic and surrounding villages. He too, just like my mother, was of simple means and of limited education, a mild tempered quiet man with an introverted personality. The age difference between them was huge, some forty eight years. So, basically he was sixty five years of age when I was born. My mother was an attractive seventeen-year-old teenager when they met and fell in love. She was the youngest of my fathers relationships, common law wives, which had come to pass but had resulted in offspring, three brothers, Joshua, Philip and Billy (William Joseph) all now deceased, and four half sisters Molly (deceased), Margaret, Jane and Sheila, currently alive and well. I, on the other hand was one of five siblings, which include two sisters, Betty and Gwen and two brothers, Clement and George both deceased as of this writing. I first met my other two brothers Joshua and Philip in the early 1960's probably around 1963 at our new home in Sable vale. I recall how they would arrive in real 'style'. Joshua drove a 1960's pink Pontiac with a white roof top and fins at the rear end, Philip on the other hand drove a green 1950's Chevrolet with a white topped roof with sun visor. These were awesome cars compared to my fathers white Opel Rekord open back 1960 pick up. That was my introduction to my two half brothers. Our relationship grew a little closer in my later years. I do not particularly like the terminology 'half brothers and sisters' although it is a factual term with reference to us being from the same father but of different mothers. To us, by us I refer to myself and my siblings from our mother. We have always viewed the rest of my fathers children as our brothers and sisters and loved and respected them as if we were from the same parents, father and mother and no less.

My parents' relationship was a happy one, peaceful and long lasting until my fathers death in April 1975. Father was always the breadwinner, he did what fathers were expected to do to provide materially, at the very least, a task he did well. However he was never emotionally involved in our upbringing he seemed always detached, distant and alone with his thoughts, passive in nature. I had always wondered whether he was that way because of the trauma he experienced during both the first and second world wars, or perhaps the persecution he and his family suffered during this same period which resulted in the loss of his immediate family as a direct consequence of the Nazi persecution of the Jewish people. I really did not know the facts. I would observe him sitting quietly on his arm chair on the front verandah staring into space in contemplation. He never spoke to us about his traumatic history; perhaps he felt it would be too much for us to bear and that we would not have understood and did not want to burden us children with it. My mother had the opposite personality. She was the influencer, the neck of the body as it were that always turned my fathers head in the direction she chose, the one who expressed her love as mothers do, who disciplined us when necessary, who administered corporal punishment when the slaps and all else failed with me. She was therefore, in my view, the 'head' of our family. My parents' relationship worked perfectly for never did we hear a voice raised, nor any arguments in our presence. It seems that they reserved such incidents, if any, behind their closed bedroom door. So, in essence, my childhood was a joyous happy experience as far as I can remember.

Dad 1928 approx.

Father 1st world war veteran. Northern Rhodesia - rear left.

Dad 1972

Dads Store in Harrismith South Africa

Harrismith today at same spot

(b.)

British Nationality and Status of Aliens Act, 1914

Certificate of Naturalisation

WHEREAS BENJAMIN LEIBE KAGANOVICH, commonly known as BENNE LEVE COHEN, has applied for a Certificate of Naturalisation, alleging with respect to himself the particulars set out below, and has satisfied me that the conditions laid down in the above-mentioned Act for the grant of a Certificate of Naturalisation are fulfilled in his case:

Now, therefore, in pursuance of the powers conferred on me by the said Act, I grant to the said Benjamin Leibe Kaganovich this Certificate of Naturalisation, and declare that upon taking the Oath of Allegiance within the time and in the manner required by the regulations made in that behalf he shall, subject to the provisions of the said Act, be entitled to all political and other rights, powers and privileges, and be subject to all obligations, duties and liabilities to which a natural-born British subject is entitled or subject, and have to all intents and purposes the status of a natural-born British subject.

In witness whereof I have hereto subscribed my name this Twenty-sixth day of May, 1932.

H. J. Stanley
Governor of Southern Rhodesia.

This certificate has been submitted to the Secretary of State for his approval and approved by him.

E. J. Harding
Under Secretary of State.

PARTICULARS RELATING TO APPLICANT.

Full name Benjamin Leibe Kaganovich, commonly known as Benne Leve Cohen.

Address Jenate Bldgs., Private Box, Bulawayo.

Trade or Occupation Storekeeper.

Place and date of birth Baratan, Soda, Lithuania, 20th January, 1888.

Nationality Uncertain, formerly Russian.

Single, married, etc. Divorced.

Name of wife or husband ———

Name and nationality of parents Benjamin and Zindl Kaganovich (both deceased) Lithuanian.

(For Oath see overleaf.)

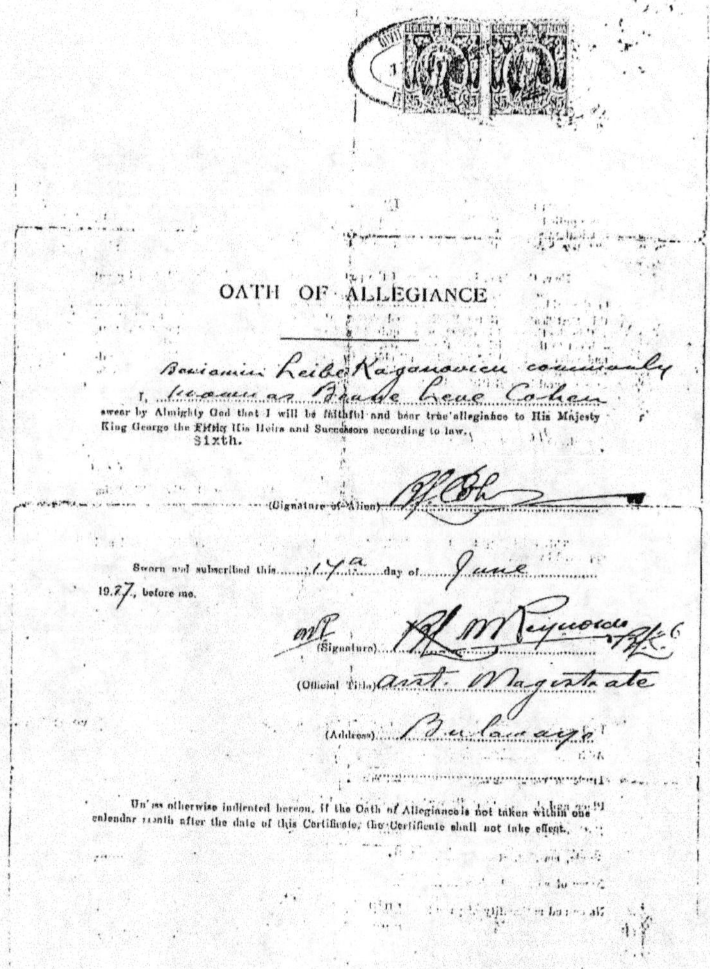

OATH OF ALLEGIANCE

I, Benjamin Leibe Kaganovicu commonly known as Baube Leue Cohen swear by Almighty God that I will be faithful and bear true allegiance to His Majesty King George the Sixth His Heirs and Successors according to law.

(Signature of Alien)

Sworn and subscribed this 17a day of June 19.37, before me.

(Signature)

(Official Title) Asst. Magistrate

(Address) Bulawayo

Unless otherwise indicated hereon, if the Oath of Allegiance is not taken within one calendar month after the date of this Certificate, the Certificate shall not take effect.

Dad's Naturalisation certificate

Fathers resting place 2023

Mum in her youth

Mum in her prime years

My Dear Mother 2023

Me and Mum January 2023

EARLY YEARS

The first 7 years of my life were spent in Farvic. My mother and father lived separately at the time. He lived in a normal 3 bedroom house of normal brick construction, built adjacent to the store whilst we lived in a separate 2 bedroom homestead with white washed walls which was in a secluded part of the village complex. It was a comfortable living space and environment. I've always wondered why it was that we lived in a separate homestead and not together with my father in his house. Perhaps it was taboo in those days as the village was predominantly occupied by black indigenous folk. We were the only mixed race, brown kids, in the village. We were, however, accepted by the whole community just as we were, kids who played with other children as part of the village make-up. I did learn years later from my mother that the reason we lived separately was simply 'The Colour Bar.' It just was not kosher for my father, a White man, and mother, a Black woman, to live together under the same roof eyebrows would have been raised. Although segregation was not legally implemented at that time as the country was part of the Southern Rhodesia, Northern Rhodesia and Nyasaland Federation under Britain. Apartheid was legally introduced in 1965 by the Rhodesian Government under Ian Douglas Smith although it was of a slightly different format than that practised in South Africa but nevertheless it was still a clever construct to subjugate the non-whites both Black, Coloured and Indian. I sometimes wondered how their relationship began, was it love at first sight? Where did they meet, was it at his store? How did the predominantly black community accept their relationship? Was my mother ostracised by them, how did her immediate family accept the situation as both she and her sister, Auntie Esther, ended up with white men, dare I ask in my old age was it intended or was it sheer innocent attraction? I did get the answer by this time of writing, it was simply physical attraction, love at first sight if you will, on my fathers side whilst living in and amongst a black community. It was like a colonisation of the villages around that part of the country in those years. Mother and Granny would visit his store once a month for groceries and it was during these visits that he noticed her and set his eyes upon her. Father later instructed his Chef to visit mother and her parents to advise them of his interest. The rest is history for here we are, the living proof of that union.

My early recollection of my childhood is when I was around three to four years of age living together with my younger brother Clement and sister Bertha commonly known as Betty. My uncle Felix, my mothers brother, lived in Colleen Bawn, but occasionally visited and spent time with us. He was a good looking boy with a dark brown, black complexion that glistened as if constantly oiled, literally tall, dark and handsome; our playmate, a creative character with astounding imagination. Our four wheeled Push Pram became a vehicle in his hands and we were the passengers of play. He used to push us around the village as a form of play which proved to be great fun for us kids. In addition to this we used to spend some play time in Colleen Bawn, where my Grandparents lived, ravaging through the village rubbish dump looking for toys, playthings that we could use as part of our play. For us it was like a treasure hunt. Unfortunately the pram finally gave up the 'ghost' as the expression goes, but, for uncle Felix this was not the end but only a temporary setback until another challenge. Uncle Felix then salvaged the wheels and created a mobile larger vehicle that accommodated all three of us children. The base frame was of robust wood construction with the rest of the body frame constructed from steel rods and chicken mesh tied together with copper wire and cabling. This was a successful project that brought us much joy as he wheeled us around the yard at high speed, as fast as his legs and stamina could go. Colleen Bawn was and still is a cement mining village under the auspices of United Portland Cement Company back in my early years. My grandfather was a Miner and the company provided housing, communal ablution blocks, public bars and entertainment areas for their employees. One thing that has always stood out with me, well embedded in my memory, was just how clean the surroundings were. People took pride in their company homes of brick and mortar with whitewashed walls and polished cement floors. My Grandmother would bake us penny-buns whenever we visited, this was a speciality of hers and how we loved them, fresh from the oven. On some weekend evenings Uncle Felix would take us to watch 'black-and-white' wild west movies which were occasionally screened by the company as entertainment for the village. It was ingenious, like an open air Drive-In cinema only this time it was a Walk-In one where all attendees sat on the ground adjacent to the screen which was a specially constructed whitewashed wall. I still entertain these fond memories of days gone by.

Back in Fravic, we spent time with our father on occasional weekends playing around his store and office whilst with keen interest observing the shoppers. He would show his generosity to the little village children who often ran around naked in his store. He would ask for their parents to come to his store before providing them with free clothes for their children if they could not afford the money or sell them at knock-down prices to those that could. He in time inherited the nickname pronounced 'Chipisa' which means to make cheap, in Ndebele. We even strangely addressed him that way as children, and father just accepted it without protest. It was only when we grew older that we eventually called him Dad. Father would then send the little 'pickaninnies' off home as he called them after a reprimand. I can still picture their facial expressions of glee and appreciation for such generosity. These same village kids were our playmates, we saw them as our friends without any recognition of their backgrounds, their environment, their appearance or skin colour, we were just children innocent of any form of prejudice. It was such a carefree innocent world then. We used to enjoy lunch with father on occasional weekends, we would be seated around his dining table and be served lunch as if we were of aristocratic offspring. Occasionally he would even give us a sample taste of his whisky. It was during one of these occasions that I met my sister Molly for the first time, she was a split image of father, the pointed nose and slim mouth, slim built and beautiful wearing a full head of hair in a beehive hair do. My sister Jane would also occasionally spend time with father, I recall my first recollection of her, it was a rather solemn encounter, she was in father's office proudly engaged as little girls go, fathers favourite as it appeared. We just looked at each other without a word, probably a look of curiosity if anything else. She was pretty and still is as of this writing now in her late 70's. My brother Billy was there too on some occasions, I recall one such occasion when he took my fathers rifle which was stored behind fathers wardrobe and like a typical mischievous boy chased us around the yard with it. Till this day I honestly don't know whether it was loaded or not, father was not amused as you can imagine, discipline was swift. Billy must have been around twelve years old then. The next time we met was at my sister Jane's house in Gweru when I was in my teens, sometime around 1968/9. Billy was now employed as a Platelayer on the Rhodesian railways and Jane a Nurse at the general hospital.

The years were proceeding at speed and soon, it was time for my schooling. It seems that my parents never considered sending me to one of the rural schools or other Christian run schools such as Bushtick or Embakwe Mission. We were ever so grateful for that in hindsight, as both Bushtick and Embakwe were Boarding Schools run by Catholic Nuns, schools that had a reputation of regimental discipline and strict adherence to rules. My parents chose, on the other hand, Mount Cazalet primary school in Gwanda some 27.5 km from Farvic. In order to facilitate this they found boarding accommodation for me with a sweet lady called Mrs Oswald who resided in Gwanda town centre thus enabling me to walk to school together with my fellow boarders, the Vogel's, Eileen, Molly and Frank. I was only 6 years old then and this was my saddest time as a child, to be separated from my parents for a time. It was an emotionally painful but necessary experience. Whenever my parents drove away, in fathers blue Bedford Truck, I would wait and watch them drive away until its disappearance around the corner. I would walk to my new abode saddened and feeling dejected and abandoned. I sometimes wonder how other children who were in similar or worse circumstances than myself were affected by the prolonged detachment from their parents during their early schooling years.

The trauma they experienced at the hands of Nuns in Bushtick and Embakwe Mission schools. This was a necessary arrangement at the time as there was no other option for all of us kids. My two siblings Clement and Betty did join me at Mrs Oswald's shortly after. For them it proved to be a short stay. Fortunately for me the total time spent was around 18 months excluding school holidays because my parents later purchased a plot of land 6 km or so from Gwanda Town in an area called Sable Vale or Bar Twenty. It was on a hill overlooking the valley plain below which had some twenty or so homesteads. We eventually moved house in 1961 into a temporary quick build of tightly placed tree trunks lined and plastered with mud and cow dung which served as mortar whilst our new brick house was being constructed. The roof was of corrugated galvanised sheeting. Our final home was completed in 1962, an attractive property comprising a large front verandah flanked by two double bedrooms, a large central lounge leading to a dining room on the west side and a third double bedroom on the east side. The back rooms included a pantry, kitchen, bathroom and rear verandah. We had an outside toilet, latrine as it was called back then, of white washed brick construction comprising a wooden box type seat over a massive pit. A pit occasionally treated with lime. It was a scary place for a child at night. Due to the elevated position, on the hill, the front steps were of practical unique design, comprising 7 rises half circle in shape. The foundation was of solid rock, attractively pointed with cement mortar, and was approximately 126 cm in height to ground level. The complete external walls were whitewashed and the roof constructed from galvanised corrugated zinc sheets. The internal cement floor together with the circular stairs were of polished concrete coloured green. My mother was a perfectionist when it came to order and cleanliness. She would often be on her hands and knees polishing the floor to a mirror finish. Our life was comfortable then, we were never in want of anything, my parents employed a gardener to care for the surrounding yard of approximately two acres including carrying out general tasks such as shopping and at times he was required to take me to school by bicycle. When my brother Clement began schooling he too was mounted / seated across the front bar of the bicycle whilst I was seated at the back carrier. When Betty's turn arrived for schooling Clement and I rode our own little bicycles to school, it was fun trying to catch up. For the internal upkeep and domestic chores my parents employed female employees who proved to be on hand for our care at times. That was the norm back then. Father had, by then, relocated his store to Gwanda town centre and would drive us to school and back having employed a driver to perform this daily routine. The business appeared to do well at first for us to afford a reasonably affluent lifestyle. As time went on and as we grew older my parents bought us larger bicycles that suited our age to enable us to continue riding to school. We were so excited to receive them, they were sporty in construction with curved shaped handlebars and vividly coloured. My one was a bright metallic red, Clement's was blue and my sister Betty's was black. We were so proud to show them off to our school friends. That was our next chapter which proved to be such fun as all the kids from Sable Vale cycled together. We often raced each other to school and back and our play break included a self made oval shaped race track which we caused by racing each other. I often wonder how our teachers coped with us returning to class bruised, battered and covered in dust. Playtime was really fun as the school was well equipped with swings, seesaws, slides, rope swings and a fair size swimming pool. Having been as privileged as we were and the fact that all this was taken for granted, never did it occur to me that my own black relatives never had the same facilities in their rural schools. It was a sad and grossly unjust state of affairs, the deliberate discriminate lack of resources in the government schooling system in black areas. It never occurred to me, at the time, that this was all part of the racial segregation apartheid system in its early stages.

Sable Vale was really a small settlement of some twenty houses situated mainly in the valley plain with ours including a few adjacent neighbours on the back hill facing the valley below. My Auntie Esther and uncle Dorward and their family, my cousins Kathy, Dawn, Mildred, Leslie and Rachel occupied the cottage dwellings at the rear of the house. Aunt Esther and my mother have enjoyed a very close bond as sisters throughout their lives right until this present time of writing. Their relationship was and still is as close as twins. They have always been together, as far as I can remember, living in close proximity to us. Uncle Dorward, Robert McLean Dorward; Jock as he was fondly known was aunt Esther's husband a white man of Scottish descent, tall in stature with a slightly freckled face, piercing blue eyes and ginger hair, a carefree individual and gifted artist who taught me how to draw as a young boy. He was employed as an Electrician in Blanket Mine situated about 6 kilometres from Sable Vale. He enjoyed his after work parties where the over consumption of intoxicating liquor was evident to us kids. He and my Father occasionally enjoyed each other's company. I recall with much fondness how he would put me on his lap, at times when we took rides to Gwanda, to steer his Blue and white Ford Fairlane. That was a special moment for me. Sadly uncle Dorward passed away in a motor car accident whilst returning from one of his after work get-togethers. It was a devastating blow to us all as kids particularly to Auntie Esther who became widowed at such a young age to care for her five girls. Occasionally my father and uncle Dorward would associate with their contemporaries in a local Pub called Ben Lewis and they would take us boys with them. I recall Clement and I playing around in the Pub lounge as kids, two little Brown boys in the company of an 'All white' Pub. It seemed normal, as there was no untoward atmosphere from their drinking friends and acquaintances, we were accepted as just kids fooling around. I sometimes wonder whether this acceptance was due to the fact that a number of my father's business associates including his cousin Uncle Solly Klein had mixed race children of their own. Some of my school friends, the Denecker's, the Vogul's and the Gallaghers were all from mixed race parenthood. Hence, to us kids that was the norm we were not aware of any racial discrimination in those days.

My next door neighbours were the Bells, a quiet family that kept to themselves. Their son Bernard befriended me as a young boy and we remained very close friends right into our adult years. He was closer to me than my own brother Clement who was a rather introverted child of similar character to our father. I was the exact opposite, extroverted, ambitious, naughty, adventurous, into everything and often faced the wrath and discipline of my mother. Bernard and I would spend hours hunting birds in the wild with our handmade catapults, fearless of wild creatures such as snakes and scorpions as we often walked bare feet. We were invincible, we thought. How often we would return home late in the evenings full of scratches from thorn trees, cuts and bruises on our feet, but no, that was not a deterrent in any way as we would return the next day. My brother Clement would join us occasionally and compete to see who would shoot the first bird. Our bird hunting escapades proved fruitless most times as we would return home exhausted, hungry, empty handed but joyful and only to repeat the same cycle the following day. Our play games were varied. We would, at times, call our friends down in the valley, shouting from our verandah, the echo of our voices would form part of our play time. Father would sometimes call us home in that manner when it was dinner time whenever we stayed out too long. It was as if a call to arms, to meet up for a game of soccer, rounders or kennicky. If we didn't have a leather ball or tennis ball, we would make one from newspapers wrapped in plastic secured by elastic bands. A game of kennicky was much fun and unique to our part of the world as I eventually discovered. Our main playground was at the home of the Nathansons whose property had the ideal play area, a flat hardened soil patch, of sufficient area to allow a soccer game, rounders and the beloved kennicky. At times we also used a disused concrete slab from an abandoned property, to play soccer, not too far from our house. We learned to play soccer and rounders at Primary School, as this was part of our English colonial upbringing but kennicky was different, an African invention together with "Intsoro" in Ndebele, a game similar to draughts, but using bottle tops on a board of specific designed pattern often played also, though called by a different name, Morabaraba, in South Africa, Botswana and Lesotho. Kennicky was played as follows: we would carve a wooden piece, similar in shape to a 'bail' used in cricket, but instead of placing it over vertical stumps as in cricket, this was placed across a slot or narrow groove in the ground approximately 20 cm long and 5cm deep. A long wooden rod of around 60cm long would then be used to flick the 'bail' cross piece as far as one was able. The rod would then be placed across the groove in the ground. The fielding team would be expected to either catch the 'bail', when flipped, in mid-air similar to catching the ball to stop the opposing player in cricket. Failing that, they would be required to choose a team mate who would then throw the 'bail' with the task of striking the wooden rod placed over the groove in the ground. If that failed then the playing team member would be required to strike the 'bail' at its location using the same rod. He would have three chances to do that. If he failed to strike it on the third go, that would be the end of his turn. The game would then continue with the next player and so forth until all payers in that team were countered out similar as in cricket. If the 'bail' was struck then the onus was on the fielding team players to catch it in order to stop the opposing team member. It was the type of game, that could go on 'forever' we often played it over weekends or during school holidays from morning to evening.

In addition to these games we used our creative minds to make Kites out of bamboo and brown paper whenever the weather permitted. The other pastime was building wire cars using wires we often salvaged from fences and disused electric cables. We designed our own car frames using 3mm steel wire fastened with thin 22-gauge copper wire. The steering wheel and wheels were made from 6mm steel rods shaped to suit. to enable the driving motion. Sometimes we connected shoe polish tins as wheel rims. Our games were endless and included creating holsters and wire guns to mimic the wild west 'good and bad guys' particularly when our normal manufactured toy revolvers purchased by our parents had run out their design life. What a laugh and excitement that was. Our parents were never really concerned about where we played because we were free and the environment was safe during those days, of course life was not always about play, we had our chores to carry out too and had to do them diligently and immediately when commanded to. We would be sent to the village grocery store to purchase whatever mum required. Occasionally we had to cycle to Gwanda town centre, some 6km or so, for groceries that were not available at the village shop, that was not my favourite task as it meant riding the complete return trip of some 10 km. In addition to that, we were required to participate in the planting and harvesting of the yearly sugar cane and mealie / maize crops, a task I hated and often tried to escape from to no avail. There were other chores too like feeding the chickens and transporting, by wheelbarrow, our daily supply of water from a centrally situated bore hole. My uncle Felix would use the surrounding clay to mould figurines and create characters which he would use as props in his storytelling. We would gather around a small bonfire some evenings to hear him narrate them. We were literally immersed in the stories that at times became our bedtime stories.

It was only some years later that the Gwanda Town council piped the water to each household dwelling yard, however we still had to wheelbarrow that tapped water in 44 gallon / 200 litre drums from the bottom corner of our property and all the way uphill to an area adjacent to the kitchen and rear verandah. This was a strenuous and often exhausting task, but we did it obediently together with our resident Gardener. Fortunately, the good weather made it easier as we very seldom experienced extreme muddy patches and slides.

Our weather system was awesome, blue skies and comfortable temperatures of 28 to 30 degrees Celsius throughout most of the year. The winter months of mid-May to Mid-August were often mild. The rainy season which usually occurred from October to April at times proved rather scary. The rain was typical, tropical downpours with extreme lightning and thunder-claps. We would cower away in-house and often went to bed early. The sound of the rain on the corrugated roof was like a sleeping pill tranquil bringing a pleasurable drowsiness to sleep. Night time was special during clear skies. My brothers and I would lay on the front verandah stairs on a clear night, which was very often, looking up to the starry heavens trying to count the stars. The galaxies and billions of stars we observed were an awesome sight which I've treasured to this very day. The meteorites darting across the expanse and disappearing into nothingness was incredible to observe. It was like a religious experience admiring God's wondrous works. The sunsets were breathtaking; in brilliant colour, shades of yellows, orange, pink to red and finally browns to black as it disappeared beyond the hilly horizon to introduce the night sky. It was as if I was observing God Almighty's artistic brush strokes.

We've always been a religious family, my mother was a very staunch Catholic and we were all baptised Catholics at an early age. Attending weekly mass was a must throughout my young years. When we were deemed old enough our parents allowed us to cycle or walk to church each Sunday. My friend Bernard and I were appointed to serve as Altar Boys during Mass. We felt so 'holy' performing the Benediction in support of the Priest during his rituals. However, we were not that 'holy' in our conduct hence we often confessed our 'sins', according to Catholic tradition, as and when we felt guilty for some wrongdoing. "Bless me father for I have sinned" was our standard, by rote, request for penance and forgiveness. I would utter my given penance of several 'Hail Mary's and Our Father' prayers in a ritualistic performance to ascertain my forgiveness only to repeat my sins over and over again. It was like an endless repetitive cycle of misbehaviour. At times my punishment and needed discipline was administered by my mother in a very literal way by applying the literal Rod of discipline. I recall with such clarity how mother would often send me to cut my own flexible stick from a nearby bush. I would have to ensure that all the nodules were pruned off to achieve a smooth clean finish. It literally became a whip in her hands as she administered my corporal punishment. She would at the same time tell me what I had done in a scolding tongue to ensure that I understood the reason for such 'terror',in my little childish eyes, it was like a two-edged sword. Such occasions brought home to me the seriousness of my naughtiness and unwholesome conduct, the fear of such punishment helped develop in me the respect for my parents and their authority, we were loved, but not pampered or 'molly coddled' as the expression goes. Despite such occasional hard discipline, a culture that was common in those days and accepted as normal, I loved my mother and still do, never did I hold any resentment towards her for such physical punishment. I deserved it, such discipline, in my view, contributed to my strong-willed personality and determination that proved necessary in my later years as I will express in my later chapters. On the other hand was my brother Clement who was the 'good' boy, always respectful and well behaved. My brother George was only a toddler in those early years. My sisters were as expected, Girls doing girly things playing with dolls. The accepted cultural norm during those early years was the saying 'children should be seen and not heard' as we were often told to play outside and keep away from adult company. I think it was their way to enable adult discussion and conversations without the prying eyes and listening ears of us children that would often result in childish gossip and laughter at the adults. I came to realise much later in my life that that paradigm was unfortunate as it created a gap somewhat in the relationships between children and their parents. I am guilty as charged for following that thought pattern subconsciously to some extent with my own children, a part of my life I truly regret. Mother, however, was balanced in the way she dealt with us children. Her hard-line discipline was balanced with many acts of love, nurture and care. I remember with much fondness how we would all, all five of us children, huddle in the kitchen area during the cold winter months, enjoying the warmth from the three-plate wood burner stove whilst mother prepared our meals. We would all converse enthusiastically about our daily activities as most families did during those years. Father would sometimes join us quietly listening-in or chipping in now and again with his 'Partois' (Chilapalapa) English, a mixture of vernacular Ndebele and English language, a unique form of language spoken only in Rhodesia at the time by all white non-Ndebele speaking Rhodesians. It was not a derogatory language at all as some may conclude but a form of communication for those that could not speak the vernacular, so was spoken by both the white, mixed race and black folk towards one another, my wife included. Father spoke to us in that way and mother communicated likewise in return with him. We children, however, spoke to him in English once we learned to speak English but for some unknown reason, till this day, I never understood why he could not speak to us in plain English as he spoke with his English-speaking associates, nevertheless this didn't bother us we thought it was just peculiar, he was just our Father in his own peculiar way.

Clement auntie Esther and I approx 1960

Family home in Bar Twenty Sable Vale Gwanda 1963

Mum George and Gwen Sable Vale 1974

Clement . Betty and me

Uncle Felix. Zephania

Uncle Jock Dorward on the right

Sister Molly 1994,

Brother Philip.

brother Joshua

Joshua and Lina

Billy in his youth

my brother Billy in happeir times

my brother Billy in happeir times

Sister Jane 2023

Sister Margaret Lisbon Portugal 2019

My older sisters Margaret and Jane 2022

Our sister Lillie we never knew about

Sister Shiela and Dad sketch

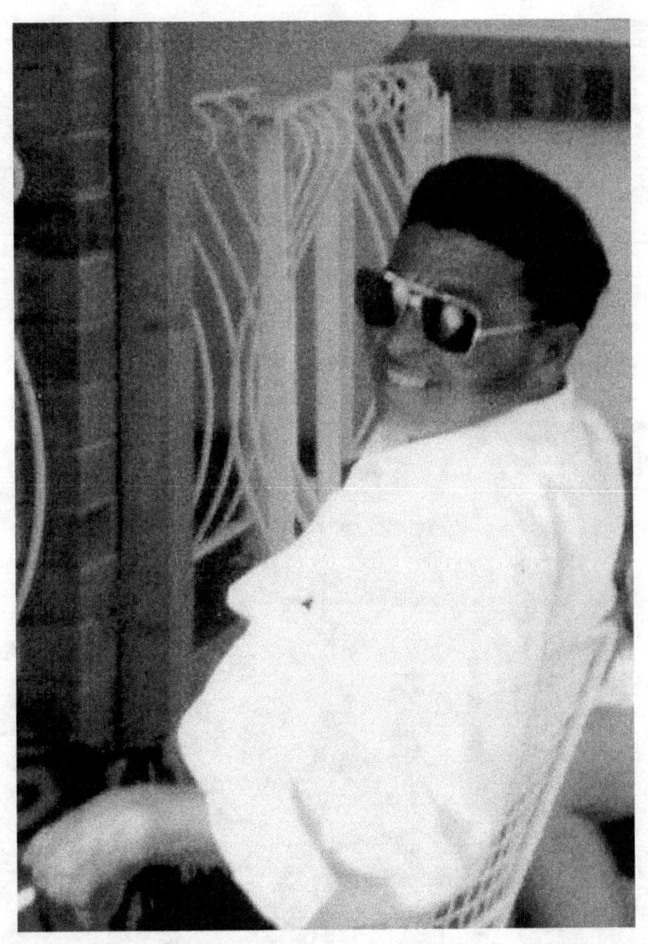

George Konson

my lifelong companian and nephew Roy Cohen 1990

My brother Clement in happier times 2000

brother George 2012

Gwen and Betty 1978

Janet and Bella Cohen

with my two younger sisters Betty and Gwen January 2023

PRIMARY SCHOOL YEARS

My primary schooling began in 1959 at the age of six. Due to residing in Farvic some 30 km from Gwanda, my parents had to find temporary boarding accommodation in Gwanda Town centre. My parents found a lady by the name of Mrs Oswald who lovingly accommodated me in my early schooling years until we eventually moved to Sable Vale around 1962. Clement joined me in my second year. This was a sad time for us, an unfortunate necessary period that enabled our schooling. I still recall, watching my parents get into the Blue Bedford Lorry and drive away. I would stand there for a time with great sadness, watching the lorry as it turned around and drove down the road until the back end of the truck slowly disappeared out of view. I recall with clarity the eeriness of the silence after the roar of the Bedford engine had long gone, I would stand there and wipe my tears down my cheeks. Dear Mrs Oswald would do all she could to comfort me.

I eventually adjusted after realising that I was not alone. I made friends with the other children who also boarded there, Molly, Eileen and Frank Vogal. I loved the walk to school, we would share stories with the other kids, laughing and playing en-route. Mrs Oswald was a kind soul who cared for us, we were never in want, we were well fed and clean. I recall how we played games such as hide and seek and skipping rope. At times we also played 'Church' . I was the priest of course, I made a chalice, using a cup, and cut newspaper folding it to mimic the starched cloth which was usually draped over the chalice in church. The host – the white wafer the Priest would offer the congregation, was a pack of X-mints. This was so much fun, that is how religious I was as a 6/7-year- old child.

In 1961 my parents finally ended my Boarding arrangement at Mrs Oswald because we moved to Sable Vale – Bar Twenty some 6 Km from Gwanda town centre. My parents had purchased a one acre plot on a hill directly facing a valley plane where some twenty properties were located. The junction road to Sable Vale was the same road that went all the way to Tuli District. We got to become acquainted with our immediate neighbours and our neighbours across the valley. I recall some of their names, the Bells, the Smiths, the West's, the Armstrong's, The Johnson's, the Bulman's, the Page's, the O'reillys, the Nathanson's, the Tembly's and the Martin's. Immediately before us were the second Johnson family, to our left were Caesar Klein and his wife Emily. Around 3-4 km to our right was the second Klein family of which we were directly related through my father. My parents and the Klein's occasionally visited each other and we children enjoyed playing together and at times rode our bicycles during these visits. Uncle Solly and Auntie Effie Klein had two sons and four daughters and we were three boys and two girls. Auntie Effie's eldest son was much older than us so we didn't have much association with him. We viewed each other as cousins because their father and our father were cousins. I went to school with some of them including secondary school and post school days. However, we lost touch with the younger girls, it seemed like they were segregated from us for reasons I never fully understood. It is possible that they were schooled elsewhere in 'white only' schools. The apartheid system allowed for this kind of action if one had the right skin tone with the correct hair texture, one could undergo a type of reclassification; from mixed race statue to white. This reclassification appears to have been practised more so in South Africa rather than in Rhodesia. I guess in Rhodesia some of these children were perhaps brought up by their 'white' grandparents hence taking their birth certificate which then enabled them to quietly intermingle within the 'white' society. That was the sheer raw evil system that I later came to understand that divided families and, unknowingly, created irreversible damage to relationships within such families. I can only think of one possible reason that parents of such families would have made such catastrophic decisions; perhaps they thought it worth the sacrifice to create the best opportunity for their children where possible without fully considering the consequences of their actions. Genetics were never understood back then the fact that a marriage union with such offspring could result in genetic throwbacks at some future time. What if that would occur, then what action would such parents take? I am now seventy years old as of this writing and the only contact and relationship I have with my late uncle Solly's and Aunt Effie's children is my cousin Lionel, a wonderful human being of such kindness and generosity not forgetting his well-known humour and gift of language with whom I am in constant contact. That separation was a direct result of the apartheid system which provided re categorisation of ethnicity in a similar way as the Nazi system of the 'superior aryan race' ideology. Mrs Klein, Lionel's mother, our aunt Effie, was a kind-hearted lady who visited my mother quite often. They became good friends as time went on. I vividly recall how she would bring us a container, some 10-15 litres, of the best sour milk ever, called Amasi (a natural yoghurt) almost every week. At times that is all we had to eat when times were difficult as my father's business began to fluctuate, took a downturn and money became tight. I recall with some sadness though that at times we ate the Pap, (an indigenous food called sadza; made from maize meal and water boiled and stirred to a thick congealed porridge similar to thick mashed potatoes) with sugar water when there was nothing else to eat. Mother would always improvise and we never complained, we were grateful to be loved and nurtured and given the freedom to enjoy our childhood, visiting our friends for playtime way into the twilight. The Woodend's were a family who resided in Vubachikwe, a Gold mining village some four km from Sable Vale. John Woodend was in my class, a very bright boy who enjoyed art as much as I did. Occasionally John spent some time with his cousin Paul who boarded by the Smith family and would also spend some time there especially weekends. It was during these times that John and Paul became part of our circle of friends. We remain friends right up to this day, together with his cousin Solly Nathenson. A little more of that later.

We played soccer, rounders / softball and kennicky at every spare moment, after school, as well as weekends. The girls played mainly games such as skipping rope, hop-scotch-and-jump, rounders, touches, and Nguni involving stone pebbles placed in twelve to sixteen holes dug out on the ground in an equal 'square grid' configuration. Pebbles from one hole would be moved about and placed, one pebble at a time, in each of the other holes until exhausted. If the last pebble fell into a hole with pebbles these would then be scooped and placed in a repeated cycle until the last pebble. The player would be knocked out as it were if the last pebble fell in an empty hole. Besides these the girls had their favourite dolls of course including the black dolls with woolly black hair called 'Golliwogs,' a name we, in our innocence, did not know was, and still is, a racist term that dehumanises black people. We did not know what it meant then, to us we thought it was just a name peculiar to that type of doll. Then there was a sand mine dump we frequented as a playground a short distance from the Gwanda to Vubachikwe Mine road, directly opposite a grocery store called 'Bar-Twenty' which surprisingly still exists as of my last visit in December of 2018. We played sliding down the red dust ridden slopes. Never did we think what our parents, particularly our mothers, thought about our engaging in such dirty filthy play because we got home with not only red faces and hair but our clothes were filthy red, covered in red mine dump dust. I really don't remember ever being scolded for that, I suppose my mum thought "Boys will be Boys'' and left it at that. All these games besides Rounders were our 'Boys' Games the girls would not join us, however on the odd occasion they did. We would all walk through shrubs and bush paths to the banks of the Mtshabezi river where we played and swam. I still recall the sandy riverbank where we would lay down exhausted after a good swim, lying on our backs staring at the wonderful blue skies and feeling the warm mid-day breeze over our wet bodies. It was great innocent fun. The warm weather was always taken for granted, it's only when I moved abroad to England, with my family in 1997, that I appreciated the blessing of the almost all year round 'perfect' climate we enjoyed in all the years in that part of the world, warmth, blue skies and the evening starry heavens that filled my heart with appreciation and my recognition of God Almighty. It was as a result of these swimming escapades that I contracted Bilharzia, (Schistosomiasis) a disease caused by parasitic worms, around the age of nine or ten. I remember being hospitalised for some seven days to undergo treatment. In terms of its impact, this disease is second only to malaria as the most devastating parasitic disease in parts of Africa prevalent in stagnant or slow flowing rivers. It was also around that time or perhaps a year earlier that I developed a heart problem. Doctor Johnson, in Gwanda town centre, was the resident doctor at the time, a kind hearted soft spoken man as I recall who treated me for this illness. It was about that time too that I developed strange symptoms, where my heart beat would be clearly visible on my skin. If I placed my arm against my body I would observe the literal movement caused by each beat. Mother eventually took me to see Doctor Johnson who diagnosed my heart condition. He described my condition to my concerned mother in the simplest of terms that I had a 'hole' in the heart, a term I later in my life understood to mean an abnormal heart valve. I was debarred from taking part in sports at school, but never listened to that instruction after school as I continued to play with my friends. It seems that as I got older my heart may have repaired itself to some degree as I was able to engage in sports in senior / secondary school from 1967 - 1971 and thereafter after some years post schooling, found fit enough to be conscripted to the military in August of 1974.

Primary schooling was serious and disciplined. Bad behaviour was not tolerated and punishment was administered promptly. Cleanliness and good hygiene were instilled in us that even our nails were occasionally inspected. Anyone found with unkempt long nails received some slaps across the knuckles. The teachers were strict but considerate and taught us well considering that my first language was not English but Ndebele. However, I was able to speak fluent English by the second grade in Kindergarten, referred to as KG2. My first year's teacher was a kind soft spoken lady called Mrs June Noach. She was the first teacher to recognise that I had an artistic flair so she used to ask me to draw 'father Christmas' and the holly branch on the blackboard during the December term of school. I still recall her words on one of my Reports, where she wrote: "A budding artist". I have treasured that insight till this day. I would draw pictures as a pastime at home. I recall one year probably around 1968/9 that I painted some pictures using acrylic poster paints on

3mm thick board to sell for pocket money. It was during one school holiday, around April, Trade Fair time – a Business Fair that was held in Bulawayo at the Trade Fair Grounds each year whereby businesses displayed their products. It was a fun time for the whole family as it went on for at least a week or two. There were restaurants, games of chance, music at the amphitheatre, random questionnaire type competitions and most of all there was a huge Fun Fare for us children. That was a must to attend, so my Brother Clement and my nephew Terence Rubenstein decided on one weekend to hitchhike to Bulawayo, some 131 km from Sable Vale, to sell my paintings for some pocket money so that we could enjoy the Trade Fair. We did succeed in hitching a ride from Gwanda town and I did sell my paintings door to door, perhaps the people who bought them just felt pity for us, we will never know. Looking back now in my old age, I would not allow my children to have done such a trip on their own, three lads barely old enough to take care of themselves let alone take on such a task. We were probably around 15 years of age, but, then again, those were innocent times when there was much love and respect in the world, when children roamed about free without fear, wonderful times that the modern generation of latter years will perhaps never understand. We did safely hike back home after that weekend of unbridled fun.

There were times though that we took innocent playful risks as kids, never considering the dangers. We would perform bicycle races around the school grounds including racing home for some 4 to 5 km on tarmac. We would on occasion fall off and arrive home battered and blue with bloodied wounds which mum would wash and treat using a dish with warm salted water on arrival. Another of our crazy games was swinging on the vertical rope swing where we would, after gaining some momentum, jump off in competition to see who jumped the farthest. It was during one of these jumps that I sprained my wrist which had to be bandaged in a sling for some time. Another of our risky undertakings was on one afternoon, after school as we walked home, we saw what appeared to be abandoned canoes on the bank of Mtshabezi River adjacent to the road bridge. This location was probably 1km from our Primary School, Mount Cazalet as it was called. My brother Clement and I together with some friends decided to have some fun by canoeing across the river with canoes we thought were either abandoned or belonged to the Police. After some minutes we heard the sound of vehicles heading to the river bank, well, that ended that episode as we abandoned the canoes and ran away as fast as we could. It's worth mentioning that during the rainy season October to April the river would at times flood and overflow the bridge, preventing all traffic for some days. However, we always went to school, never missing a day, as there was available a suspension walkway bridge spanning the width of the river hence allowing us to walk across to attend school. This was another opportunity for 'naughty' boys to scare the daylights off the girls by manoeuvring the narrow bridge from side to side creating an unbalanced ripple motion effect, and how we loved to hear the girls screaming with fear. That was some of the 'silly', innocent childish games we engaged in. In today's world that would be deemed a health and safety extremely high risk incident, we however, viewed it as safe as the bridge was claddered on both vertical sides and floor walkway with corrugated metal hence impossible for any of us children to have fallen off.

Our schooling was proactive, as there was provision to be part of the Boy Scout and Brownies after school clubs, whereby we would engage in wholesome activities learning various skills including how to tie the various knots such as sheepshank and reef knots which I occasionally use till this day. One day our Scoutmaster and Brownies Captain arranged a climb of Mount Cazalet, which is some 1098 metres above sea level, this was a colossal feat for us children as we thought back then. That took the whole day, but what an occasion of fun. After finally reaching the summit I remember carving our names as a permanent remembrance on tree bucks at the mountain peak and enjoying our packed lunch whilst we viewed the traffic below which appeared like little 'dinky toy' cars, it was an exhilarating never to be repeated experience for a young boy.

Education wise, the curriculum was satisfactory. I did well during my primary years achieving one of the top three grades. It was as if we had pre planned turns to be top of the class, my competitors were Charmaine Noach, my Grade 1 Teachers daughter and Manjula Naik a petite quiet little girl of Indian ethnicity. Occasionally her dad, a shopkeeper businessman, gave us a lift / ride in his green and white 1957 Chevrolet impala. It was an awesome ride for a kid. They lived in the street adjacent to Mrs Oswald where I boarded, so at times we were privileged to spend the afternoon watching black and white early television programmes. Our class generally got on very well during those school years, I was always under the protective arms of my friend Bernard Bell, a well-built boy a year older than me. He was literally my next-door neighbour and protective 'Bouncer', we were always together right through to secondary school and beyond. I finally completed my primary schooling years in December of 1966. The following year was my next chapter, Secondary schooling.

SECONDARY SCHOOL YEARS

My secondary schooling years began in January 1967, I recall the anxiety and excitement that I felt prior. My parents initially planned to send me to Maritz Brothers College, a multiracial All Boys boarding school, in Kwe Kwe, however , that did not materialise for some reason. I guess the reason was a financial one. So, there was a change of plan with the decision being made to send me to Founders High school in Bulawayo, a government funded school for Coloured / mixed race children. There were other multiracial schools such as The Convent in Bulawayo and Saint John's High in Salisbury / Harare. It was exciting to drive up at the end of 1966, just before Christmas. with my parents to Bulawayo for the purchasing of my school uniform at Hassamels Store in Grey street now called Robert Mugabe way. It was exciting to try on the shorts, shirts, socks, shoes, a new tie and finally the maroon Blazer with a sew on badge. It was of interesting design, a pick overlaying an open book with the motto "Truth is ever Simple" embroidered on it. It was a motto I never considered or gave any thought to, neither did my parents nor any of my Teachers and school colleagues ever discuss its true meaning and application. I guess the pick and open book symbolise study hard work through education prerequisite to success. The emphasis that "Truth is ever simple" was to teach us to be truthful at all times but the full understanding of that motto only came to me many years later in my adult life, I will expand on this point in a later chapter. We completed our shopping trip that evening, drove back exhausted but satisfied.

The time soon arrived to get ready for my secondary schooling in early January of 1967. Father bought me a black steel trunk to pack all my requirements such as my clothes, uniforms including casual wear plus all my necessary toiletries. I felt a mixed bag of feelings from apprehension, concern, sadness and curiosity for the unknown. The final touch was painting my name and address in white attractive Gothic alphabet style letters which I copied from the current newspaper heading. I proudly painted the words 'Francis C' kind of misjudged the spacing so could not fit my full surname. That error soon generated much ridicule and laughter from my Hostel school mates, but I took it on the chin, joining in the laughter as recognition of my stupidity. Lastly below my name I painted the necessary full address in case of loss: Plot 16, Sable Vale, Gwanda. I was now ready for father to drive me to the train station. How we loved those train journeys, we played games with other school children of the same age group across ethnicity and we chatted away excitedly during the 3 to 4 hour journey which seemed endless. We usually arrived in Bulawayo late afternoon to be picked up by the school bus and driven to our destination, the hostels, Georgia House, Saint Elizabeth, where my brother Clement and I went and the girls hostel where my sisters went. Schooling was regimental with strict time frames to adhere to, from the awakening hostel bell, breakfast and the walk to school. The school curriculum was a British system with various qualification periods in between, Form 2 Leaving certificate through to C.O.P. (College of Preceptors) G.C.E. O level, M and A Level examinations. The curriculum was further divided into various levels based on one's measure of intelligence and subject material. The academic stream was designated A1 and A2, with the technical streams being B1, B2, C1 and C2 down to G. I was graded C2 when I began my secondary schooling in January 1967 but by end of that year I had successfully progressed to A2 the second highest grade. My favourite subject was Art, of which I excelled just as my primary School Teacher had predicted. I loved drawing and painting, it was my natural inclination, a gift as people say. I was doing well and my parents were proud of my progression.

Boarding life was disciplined, breakfast, lunch and dinner times were strict and enforced. Study time was one hour long after lunch and on every evening after dinner, this time was increased to 2 hours during exam periods. Bedtimes were set and enforced based on junior level, forms 1 and 2, and senior levels forms 3, 4, and 6. Weekends were fun as we were given a free day, Saturday, to visit the city centre, go to movies or do whatever we wished provided we were back at the hostel by

5:30pm. I used those occasions to visit my brother Philip and his family. my sister Molly and her family including my sister Margaret as they all lived in the coloured suburb called New Thorngrove. A suburb of rather substandard, quick construction comprising red brick, zinc doors, asbestos cement roofing and unplastered walls. The rooms were tiny and cramped which made living difficult for large families. This was the legacy of apartheid as such homes would never have been built for white folks. Sundays began with compulsory Church attendance until lunch time. I attended the local Catholic Church at the time all throughout my schooling as I was baptised and confirmed at a very young age. It was a chore I disliked, full of ritual and little substance, arriving back at the hostel with red sore knees. I suppose it kept us in the 'fear' of God although it didn't work on some occasions as we ran amok. My 'partner in crime' was my friend Roger Birdas, a good looking boy from Mutare (Umtali as it was known back then) . We were dormitory mates, our beds and cupboards next to each other. We attended the same class and were in the same grade A2. We were inseparable throughout my secondary school years. He was clever and funny, a natural comic, he had me in tears most of the time. We practically laughed our way through senior school never taking anything seriously. It was as if we went to school because we had to. At times he was annoying, we would get ready for school, get dressed, have our breakfast and head off to school, school was within walking distance of a few hundred metres, only to realise that he was wearing my khaki shorts. I would laugh and say "hey! Roger you're wearing my shorts!!" he would just laugh back as it was part of the fun as friends, we shared and shared alike. As far as the girls were concerned, we were the 'bad boys' and they loved our attention. It was all part of the fun and games. I must confess that, at times, we were really off the rails. There were two extreme occasions I recall where we were severely disciplined by the School HeadMaster by the name of Gustav Solomons. He was a short dark man of west Indian ethnicity that had a bit of a strange walk, a sort of side-to-side sway. We would recognise him, from his walk, a fair distance away, a mile away as the expression goes. The first occasion of our misbehaviour was when we went drinking alcohol at a bar called Mborombo in the old suburb called Old Thorngrove. It was a public bar for 'Black' people as the apartheid system went on. We drank the indigenous beverage known as Chibuku, a milky, grainy traditional sorghum beer drink with much of a kick; the main grains being malted sorghum maize and millet. I don't recall physically going to order the drink from the bar counter as we were school kids, of mixed race and in school uniform, I guess we probably asked a passer-by or one of our Black 'friends' to buy it for us with our pocket money, which they always gladly obliged. We would order a 'skull' or two, as it was called, a one or two litre measure container, and would share it between the three of us, Roger John and I. On that occasion! We really overdid it as we arrived back at the hostel in a right old state of intoxication quietly sneaking into our dormitory. I don't recall how we got away with it then. We did it again the second time and got caught. That weekend we were to attend a concert at the school Hall and we attended it in a drunken state. This time it was, again Roger and another friend called Desmond Dusart who 'acquired' a bottle of 100 Pipers whisky from his father's wardrobe which we gladly drank in preparation for a fun evening. It seems, on this night, we were not the only ones who attended the function intoxicated, it was half the hostel I think, it seemed so anyway. The next Sunday morning we were all summoned to the headmaster's office where we promptly received six of the best caning ever. We couldn't sit properly for days. Mr Solomon, the school headmaster, was a very strong man, though short in appearance, but was able to deliver the severest of strokes with a cane. It was surprising that we were not expelled from school, till this day I do not know why we didn't; Perhaps our parents intervened and appeased the situation. The paradox on that occasion was that one of my paintings was hanging just above the headmaster's desk. He had obtained it from my art class some weeks earlier and thought it was worthy to be displayed in his office. It's just ironic that the theme for my painting, which was done in a collage format, was 'Our Generation' which depicted young people in different modes of behaviour befitting the classic 1960's but here I was on this occasion bending down to be caned for the typical 1960's misbehaviour I had depicted in my artwork. The caning achieved the desired effect as we never drank intoxicating liquor again.

Most of us adjusted well to boarding school; perhaps it was due to good management, order, balanced discipline, quality meals and a measure of freedom. All of us Hostel Kids got on really well, we made fun of each other without malice and gave each other 'nicknames'. My friend John was 'Woody' his cousin Solly was 'Gus' I was called 'Cuckoo or Fowl' befitting my surname Co-hen. In addition to that, some of my friends made fun of my speech impediment. I suffered from an extreme stammer when I was a child, and I never understood the psychological reason for it. My friends, particularly Bernard Bell, would make the situation worse by making fun of me. I never took him seriously though – he was my 'Bodyguard' and very close friend and neighbour. I stammered through school especially when trying to read cold print, certain words were triggers for me. It was so bad that every time we were introduced to a new Teacher I would ask my friend Roger Birdas to tell them my name as I was too embarrassed to say it myself, not only that, but also became flustered and sweaty due to the sheer effort. It took me many years to overcome it as I will explain in a later chapter.

End of year was especially exciting as the hostel Staff permitted and arranged inter hostel parties, the school also occasionally arranged end of year talent shows which proved to be full of fun and laughter. A number of us participated in these shows, my friend John Woodend acted out a scene as a Ndebele News Reader, on one of these occasions, it was hilarious. My classmates and I, on the other hand, formed a Music Band comprising my friends Jack Hamilton on lead guitar, Arbeneza Garnie on rhythm guitar, I on bass guitar and finally Paddy Watson on drums. Jack was our band leader, a gifted guitarist he was and Paddy organised it all via our Music Teacher Mr Budd. He was a typical English gentleman, a larger-than-life figure as I remember him who instilled the love of music in us. We drew crowds of curious onlookers, fellow students including smiling giggly girls at every after-school practice session. It was so much fun as we belted out various rhythm and blues songs of the day. We were only sixteen years old then. This performance gained us a measure of popularity amongst our school contemporaries, we were basking in the limelight. In addition to that my friend Bernard and I were part of the school choir. We sang tenor and I occasionally played the Cello (4 string bass). We participated in inter school concerts, I recall, on one occasion we took part in 'Handel's Messiah' concert which was an exhilarating occasion. Our Choir Teacher, a dear Mrs Smith instilled so much music appreciation in us which included listening to the great Classic Masters such as Beethoven, Tchaikovsky and Wolfgang Amadeus Mozart. She was so proud of us. We loved it, and never missed choir practice. My secondary school years were filled with much joy, mixed with occasional juvenile misbehaviour. Sadly, our school band was dismantled because of an unfortunate incident that occurred with my friend Jack. He suffered a brain haemorrhage on a weekend out at Matopos Hills with some friends. It was supposed to be an innocent get together BBQ (Braai) with friends but it turned out to be a nightmare as he was rushed to Mater Dei Hospital in Bulawayo for an emergency operation. We learnt of this at school as advised by our class teacher. It was a devastating blow for Jack and his family. Jack survived but was partly paralysed, the whole of his left side became dysfunctional and that resulted in the loss of the full use of his hands.

I would visit him at his home occasionally and witness the very sad scenario. Jack would attempt to hold and play his guitar to no avail, I could see the sadness in his eyes and the deluded determination to one day have his ability restored. It never happened. My life took another turn from there, it was then that I learned the unhealthy habit of cigarette smoking sometime in 1970 when I was about seventeen years old. It was the 'cool' thing to do back in those days, and I foolishly did it to my parents' disappointment. I sadly twisted my father's arm to give me written permission so I could smoke at boarding school. The Hostel Staff permitted us to use a separate prep room as a smoking room. Fortunately, I eventually gave up the habit in 1979 after a bout of malaria.

Looking back, I must say that I enjoyed my school years, they were filled with joy, happiness, friendships, much fun and the correct measured discipline. We were daring risk takers at times but felt secure as kids because there were strict measured guidelines and time frames for everything. There was a time for homework, play, games, sports, swimming, inter-school sports and athletics. I enjoyed athletics as I qualified as a 100 metre Sprinter and 200 metre relay participant. Soccer was a must too, I was kind of 'good' enough to be picked for the second senior school team, I was the right winger and loved it, but I was not that good, anyway, hopeless perhaps is a better word, it was just a game of fun as far as I was concerned. Other than that, I was known as 'The Artist' for my talent and creative artwork. It gave me a sense of achievement, pride and popularity. We would go through phases of behaviour at our Boarding Hostel, guitar playing was one of them, a group of us from the same and adjacent dormitories learnt to play the guitar. We were influenced by three Mu-ta-re boys who were musicians who taught us the basic guitar chords, we played a number of Blues songs which basically comprise three simple chords. These were really fun times as we would sing and play. The next phase was just out of the normal. We suddenly began to tattoo ourselves using a flame sterilised needle and black ink. I don't recall who it was that started us on this road but nevertheless a few of us thought it was a macho thing to do. I had a tattoo of a ship's anchor created on my right upper arm; did I choose that to depict some bad boy 'pirate' image? I don't really know; did it cross my mind that this reckless act of a fifteen-year-old boy would upset my parents? No it didn't. I was just a naughty carefree kid too self-involved to consider these things. This tattoo is an indelible mark on my body, a constant reminder of my misbehaviour during my schooling days.

I eventually completed schooling in December 1971 having achieved sixth form Metric Level equivalent to one year A level standard. I could have achieved better academically if I had worked harder and taken my education more seriously as my friend John Woodend and colleagues such as Sam Ameer and Ashock Morar and others who went on to obtain degrees in Agronomy and Engineering. I was not disciplined enough to take my schooling seriously. My parents had no idea about careers, nor did they understand the education system, nor were they sufficiently schooled to guide and encourage me, hence, their role it seemed was to send me to school to acquire an education. I really had no idea of what I was going to do, what direction I was heading, I was on my own to do what I thought best. The thought of the possibility of being an Architect crossed my mind, but it proved to be just a thought. I remember attending an interview with the headmaster just prior to starting my 'O' level syllabus where I requested to do Technical Drawing as a subject which I was good at and enjoyed. Sadly, or should I say, unfortunately, I was not permitted to do so because of the fact that I was in an A (academic) stream which did not include that particular subject in its curriculum. I was not given the option to downgrade to a lower 'B' Technical stream either. Would I have accepted that downgrade if I was offered? I really don't know, perhaps my own selfish pride may have gotten in the way. I guess my Headmaster Mr Solomons, thought it proper to help me out during my final year of schooling as he organised an interview for me as a Trainee Commercial Artist at an Art Decor Company based in Bulawayo city centre.

My interview was rather odd I thought, as I was asked whether I was capable of drawing a radio that was placed on a table in front of me. Having achieved a distinction in my G.C.E. (General Certificate of Education) I just wondered whether my 'future' would be Employer was undermining me due to my ethnic background by asking me such a question. Surely my distinction qualification should have convinced my interviewer that I was quite capable. Anyway; I had to further produce 'Advertising' type lino print samples at a later date to be reviewed during my second interview. To my glee I did have a successful second interview at the end as I was invited to start work sometime in January of 1972, but for some unknown reason or reasons, to this day, the company either relocated or went into liquidation as it was no longer at the original address where I had attended the interview. So, that was a sad occasion for me, an unexpected and unfortunate turn of events. It's funny, true but strange which direction life takes you because soon after that I joined the Rhodesia Railways and trained as a Train Guard after my Fathers advice. There was nothing else it seemed for us mixed race (coloured) children as I soon discovered especially if one's father was an obscure unknown shopkeeper in a little town like Gwanda. It seemed that all the mixed-race / coloured kids ended up on the railways to be employed as Shunters, Firemen and Train Guards. The occasional 'one-in-a-bucket' kid of colour who made it in a skilled Trade apprenticeship was one who had the good fortune of having his father employed by the Rhodesia Railways. The fact of the matter was that, in the apartheid system all the high paying jobs, whether in skilled trades or commercial and managerial fields were all reserved for the White folk. My kinsmen of both black and mixed ethnicity were to contend with the lower skills. Sadly, the majority of our black relatives had to survive with the crumbs; the 'lower' mundane labour jobs which often included unskilled hard labour, Gardeners, Domestic workers and municipality grass cutting work or other labourer type jobs, shop assistants and the like. Ironically Bus Drivers and Heavy goods Vehicle Drivers were viewed as lower skilled employment only 'fit' for my Black Kinsman. It seemed that the only multiracial across the board opportunities were the professions such as Teachers, Nurses, Engineers and Doctors as these were necessary as the system demanded to cater for the exclusivity and separation criteria of apartheid. Often the, Black and Coloured, kids who made it in these professions were from affluent backgrounds and were fortunate enough to be schooled in most cases in private non-racial biassed schools. They thereafter were able to progress to teacher training colleges and universities. It's odd though, as I soon noticed, that coloured people, I mean mixed race people, were never employed in the Police Force for reasons I never discovered. Was it lack of interest from the Coloured Community or was there some other government legislated prohibition?

That was my introduction to the Apartheid system of racial discrimination. Did my father know something I didn't know, that my only hope at the time was to find employment with the Rhodesia Railways. I soon understood the reason why my schooling both at primary and at secondary level comprised Kids from mixed race ethnic backgrounds only. Our only interaction with White Kids was occasionally during school sports, mainly Soccer, Netball and Tennis. We didn't give that much thought when we were in school, it was just accepted as normal and perhaps that was the only school we qualified for, so I thought, as Maritz Brothers College, Saint John's College and the Girls Convent were the only multi racial schools available. Little did I know that that was part of the Apartheid system of racial segregation. Never did we even consider, nor did it come to mind the reason why my Black family members, cousins and uncles all attended schools in their respective rural domains and townships. There was no interaction with 'black' schools whatsoever, it was as if they didn't exist to the many. I soon discovered the reasons.

Me in boarding school 1968

SEGREGATION AND APARTHEID AWARENESS

When did I become aware of this issue of apartheid, the Colour Bar as it was called in Southern Rhodesia? A system of being literally debarred from enjoying a free unbridled lifestyle, a lifestyle that many take for granted today such as purchasing a house in an area of choice, unlimited education, facilities, entrance into clubs, restaurants, entering the Job market of choice as equals etc. All that, where one lived, schooled, type of employment one engaged in and entertainment venues one attended, was based on the colour of one's skin. The answer to the question: when did I become aware of the colour bar / apartheid system? It was sometime after 1967 during my secondary schooling. We were oblivious, most of the time to the details of the political situation in the country. We were just kids. The fact that around 1964 Ian Douglas Smith became the then prime Minister of Southern Rhodesia and later engineered the unilateral declaration of independence from the United Kingdom following a long-drawn out dispute with Britain over their demands for black majority rule was to us just another cog in the wheels of politics, another newspaper headline. Little did we know the implications of that situation. It was shortly after that that his predominantly 'white' led Government introduced, by legislation, the system of apartheid – a colour bar, a racially divided system of separation of the races, a system of white privilege racial bias and class distinction.

The whole nation was subdivided into three ethnic 'boxes' marked Black, White and Coloured as it were, a type of caste system with the lowest being black, and highest being white with coloureds, people of colour, in the middle. The Land Tenure Act, a segregationist law which superseded the land Apportionment Act in 1969 unfairly apportioned housing areas and designated them African / Black, Coloured and European / White. I will state for clarity for you dear reader the extent and gravity of this law in terms of the segregated suburbs in and around the city of Bulawayo where we resided. Of course the segregation was countrywide but my experience is in the city of Bulawayo where I grew up. The 'Black suburbs' as far as I can remember were as follows: Mzilikazi, Mpopoma, Magwegwe, Makokoba, Empandeni and Nkulumane. These were termed the western Suburbs, they were huge in terms of population, many of the properties were small brick dwellings, well-built but of simple construction of approximately 12 square metres plus. I must give due credit to the Rhodesian Government at the time that built these properties to a reasonable standard not like the shanty towns of corrugated zinc sheets that are so prevalent in much of the black areas of South Africa such as parts of Soweto, Cape town and Kimberly, areas that I witnessed first hand in the 1980's and 90's. The apportioned Coloured and Asian / Indian areas in the city of Bulawayo were Old and New Thorngrove, Rangemore, Trenance, Forestvale, some pockets of houses on the fringes of Bulawayo including some rundown Flats in Main street and twelfth and fifteenth avenues, then, of course, there was Barham Green a suburb predominantly occupied by Africaans speaking Coloured peoples of South African origin. The European / White suburbs were North End, pockets of houses along MacIntyre avenue, Sauerstown, Queenspark, Tegela, Paddonhurst, Romney Park, Suburbs, Parklands, Bradfield, Hillcrest, Ascot Mews, Ascot high rise apartments, Riverside, up market City centre Flats, Hillcrest, Famona, Morningside and Hillside. Some of these suburbs such as Hillside and Morningside had palatial properties with swimming pools and the occasional Tennis Court for the Rich upper class one could say. Multinational Businesses were foreign owned and managed by white folks including most Farms and the agricultural sector, people of colour had the odd clothing stores along the fringe streets of Bulawayo including School uniform providers like Hassamals and Esats which were Indian owned. In a nutshell, this was the general make-up of apartheid Rhodesia, a configuration that applied throughout the cities and towns in the country. Salisbury / Harare, the capital city, on the other hand appeared to offer people of colour a little more choice; perhaps this was because of being the Capital City and hence occupied and visited by internationals. Bulawayo was more divided I guess because it is situated nearer to South Africa and had strong business and cultural links with South Africa in those days. Apartheid was the most degrading, dehumanising, soul destroying, oppressive system ever invented by humanity, it degraded the black indigenous people, my kinsman and family, to a people 'without history' ignoring and rewriting the black histories of the Great Kingdoms of Monamatapa and that of Great Zimbabwe to the extent of denying the fact that Great Zimbabwe was built by Black Africans of Zimbabwe. I recall with such clarity the infamous statement of the Apartheid Prime Minister, Ian Douglas Smith who once said "never in a thousand years" regarding black majority rule. This system of Apartheid was basically a system of rule by the minority for the benefit of the minority, the majority were to be subservient to the minority. It was a system of control and white privilege. Everything was in the hands of white folks, the economy, all major businesses, the housing market and property management, the employment market, everything! The front end desks were manned by white secretaries, Supermarket Tellers were white folks, so you can imagine who they served first in the shopping cue, Property Estate Agents were managed by white folks, the jobs market was controlled by white folks, our chance for a decent job were limited because first preference was given to white folks then us people of colour - second class citizens - our black folks were at the lower end of the apartheid spectrum and kept in subjugation to do the mundane labour jobs. The only decent forms of employment at better salaries for our black folks were the military and police forces and prison wardens. The Bosses, people of higher rank, whether in the Police Force or military were white folks, they were in control. Suppression of the masses was at a colossal unimaginable scale at every level of society. The world had forgotten us Rhodesians as they seemed to concentrate on ending the Apartheid system in South Africa. Apartheid in Rhodesia had to be dismantled as well, in time. The end came in less than twenty years from the utterance of the words "Never in a thousand years" as I will discuss later in this and other chapters including its effect on the whole populace.

My parents initially enrolled me into a multiracial Boys only private school called Maritz Brothers college based in Que Que / Kwe Kwe a small town in the Midlands of Zimbabwe. Unfortunately my father could not financially afford the fees hence he pulled the application and enrolled me into Founders High School a government funded High school for Coloured / mixed race children in Bulawayo. At first I merely thought that it was just another cheaper option multi-racial school until I noticed the ethnic composition – Mixed race / Coloured, Asian, both Indian and Chinese ethnicity. It was a segregated school in the apartheid structural machinery. Every school term, three terms per year, differed in terms of the curriculum progression but remained the same in its structural components such as hostel life, sports, weekend activities, start of term and end of term events. I completed my secondary schooling in December 1971 as already described. It was a daunting time, a blank canvas in my life. What was I to do? My parents eventually, early in 1972 organised accommodation for me with my Auntie Iana and uncle George Edwards who lived in an attractive property at the edge of the city centre. I had applied for a job as a Train Guard as encouraged by my father, and was successfully offered employment. My recruitment began early 1972 hence my permanent move to Bulawayo. That was the beginning of my independent life as a young seventeen year old boy. Back then the legal adult age of majority was twenty one years, so basically I was still a child. My siblings were still in school, my father eventually became bankrupt shortly after that. In time I became the breadwinner of the family, not by choice but by necessity. It was culturally expected though, that the first born would have to take up the responsibility as family provider when there was no other option as father could no longer provide. I do not recall whether my parents received any financial assistance from social welfare, what I do know is that my father received some help from the Jewish Guild Society, a charity organisation, based in Gwanda. Life became difficult for my family from that time onwards. I took my responsibility seriously as a God assigned role. Was I too young to take up such a role? Was I mature enough? Such questions did not even come to mind. I just took my new role on the chin, grabbing the 'bull by the horns' as the saying goes with a resolve to do my utmost to fulfil it. I would set aside and contribute a portion of my salary each month for the care of my family from that time onwards, a promise I have carried out right up to this present time of writing for the care of my elderly mother who is now at a good old age of eighty eight. I promised to take care of my family until they reached their own independence and hence were able to also contribute likewise towards the whole family's livelihood.

Working as a Train Guard was challenging for such a young boy; however, I was determined to do my best. The training included vigorous manual instructions from the curriculum, classroom scenario, together with practical exercises in the field such as marshalling of Goods trains in their respective yards. Night shift was not fun particularly during the cold winter months of June through August. At times the Shunter, a goods wagon Marshaller, and I would huddle in the Train Driver's cabin for warmth. The smell of the steam from the heated coals was a soothing experience. I didn't fancy being a Fireman, it was a physically demanding job. My job training period was about six months and I was thereafter posted to the city of Gwelo, a city in central Rhodesia now known by its original pre colonial name Gweru, some one hundred and fifty kilometres north of Bulawayo. We were accommodated in specially built units, for workers of mixed-race ethnicity, the only time we shared the same workspace with white fellow employees was in the Guards Room and canteen. The ablution block was segregated with the following designation Black, White and Coloureds, however, the Canteen was surprisingly multiracial and served healthy hot meals to all Railway employees. Our work shifts were not by choice or preference as sometimes awarded to our white colleagues, we did what we were assigned without protest and viewed the fact that we were employed as more important as it provided monetary benefits for our families, the salary was very attractive for a young man as one could work overtime as and when one wished. We were given regular time-off after several shifts which enabled us to visit our families or go on short holidays. The general benefits of my Railway employment were good and included medical aid and a generous pension scheme.

For recreation, during off work hours, we frequented the non-white, 'Blacks and Coloureds only' public bar at the Queens Hotel in the Gwelo / Gweru town centre where, besides drinking, we played darts and billiards. This was our main past-time between work shifts. I enjoyed my life in Gwelo, a quiet peaceful city back then. Work was kind of routine, it included marshalling of the wagons both goods and passengers as required and being responsible for the timely running of the train. The main line between Bulawayo and Harare operated on a Centralised Traffic Control system, an electric traffic light system similar to road traffic, however, the branch off lines such as Bannockburn, Shabanie, Mashaba and Selukwe operated on a 'Paper Order,' system which detailed the Sidings and crossing time frames. It worked well in my view as there were no reported accidents during my service. The off main line operations were very scary for me, as I was only around nineteen or twenty years old. The only light you had was the 'Guards' lamp, a battery-operated torch like lamp that enabled 'Green, amber and Red' traffic light operation – go and no-go type. The rail line and surrounding area were not lit besides the natural moon light and starry heavens which afforded one a little bit of comfort. A cloudy night was scary, black as pitch, and included the night sounds and shrieks of wild animals and creatures including the 'toots' of owls. I often thought of being attacked by some wild animal during these operations whilst the Train Driver and Fireman enjoyed a measure of safety in the Steam engine. I must admit though, that was just my imagination running away with me as my experience was mostly uneventful until one night when I caused a major Shunt accident which unfortunately ended my employment on the Railways in around October of 1973. I recall that incident with much clarity.

It occurred on one night during a change-over shunt at a siding near Que Que / Kwe Kwe, an Iron and Steel manufacturing Plant named R.I.S.Co (Rhodesia iron and steel Company at the time).

We stopped at this particular Siding where I had to drop off some empty wagons. The Centralised traffic control (CTC) System automatically operated the red traffic light to enable the shunt operation. I had to uncouple certain wagons and redirect the Driver away from the main line by operating the first set of points. The second set of points were to permit the empty wagons to be directed to a certain line location where they would be uncoupled and left at that position. It was unfortunate that I decided at that moment to wave the Driver on without first performing the change of direction of the points. I thought that I could outrun the reversing train as I was already at the ready with the points keys. I recalled my school days as a sprinter, so I was convinced that I could out run the train key in hand to unlock the points and turn the line change operating lever before the wagon wheels got to that turning point. Unfortunately, it appeared that I was a little too late according to the Incident Tribunal which was held some weeks after the incident. I argued though, that I performed that change in time, less than a minute, in my view and that the points were faulty resulting in what is termed 'Split Points' where the wagon wheel literally runs in between the rail rather than on the rail. The end result was a colossal crash where one wagon dragged the other causing a major derailment. The next thing I saw was a wagon at a vertical ninety-degree position whilst the train was still moving, dragging the other wagons with it. The train wagons became like a mangled chain. I ran for my life flashing the red-light signal on my torch to alert the Driver who eventually saw my flashes of light and stopped the engine. The chaos was soon evident with wagons strewn across the entire station. I escaped unscathed, a little shaken but otherwise ok, a traumatic experience for a twenty-year old kid as I had just turned twenty. The chaos lasted some twenty-four hours at the very least as all train operations on that Bulawayo to Harare line were stopped with immediate effect to enable urgent line repairs and the removal of the debris and mangled wagons. That! was the end of my career with the Railways as I opted to abscond rather than face the result of the Tribunal. I think I would have lost my Job anyway as the damage in terms of cost must have been massive. My life from that point took another turn. I had no idea as to what was next, it never occurred to me then, just how closely I had escaped an early death by the 'shear skin of one's teeth' as the proverbial saying goes. I left it to fate, as I believed at the time, as if it had been written and I had no choice in the matter. I packed my bags after the Tribunal and caught the next train to Bulawayo without telling a soul, not even my friend Anthony Meyers who was also a train Guard of the same intake as me, assigned to the same city and Railway Quarters. I cannot recall whether he was on a shift on that day hence the reason I was unable to tell him of my decision to abscond.

I arrived in Bulawayo and lived for a short while with my Aunt Ina and husband Uncle George Edwards with their sons Brian and Joe and sister Rosemary. Rosemary was the eldest and seemed to be the odd ball. I would see her every now and again and observed that she was never associated with the mixed race / coloured community. I knew that because the community was small, we all frequented the same places, went to the same schools and enjoyed the same entertainment areas so I drew the conclusion that Rosemary had rejected her own background community and associated herself with the white folks perhaps because she could. She was light skinned and blonde. I understood the reasoning, for better opportunity, livelihood and privilege. At least she did not disown her mother I thought. My life then was in limbo, I had no clue as to what to do next, I kind of stumbled into the next phase, it seemed like I was left to fate if one believed in such a philosophy. My weekly routine at that time was spending time with friends at their homes where we would smoke cigarettes, listen to music and enjoy each other's company. Some of my friends smoked cannabis known as Imbanje in the Ndebele language, I didn't care for it, although I did try it; it was not my thing. We became adventurous over weekends going to our favourite Bar ' The Skittle Inn' as it was called, a segregated Bar located in thirteenth avenue in Bulawayo, with sections designated Coloureds in one room facing the west side and White folks in the opposite east facing room. These bars were really just drinking and gambling dens for adults only. No food was made available, just alcohol. There were, though, many attractive restaurants and hotels in the city centre and on the outskirts of the city, but these were reserved for 'whites' only. One evening, after having a few, my friends and I tried to enter the Cecil Hotel, a posh whites only bar only to be told in no uncertain terms, that the only area we were permitted to enter was an underground Bar sign posted 'Coloureds only'. That was the kind of humiliation we were subjected to during the Rhodesian era. The only other non-white places we frequented were the Waverley Hotel, Great Northern Hotel and the   ex-Servicemen Club for Coloured peoples situated on the western part of the city between eleventh and thirteenth avenues. Black folks drank along with us at the Waverley and Great Northern Hotels. It was just natural to us with no incidents or clashes. The traditional beer called Chibuku was consumed at a Bar called Number Five and one called Burombo situated in a suburb called Old Thorngrove on the outskirts of the city. Friday and Saturday nights were fun as we attended dance Halls to enjoy live music and dance with much drinking from eight in the evening until two o'clock in the mornings. These were regular occasions during those early seventies held only in the Coloured suburbs of Barham Green, Trenance, Forest Vale and Rangemore. Occasionally they were also held at Westgate, a Railway Employees suburb situated west of Bulawayo city centre. The music was awesome from disco to Rhythm and Blues and Soul music which proved to be my favourite. We danced and literally drank our 'troubles' away in the climate of 'wine, girlfriends and song' only to wake up the next day with a headache to face the same issues still waiting at the door of life. It was during one of these weekends that I met a chap called Charlie Mcleod who advised me about an Engineering Company he worked for known as R.E.S.C.Co. (Rhodesian Engineering Steel Construction Company) was recruiting 'Operators'. The 'Operator' Job role included the following tasks: To operate drilling machines, saw cutting and steel section cropping machines, guillotine cutting, Overhead Crane operation, profile cutting equipment and template marking of steel plates. I casually asked Charlie to organise an interview for me, which he gladly did. The 'Coloured' community was small and kind of close knit so, many of us knew each other reasonably well as we frequented the same places for entertainment, the same bars and the same dance halls. I am ever so grateful to Charlie who afforded me an opportunity, another junction on my life's journey. To my surprise I was offered the job as a Template marker and Profiler, that was in early 1973. It was then too that I had to find more suitable accommodation nearer to work. My friend and Primary School Mate Burns Gallagher offered me a place at his residence in Barham Green which was walking distance to work. Burns had gotten married to Noreen Lees at the time and had settled in Barham Green, a middle class coloured community suburb. It soon dawned on me, whilst living in Barham Green, that the Coloured Community there also practised class distinction as some seemed to look down on us because we were from an obscure part of the country and from mixed race parentage. Much of the community in Barham Green were of South African heritage so perhaps felt 'superior' in some way. That did not bother me somehow, I just could not understand that mind-set as I was not brought up that way. To me people were just people whether black, white or brown and deserved to be treated as equals as part of the human race spectrum. It seems that the whole apartheid system filtered down to the community as divisions became apparent in the whole community. One was then assessed and categorised by the different shades of skin tones, it was as if, the lighter shade you were the more accepted you were. If you were dark skinned, you were unlikely to date a lighter skinned girl. Yes, you might be thinking how bad that was, yes it was, and that was our reality during the apartheid years. I recall with such clarity one occasion in 1976 when I was dating my wife who is light skinned of a white Irish father and coloured mother, a girl of my dreams beautiful in all ways not only in appearance but with a beautiful personality too. I had taken her out for a drink at a bar in Barham Green just as we were attending one of the weekend dance Hall sessions. An acquaintance of mine, 'Tuppy' Vanbeek, together with his brother sat opposite me and looked at me and said " Francis, which witch doctor did you go see, how did you find a beauty like her?" well! I was more dumb-founded than anything else and laughed it off to his surprise. 'Tuppy' and his brother were one of those funny entertaining characters well-liked by all though, so I was not offended by his remark, just bemused. I recall on many other occasions being stared at by both my fellow kinsman and white folks, stares I ignored. One other occasion worth mentioning occurred in December of 1984 when my wife and I went on holiday to South Africa. We had two children then our daughter Francine and our son Benjamin, a handsome blue-eyed boy. I mention this, not in a prideful, class distinctive sentiment but as to convey the experience, the reactions and inner emotions I felt on this occasion. We were driving back to Bulawayo and stopped at an off-road restaurant for lunch somewhere past either Johannesburg or Pretoria. We walked in with our children in hand and sat down at a vacant table. It did not occur to us whether this was an 'all white' only restaurant, we just walked in. My wife went to the counter and placed our order whilst I sat with the children. I looked around only to be stared at by the all white attendees, I wondered whether they assumed my wife was white but no one said a word. I ignored the uncomfortable glares, the 'air was so thick you could cut with a knife.' We consumed our meal and thereafter drove back to Bulawayo. I guess everyone was taken by surprise and served us without incident. There was this feeling like You are not supposed to be here. Another occasion was when my wife and our two children travelled by train to Pretoria for a short shopping trip. I think she went to purchase a sewing machine hence travelled outbound on her own and was joined by her twin half-sisters on the return journey. On this occasion I was not able to go with her at the time because it was sometime during the year when I could not get off work. Engineering companies always closed for two weeks every December hence we always travelled to South Africa to enjoy seaside holidays every year from 1980 onwards. Therefore, on this occasion she travelled with her sisters. She was, however, offered and booked on a first class coach whilst her sisters had already travelled ahead booking on the second class ' coloured' coach. Yes, you guessed it, that was a most amusing experience. I suspect Desiree and Denise were dismayed to discover that my wife and the children were travelling on a first class 'whites only' coach whilst they were separated in the second-class coach. Perhaps they felt even a little upset, but they took it on the chin. I guess they would probably have accepted the 'white privilege' comforts if they were in a similar position and able to. My wife accepted the offer without question for the sake of a comfortable journey for herself and the children. Why not I thought when she told me. I guess the staff assumed that she and the children were white as first class was a 'white only' carriage. More of that later. Dating across the racial divide was taboo and often would have resulted in rejection and animosity from all sides.

1973 was the beginning of my career in engineering, a career I loved and experienced with such passion until my retirement in the UK in November of 2018. As I have already stated, Charlie Mcleod opened that door early in 1973. R.E.S.C.Co was a very successful engineering business specialising in Railway Rolling stock, manufacturing of mining equipment including heavy structural steel fabrication and installation. The Rhodesian mining sector was very productive so most engineering manufacturing companies in Rhodesia were very much involved in this sector. It was a flourishing well-paying industry, jobs were plentiful, in fact the 1970's and 80's have proved to be the most lucrative and economically viable and the most successful years of the country to date. It was the best time of our lives; life was great and affordable as we enjoyed one of the highest standards of living in the world. I will elaborate on that a little later.

I started work promptly with much excitement and enthusiasm. Our working environment was good, the hours were good with availability of overtime over weekends. The company had two separate divisions one specialising in Rolling stock, the London Road branch, and the other in heavy Structural steel fabrication and welding based on Leamington Road industrial complex. I worked for both divisions starting at the Railway Rolling stock branch. The work was labour intensive and our chargehand was a real slave driver probably due to demanding production targets. I was always punctual and a diligent employee. Our main role was assembling and riveting wagon piece parts both hot and cold riveting. It was strenuous work, but we coped as young strong able bodies. After about a period of 6 months I was transferred to the Structural Steel division on Leamington road and assigned to template marking and gas cutting of steel plates in preparation for assembly by qualified boilermakers / Fabricators. We worked mainly in the open uncovered yard where sometimes it became unbearable due to the hot climate as the steel plates heated up making it quite a challenge to perform our tasks, nevertheless we managed. The work was a little more challenging as we had to mark and profile cut various shaped plates of different material thicknesses, particularly odd shapes and thicknesses mainly above 12mm which could not be cut by guillotine. Our Foreman at the time was a gentleman named Victor Hugo, a soft spoken individual who treated us well with respect and dignity. After some months working in that role, I decided to request for an apprenticeship as a Boilermaker after observing the interesting manufacturing of various shaped components and structures. I was fascinated with the manufacturing process that began from hand drafted drawings / blueprints to the finished painted components and structures. I fell in love with the skill set. I noticed too that all the Boilermakers / Fabricators were white and the welders were mainly black with some, a small number, being of Portuguese ethnicity. I wondered why none were of mixed background, coloureds, I soon discovered the reason.

One morning I had resolved to speak with my Foreman Vic Hugo as he was called in short. I approached him privately in his wooden cabin office and said "Excuse Mr Hugo, (first names were not viewed as appropriate to our white masters as it were) may I speak with you for a moment" at which he responded "sure young man" I continued "is it possible to apply for an apprenticeship as a Boilermaker?" Mr Hugo looked at me with an empathetic glance, put his arm around my shoulder in a fatherly way and politely said "Sorry son but this company does not employ non-white people as Boilermakers." You can imagine my disappointment and feelings of rejection. I was gutted, my background including my educational status did not matter, it was my brown skin colour that mattered as that was the problem.

I continued, though, to work there for some months thereafter until another door of opportunity opened.

For the sake of clarity and to enable my non-technical readers to understand these trade skills I shall attempt to explain as follows so you, dear reader, will have a better appreciation. Steel structures such as bridges, Grain silos, mining conveyor systems, Towers, buildings etc are evident throughout the world and taken for granted by many. We see them every day and admire their beauty. Famous suspension bridges and Victorian railway stations are examples of fabricated, forged, welded and bolted constructions manufactured and erected by Fabricators. Many components in mechanical systems are fabricated, welded and precision machined components. It is truly an art, a creation which begins with the Design Engineer, either Mechanical, Structural or Civil. The Boilermaker / Fabricators role, skill set is to take the design from its cradle, the blueprint, to a finished product. The knowledge base includes a good understanding of geometry, trigonometry, the transfer of the information from the blueprint to the steel sheets / plate and sections which is enhanced by intuition and artistic talent. Also included is the cutting, bending and forming of such materials into complex shapes followed by the assembly of such piece parts which are held together by the welding process into finished structures and or components. The understanding of the operation of machine tools used to bend, roll, cut and the straightening operations is crucial to the manufacturing process. The understanding of welding technology is also a key aspect of the role. Since the welding process involves great heat transfer distortion occurs and it, again, is the Boilermaker / Fabricators role to control such distortion by manufacturing preemptive holding tools, jigs and fixtures in order to produce structures and components that are finished to design tolerances and dimensions. The Welder's role on the other hand is a relative one which is to fully weld the fabricated structure or component not only to achieve sound welds free from defect but to weld in such a sequence so as to reduce distortion. Great skill is required to achieve this across the various range of materials from carbon steels to exotic materials that require different levels of welding application, such as eye to hand coordination and heat transfer and control and a good understanding of welding technology and electro mechanical welding equipment. I was in awe to discover many years later during my studies of the Bible that the 'first' man to manufacture steel components / forgings is actually mentioned in the Bible book of Genesis, a man by the name of Tubal Cain. See Genesis 4:22 *"Also, Zil'lah gave birth to Tu'bal-cain, who forged every sort of tool of copper and iron. And the sister of Tu'bal-cain was Na'a·mah."* I trust the aforementioned explanation and effort in clarity will help my readers to understand and appreciate this aspect of my life which is deep within my DNA and artistic flare.

Back to where I digressed. This time, around 1974, my late friend Stanley Woodend, had recently had his apprenticeship transferred from one engineering company to Morewear Industries, just off Khami road down eleventh avenue extension, a large Engineering business employing over a hundred and fifty shop floor staff comprising Boilermakers, welders, machine Operators, overhead Crane drivers, sand blasters, spray painters and other labour type personnel. One day, Stanley told me that the company had recently purchased a top of the range – super-duper three headed gas profile cutting machine imported from Japan and that the company was looking to employ a profile cutting Operator with experience in gas cutting using at the very least the conventional straight line profile gas cutting type equipment. Stanley told me he would organise an interview for me which he kept to his word as I was shortly thereafter called for an interview. I was ecstatic!! another rung on the ladder of progress. My interviewer was the work foreman, a man named Alan Smith who asked me whether I could operate such a machine. He took me to physically view the machine which was situated in a strategic 'preparation' area of the factory and asked me a simple question "Can you operate this machine?" I did not hesitate with my response, I resolutely answered "Yes I can." of course I had never seen such a piece of equipment ever, it was bright red in colour comprising a fixed console on the right half of the kit, with a long arm extending on the left half which supported three extended vertical and horizontally adjustable gas cutting nozzles. Below that was a flatbed approximately 1.5 metres square which had a perspex sheet placed over a machined flat area, following that was the rest of the bed which comprised steel plate supporting slats evenly spaced and secured in slots to a distance of approximately 3 metres to enable replacement after use. The area supported standard sized steel sheets of 2.4 x 1.2 metres width (8 x 4ft). The nozzle arm could traverse along the entire length of the sheets and beyond. The console had a lever arm which the Operator would manipulate in order to position the nozzles to the correct cutting dimension just above the steel plate – 2-3 mm depending on the plate thickness and nozzle size. The lever enabled an electronic photo eye mechanism attached to pick up detect the marked shapes on an approximately one-metre square sheet of template paper snugly placed under the perspex sheet. All steel plate profiles had to be either hand drawn or marked using smaller templates in black ink or marker pen on the larger template paper. I was intrigued, this was really a state-of-the-art piece of kit in 1974. Prior to that, engineering companies used a magnet type profiler over a steel plate template to cut steel profiles, really archaic at that time, so this three headed profiler was a game changer and I was the first employee that would make that happen. Alan Smith offered me the job almost immediately; I assume that he was impressed with my enthusiasm and positive attitude although I had never seen that type of machine before. I soon handed in my notice at R.E.S.C.Co and moved on to greener pastures at Morewear Industries sometime in early 1974.

I began work promptly on a Monday after working my notice period at R.E.S.C.Co. My ex-Foreman Vic Hugo did not seem surprised at all but just wished me well in my new role. Morewear was a different layout, a huge rectangular shaped building of some 5400 square metres of working factory space traversed by four overhead cranes ranging from 10 to 50 Tonne lifting capacity. It was a noisy atmosphere filled with sounds of steel banging, drilling and punching presses, whining overhead crane sounds typical of a steel Fabrication shop. The workforce was typical across the racial divide made up of white Boilermaker tradesmen, black Welders and black labourers.

Machine operators and overhead crane operators were predominantly people of colour. This was apartheid at ground level. At one end of the factory was a separate raw steel sales department which functioned independently. The office, stores area and ablution blocks were situated alongside the factory length. In addition to all that was a massive yard space which included a sand blasting area of-set from the finish painting and despatch area. This was ultimate engineering to me at the time, I was in awe filled with excitement and enthusiasm to join a work force of some one hundred and fifty personnel. The toilet facilities, changing rooms and 'tea room' were clearly segregated and contained wall plaques painted with the words whites, coloureds and blacks. It's strange how our black work colleagues and black people in general were referred to as Africans as if we were not the same white and coloured Africans, indigenous to Africa. I could not work that one out and wondered if anyone else could. My friend Stanley Woodend was the only coloured qualified Boilermaker on the shop floor at the time and he was proud of it and proved to all to be a highly skilled able tradesman. I worked diligently too in my job role and gained mastery over the machine operating it with great skill to the satisfaction of my employers. Due to the address of Morewear, down Khami road, I had to find more practical accommodation and so moved from Barham Green to board with a wonderful lady Mrs Mary Manuel in a flat in Fort Street between second and third avenue. I shared a room with her two sons Vincent and Victor Manuel together with my primary school friend Winston Gallegher. Winston and Vincent were my very close friends at the time and Vincent was the one who introduced us to his mother who kindly welcomed us. Vincent worked on the Rhodesia Railways as a Shunter and Vincent was a Plasterer in the building trade so, we all had secure jobs. Life was great, weekends were filled with adventure, smoking, drinking and partying was the regular thing and we very often over indulged. We were a happy peace-loving bunch until one day a large contingent of Police invaded our accommodation during early parts of a Sunday morning. They obviously thought otherwise on that occasion. We had just come from a dance hall session at Barham Green probably around

3.o'clock in the morning and had gone to bed in an intoxicated state only to be woken by shouting and banging noises from the Police at around 5' a.m. We were in a daze wondering what had happened and what we were being arrested for. We were promptly handcuffed and driven to Bulawayo central Police station. We realised that the Police had surrounded the building to prevent any attempted escape. We were subsequently booked in, stripped of our belongings, searched and escorted into different cells. We were not charged with any crime, it became apparent though that we were suspected of carrying out some heist, a gang robbery and hence imprisoned whilst further investigation was being carried out. We were in shock, and instantly sobered up trying to make sense of it all. I was thrown into a cell which already held ten black guys. It seemed that there was no apartheid at that moment, there were no separate cells designated Blacks and coloureds. We were put all together in one holding cell sharing one toilet hole, it was a humiliating experience. I refused to eat the meagre meal they supplied. Eventually we were released around 3.o'clock that afternoon to be told it was a case of mistaken identity and false information from our accusers. We were once again free to return home a little dishevelled and humbled.

That Monday proved to be a new week for new experiences and soon our negative experience was in the past and forgotten. I must comment here that the Police were highly feared during those days, we always viewed them with great respect and fear as respect for authority was instilled in us as kids and so it was the accepted culture of the day. We once again resumed our normal activities of work, partying over weekends and drinking at our favourite pub 'the Skittle Inn'. We were mobile as our friend Vincent owned a car, I was only an unskilled machine operator at the time so could not afford one. This was my life for some months until I received a brown envelope stamped with a government of Rhodesia mark. It was my military 'Call-up' papers informing me to report to Llewellin Barracks, situated in Bulawayo North Province, in the month of August of 1974. A full-scale guerilla war had been raging since 1967 but was fought in the rural areas between a combined guerilla army of Zanla and

Zipra forces on one side against the Rhodesian armed forces on the other. City life throughout the country was not affected, people continued with their daily activities, they went to work as normal, children went to school, weekends were normal like any country in the world. Tourists from other lands did not have a clue of what was actually occurring. The country was a very popular destination for mainly British, American and South African tourists. It was as if there was no conflict. My Bosses soon required that I train others to operate the Profiler as my conscription was for a twelve-month period that would run consecutively from August 1974 to August 1975. I did not give it much thought at the time as this was a common arrangement for all white and coloured men from eighteen years and above. Ours was a forced conscription whilst black men joined the Rhodesian army by choice. They were assigned to the 'Rhodesian African Rifles regiment, a regiment formed in may 1940 in the British Colony of Southern Rhodesia. It was a paradox, I often thought, that this regiment would be engaged, during the liberation war, against their own kith and kin on the Guerilla Forces side. Perhaps the reasons were contractual or purely out of Job necessity. The white boys were assigned to either the Rhodesian Light Infantry or Selous scouts regiments. We were, on the other hand, conscripted to form the first Coloured protection company C.1. Prior to that all coloured men were conscripted into the Transport and Supplies Regiments at the beginning of the war. With regards to our Jobs; all jobs were secured by Government legislation, we received our salaries from both our employers and from the military so, from a financial point of view we were well remunerated. So, began my next chapter.

MILITARY CONSCRIPTION - 1967 TO 1980 GUERILLA WAR

Military conscription, the call-up as it was referred to, was a time of excitement and apprehension for most, like coming out of one's manhood culturally speaking. Wearing the military uniform was viewed as glamorous, one suddenly appeared attractive to the ladies for some strange reason. Perhaps it was the well-polished boots, the well fitting berets or G.I. caps, the shiny brass buckles on our belts, well pressed, in some cases, starched camouflage uniforms that did it. The ladies couldn't resist it seemed. It was not the case of going to fight for 'my country' scenario. None of us were into politics nor did we give the reasons much thought, for us it wasn't the case of going to fight for one's country as we were an oppressed people, we were just fun-loving boys and accepted the call-up as part of the whole 'growing up thing', the macho thing all were expected to do when coming of age; military service. We had to have haircuts prior to reporting which proved a disappointing task as it meant the end of our well-groomed afro hair styles which was the fashion in the seventies. I packed my bags with a change of clothes and included some toiletries as I thought necessary. I was ready and reported to Llewellin Barracks in Bulawayo. A military base just a few kilometres from Bulawayo off the Bulawayo to Salisbury / Harare road. I reported as required promptly early on a Monday morning. This was the day of all days, the day that was always spoken of in the streets, the day of reckoning, the day to prove one's manhood.

The day was abuzz with activity, we arrived in different modes of transport, train, buses, taxis and cars some from afar as Umtali (Mutare), Salisbury (Harare), Que Que (Kwe Kwe), Gwelo (Gweru), Sinoia (Chinoy) Fort Victoria (Masvingo), Shabani (Zvishavane) and elsewhere. It was interesting to note that some of us came from the same school, Founders High School in Bulawayo and others from Morgan High school in Salisbury / Harare. My close friend Bernard, my all-time neighbour from primary school days was there too. He was there to protect me it seemed, my bodyguard, as he always did when I was in primary school. I felt safe, safe from an unknown enemy. Bullying was rare in those days, the culture was one of respect and friendships, we greeted each other as expected as if we were of a kind of species, like dogs that sniff each other in greeting, even if we didn't know each other it was the typical cultural hospitality, 'a love of strangers' that we were accustomed to and learnt by observation as kids. It was typical of the African spirit, I guess, the hospitable nature that I witnessed as a kid. Our welcome from our Military Instructors, from hardened experienced soldiers, was a stern one, no smiles, no handshakes, just commands that were screamed at us. It was an awakening! Roll call was swift. We were soon marched in single file to the barracks to obtain our uniforms, the complete kit; from underwear to socks, boots and kit bag. The first day was a scary introduction. We soon learned that our Instructors were not our friends, we were not on the road to Tipperary as the song goes; this was a road to uncertainty. The day went fast. We were fed, medically examined and allowed to rest for the rest of the day in preparation for a vigorous three weeks program of training. The normal training time frame for Rhodesian soldiers, in general, was about three to four months ours was a condensed program of three weeks. It was a gruelling schedule, a vigorous program not for the faint hearted literally speaking. It began early in the morning. The Instructors would shout wake up calls. We had no alarm clocks to go by; they were our alarm clocks. We were soon divided into four Platoons of around thirty plus men to form the total company of some one hundred and twenty soldiers.

Training included, weaponry, shooting rifle range marksmanship, attack mode target practice, assault course, map and compass reading. We were taught how to disassemble, clean and reassemble our rifles in quick time, and being told repeatedly to view our rifles as our 'wives' or 'girlfriends' in terms of taking care of them and being with them at all times as they would mean our very lives in battle. Grenade throwing was also included as part of the weaponry training. Some of us were, at a later period, given specialist training as Military vehicle Drivers, Medics and radio operators, "Pronto's",as we were called. We were not trained in hand-to-hand combat techniques, we assumed this was because the war was not a conventional one but a guerilla war, out in the rural bush areas fighting an invisible enemy. The days were crammed with activity from waking in the morning until bedtime. Time frames for the various activities were well planned and strict. Forty press ups was the norm each morning only to be grilled later in the day by completing the 'Assault Course' - a trail combining running and exercising. It really turned us from boys to men in a short time. Breakfast, lunch and dinner times were observed timeously and were often deliberately disrupted by our Instructors. At times you just about got a mouth full, when we were 'screamed at' that breakfast or lunch was over. We soon learned to eat quickly with less conversation as we never knew when we would be told to stop eating. I must admit though, that we were well fed, the menu was varied and of awesome quality; pure home grown organic. Rhodesia had a thriving agriculture in those days, we had an abundance of food with the surplus produce being exported to neighbouring countries. Our grain silos were overflowing, it was like the land of 'milk and honey' Africa's BreadBasket metaphorically speaking. In between the military lectures and practical demonstrations we engaged in strenuous physical muscle building exercises and stamina. We either marched or trotted, 'doubling up' as it was called, from activity to activity whether to and from meals as well, as uncomfortable as it proved to be. We never walked, we marched or jogged everywhere. That was our daily routine, trotting about in two or three aligned rows. We eventually learned to march in sync, parade style. The only respite was during lectures and bedtime of which was at times short lived as we were awakened in the middle of the night to be doubling-up around the barracks as and when the Instructors thought fit just for their amusement. Our training also included a particular way of bed making, the triangular corner fold of the bed sheets and the way they were to be tucked under the mattress. Inspections were regular so as to maintain order and tidy barracks. All this vigorous training paid off at the end as we were then ready, confident and most of all physically fit as twenty-kilometre full kit marches were proving to be second nature.

We did have some funny episodes at times, I recall one particular incident at the rifle range, shooting target practice range. There was this fellow by the name of Cloete who was positioned next to me on my left side. We were on our bellies with our rifle butts secured against our shoulder blades firing away at the target some distance away. The doppies, or bullet casings, would automatically eject during the shooting process, this was of course, normal and we had been made aware of it but somehow my 'friend' Cloete had not paid attention. He obviously sees these casings being ejected and he decides to put his leg up as a signal to the instructor. The Instructors were of different ranks from Corporal to Sergeant, staff Sergeants and Sergeant Majors, all white, tanned muscular bodies, chiselled faces with interesting moustaches. I think my artistic eye perhaps made me naturally observe, in detail, their appearance. Their camouflage shirts were always well pressed tucked-in their underpants, as we were taught, creating a crease free bodily contact. Ironically, I still do that at times showing just how embedded our training has proved to be. The Instructor then calls us to stop firing and walks up to Cloete and says to him "what's the problem soldier"? Cloete replies "Sir!! I am firing towards the target but, how come the bullets are falling next to me?" We roared with laughter only to hear the Instructors' loud mouthed rant in response in the most colourful language of the day. Cloete proved to be the joke of the day and many days thereafter. Such occasions were taken on the chin by all without feeling offended.

We were afforded some time off on weekends to enjoy the company of visitors and to listen to a radio program called ' Forces Requests' where greetings from loved ones were aired with the accompaniment of music. It was a very popular radio program throughout the war years enjoyed by all the Rhodesian military forces. Another, not so funny incident occurred on one Sunday. I cannot recall whether this was the first Sunday during our training or some other Sunday when we were required to attend a church service conducted by a certain Army Chaplain by the name of Rajah who was from an Indian ethnic background. I mention his ethnicity as it was rather unusual at the time to have a church Minister of that background. I recall that some of us, in our Platoon, declined not to attend as we viewed the service as incompatible with what we were being trained to do. The question we were considering was, How can God be said to be with us when we are being trained to take a human life? Were not the other side, the guerilla Forces the so called 'terrorists' as they were referred to also being told the same thing and if not, did they not also experience an episode of conscience? Rhodesia, now Zimbabwe, a predominantly Christian Country at the time and still is today so both sides of the conflict claimed to be Christian or belonged at least to some other religion such as Islam and Hinduism. What happened to the Christian tenets taught by our Lord Jesus of Love thy neighbour, the golden rule, and the sixth commandment "Thou shalt not murder" or the sacredness of life I wondered? This issue became a dilemma of conscience for me and others. I recall that there were two or three boys who were Seventh day Adventists who refused to carry a rifle, a stand I thought was rather odd a compromise in my view. We soon realised that our refusal to attend the service was not taken lightly by our Instructors as we were subsequently severely punished by over-the-top physical exercise for having the audacity to refuse to attend. The end result was that some literally succumbed through sheer exhaustion and we eventually succumbed and attended the service to their satisfaction. For me, it was just a physical presence as I was not spiritually engaged. I felt that the whole thing went against the grain of my conscience, nevertheless the incident was soon a past event and forgotten. I did discover, though, in my later years that there was one Christian denomination that remained neutral and refused to participate in this conflict. I shall expand on this in my later chapter. The day of our deployment soon arrived, we were fully kitted out, backpacks, kit bags, full webbing and of course our 'wives' the automatic weapons and boxes of munitions. I did notice though, that our weapons were different from the white soldiers, ours were named S.L.R's (self loading rifle) and Bren submachine guns and that theirs were FN's (Fabrique Nationale) of similar configuration but different. The FN;s had a snout, which looked similar to a short silencer, at the end of the barrel and ours had some curious evenly spaced elongated slots approximately 50 mm long around the barrel. Both rifles carried a twenty-round magazine. Our webbing too was of substandard World War two kind with metal water bottles whereas theirs was of modern design with padded over shoulder straps and plastic type water bottles, obviously lighter in weight, located in a webbing pouch. I clearly recall my thought pattern then; I couldn't help thinking whether this was another example of racial bias where we were viewed as not deserving of the best kit being classed as some sort of inferior second-class soldiers to be given inferior weapons and webbing. If that was a full-scale conventional war we would have been 'cannon fodder' as I truly believe we received inadequate training, I thought it not possible to condense three to four months of normal training to three weeks and still do it justice, of the same quality and substance. I think apartheid just made us conscious of these differences and it created, in my view, this childish concept of comparisons. We were eventually given the upgraded padded webbing with plastic type water bottles in the later years when we did post National Service call-ups sometime around end 1975 to 1979. We completed our training as scheduled and had a passing out parade proudly marching in sync for the public, fully kitted and ready. The Seventh day Adventist boys were given no choice but to carry a weapon too. I clearly recall Major Jardine, a short well-built man with golden brown moustache, our commander in chief making it clear to them, during one of his final lectures, that they were going to be deployed with us with or without weapons.

We were soon on the road in convoy to our assigned destination Mount Darwin and Bindura locations north east of Salisbury (Harare) some 522 kilometres from Bulawayo, a journey of around seven plus hours. A convoy of some thirty trucks or so. We were totally exhausted, physically and mentally when we arrived, not only from the strain of sitting on steel military type benches on the trucks but also from fear of the unknown in rural territory we had never visited, the dreaded landmines were of concern. Fortunately; we made it without incident. We camped for the night at Mount Darwin and the next day proceeded on our journey to our final destination in Ruwa where a base camp had been constructed in advance for our abode. That remained our base camp for the duration of my National Service the entire 12 months until August 1975.

The Ruwa base camp was situated on a small hill outcrop which gave us some protection and advantage against attack. It was fully kitted out with a barracks, ablution block, kitchen, canteen, radio communications room, medical facility, helicopter landing pad and our captain's quarters. There was also sufficient surrounding area for equipment storage including military vehicles, ammunition storage, water bowsers and a separate exercise and parade area. Our exercises included daily physical fitness training and upkeep with random 'Stand two's' callouts, which were perimeter guard duties at specially designated posts. We were self-sufficient, well fed and satisfied.

Our main role as a 'protection' company was to look after government Civil Engineering equipment and facilities together with protecting the workforce. At times we were deployed to look after the 'protected' fenced off villages. In reality this was a military control stance to monitor the movement of the villagers. We were deployed in a cyclic arrangement platoon by platoon and section by section, a section comprising six or seven soldiers, in different sites all around Bindura and Mount Darwin, a town in Mashonaland Central Province in north-eastern Rhodesia / Zimbabwe. My soldier job role was a Signals pronto. A radio operator reporting to base camp and receiving and transmitting communications from base camp and from and to one another as per assigned call-signs. HQ was call-sign Zero. Whenever we rotated back to base camp a number of us Signal men were deployed to man the Relay Station located some distance away on the highest hilltop. We were flown to and fro by open helicopters we nicknamed "Choppers" to spend a week at a time. Sometimes we were left there for two weeks when circumstances demanded it. We had ration packs and sufficient water in twenty litre Jerry cans. I still remember with such clarity the daily ration packs which typically comprised tins of Fray Bentos, we called

Bully Beef, beans, powder form mashed potatoes, orange juice, salt and sugar sachets. At times we purchased mealie-meal and vegetables from the surrounding village shops. Some chaps brought their own spices like curry powder to flavour the bully beef. The signal Relay station was varied. There were quiet days which we spent lazing about and then there were challenging occasions when we relayed 'contact' information, a contact being a description of the shootouts, military engagements between the Rhodesian and Guerilla forces on the ground. The relays involved passing information between the Rhodesian forces on the ground to headquarters based in Mount Darwin in an effective, accurate and timeous way in order to be promptly acted upon. It was as a result of such effective and prompt action on one occasion that I was awarded the Lance Corporal single stripe which I was proud of. We were flown down in an exchange arrangement as scheduled by helicopter on completion of our assigned tasks each week. It used to be quite an occasion, feeling relieved and exhausted to be back at base camp. The first thing we did was get into a hot shower to cleanse ourselves, getting rid of the one / two weeks filth and stink of which we were so accustomed to that our noses didn't seem to work, as we could not smell ourselves. You might, right now, be thinking, other than that, did you experience any close encounters, attacks or unusual incidents and dare I say occasions of relaxation and fun?. Yes! There were such occasions.

There was one occasion when we were camped at a place called Dotito. It was a calm night. Our military truck was parked in between thick bushes and camouflaged; completely out of sight. There were eight soldiers. We slept in a dugout 'V' apex shaped tent as was the norm. My spot, as pronto (signalman), was at the front of the open tent with the signal radio placed just behind my head. Our rifles were always at our side as we were trained: cocked, safety clipped, and ready for engagement. The night was calm. Typical of a tropical climate; warm. The star-studded sky and moon were a welcoming canopy over us. We felt like we were protected by the Almighty. My friend and schoolmate Clarence Bosman, our truck driver, was on guard duty at the time of this incident. Clarence was a very entertaining chap, we were often in stitches with laughter. He was of slim build: handsome with such a smooth complexion that never needed shaving. We always wondered about that. He had a peculiar way of speech with a bit of a stammer but was gifted with a very fun-loving personality. He was nicknamed Kobaas from school days. I never knew what the word meant or who for that matter gave it to him in the first place. It just suited him. Anyway, he was on guard duty that night at a particular time. We did two hourly shifts as per the norm. The next thing we heard was this hair-raising scream " snaaaaake!!!" and I immediately felt a thud on my chest. Apparently the snake: a six foot black mamba or cobra, had made its way along the top piece of tree trunk that supported our tent at its apex. Clarence was seated probably about a metre away from it when he suddenly turned his head to be confronted face to face with it hence the sudden scream which caused the snake to fall off in fright and somehow landed on my chest. My reaction was instant. I literally flung my blanket together with the snake and jumped out of the tent at great speed. My fellow 'sleeping' comrades also vacated the tent in quick succession behind me. We spent the rest of the night at the back of our military truck. As soon as it became dawn, we hunted down the snake only to discover that it had crawled under the base sheet of our tent. We eventually shot it dead when it came to view. We felt a sense of relief. We retrieved it from its hiding place, lifted it up as if it was some trophy to be displayed with pride and discarded it like a piece of trash. A snake in African culture is no pet, it's a creature to be destroyed. Perhaps this dislike of snakes has always been a mindset from the Biblical account of Adam and Eve who were deceived by 'the snake'. The experience was somehow leaked to our resident military commander, Colonel John Parker who was based in Mount Darwin. We understand, on feedback, that he viewed the incident with some humour and as a waste of rounds (Bullets). Whenever I have relayed this story to colleagues and to my own children it has been viewed with horror and with expressions like "What!!!" To me it has been just another incident in my life's journey, absolutely terrifying it was though.

The realisation of the reality of the war came to me on two occasions. The first one was when we were in a small convoy of three or four trucks heading to Mount Darwin from our base camp in Ruwa. We were either being deployed there in convoy as a replacement Platoon or to obtain replenishment supplies. I was on the last truck and suddenly we heard this deafening loud bang followed by a plume of dust and smoke which obscured the vision of the truck immediately in front of us. We all shouted "de-bus"! A military term to 'get off the vehicle'. We had trained for this occasion several times so we knew exactly what to do and what positions to take on the ground in preparation to face a possible ambush. The reality of the scene became evident once visibility had returned when the dust settled. The front truck had hit a landmine on its rear wheels. We were fortunate as all were unharmed. We lived to tell the tale.

The second incident is a situation that occurred when we were based in Mount Darwin headquarters. A message had been conveyed to us that a net load of 'terrorist' bodies was displayed on the slab. As you probably know dear reader one man's terrorist is another man's freedom fighter hence for the majority in Rhodesia these were Freedom fighters who had met their sacrificial death in the hands of the Rhodesian military. The slab was an area of concrete in proximity to the military base used to display dead bodies to shock and awe the public. This was the reality of war, dear reader, no niceties but just plain horror. The Rhodesian military would do this from time to time and would forcefully arrange for the villagers to view as a warning to them as if to say, "you mess with us, this is what will happen to you." A number of us decided, out of curiosity, to tag along with other soldiers to view, a decision I have regretted ever since. The memory has become hard wired, indelibly marked like a branding iron in my brain till this day. It is a memory so vivid in my mind as I am writing at this moment in time, some forty-eight years later. The incident brought home 'man's inhumanity to man' a consequence of his greed and twisted ideology. There are no heroes in war as far as I am concerned. I kind of felt a dread regarding the automatic rifle I was holding, its sheer destructive capability. The horror of it all caused some in my platoon to refrain from eating meat for some time. At the end of it all I swore to myself never again to satisfy such a negative curiosity.

Other than this incident we had occasions of enjoying a party atmosphere at our assigned base camp whether in Mount Darwin or Ruwa. We had occasions to enjoy a drink and to share our stories with much humour as we developed close friendships.

Racial segregation in the military, this apartheid ideology, was evident everywhere we went. The higher-ranking officers were all white soldiers, mixing across the racial divide was not practised even in war. An example in mind was on one occasion when we were deployed in Mount Darwin. We soon discovered that the Army; the Rhodesian Light Infantry command, would bus-in white girls from Salisbury / Harare on weekends as entertainment for their soldiers. Entertainment that included alcohol and music, a kind of dance floor scenario. On this particular occasion we requested to join the party. After all, we were supposed to be in it together, only to be told in no uncertain terms that we were not allowed as this was a 'Whites Only' engagement. I must give credit at this point to Colonel John Parker who was the resident commander at the time who, when informed of our complaint, gave the direction, the order, a command, to allow our attendance. We developed great respect for the man from that day on as he went against the current grain to view us as equals. As a result of his action on that day Colonel Parker was often invited for special curry lunches whenever he visited our base to give us a morale boosting 'pep' talk. He would drop in by helicopter each time. His visit was like a celebrity homecoming event every time. He maintained this special relationship with our unit right to the end of our National service in 1975.

The end of our one year's National Service time soon arrived. We were relieved and excited to return to civilian life once more. We were soon in convoy, the long road home to Bulawayo. Our excitement was soon to be dampened by an unpleasant racially motivated incident en route. We stopped at a small town called Enkeldoorn to enjoy some freshly made, hot fish and chips at a particular restaurant. We debussed from a convoy of military vehicles having parked just opposite the restaurant in full view of the all-white attendees, patrons at the venue. We assumed that they would at least cheer us or display friendly greetings; after all we were engaged in a war to maintain and support their privileged lifestyles, a situation we did not agree with. To our dismay we were told, as we entered the restaurant, that Coloureds were not allowed in and that we would only be served through a small hatch, aperture, behind the restaurant's kitchen, the 'back door' as it were. Yes, a shocking incident, the sheer audacity of it all! We, as usual, accepted our plight although we were angered by the callus approach: we were too hungry to cancel our patronage. We paid for our meal, hopped on our trucks and made our way home feeling rather dejected and rejected simply for being the 'wrong' colour; non-white. We were dismissed as irrelevant folks.

We had done our stint. 12 months of military service had come to its end, we were looking forward to getting back to civilian life, to our jobs, families and friends. For me it was the beginning of another chapter, I needed to find new accommodation as my two closest friends Winston Gallagher and Vincent Manuel had died in a tragic motor car incident some months earlier. We all lived together with Mrs Manuel, Vincent's mother, a pleasant, lovely lady who took Winston and I in as her extended family. She accommodated us without prejudice and always treated us fairly, she made our stay comfortable, it was our second home at the time. The reality of their death hit home as soon as I arrived. I was alone, sleeping in an empty bedroom. As we had shared the rather large bedroom together, I was met with four walls of silence every night. It was an unbearable experience. I replayed that day in my mind over and over again, it was like a stuck record continuously repeating the same lyrics.

The tragic incident took place during one of my rest and recuperation weekends. Our national service afforded us two weeks rest and recuperation, termed R and R, after every two months of service throughout our year's service. These were always exciting times to visit our families to do the things we did, the free flow of alcohol, the partying, the music and the great friendships. It was back to the old adage, wine, girlfriends and song scenario as the saying went. You see, I too had a girlfriend in Salisbury / Harare at that time prior to meeting my beloved wife, so I had arranged to visit her that weekend which happened to be the last weekend of the two week R and R break. It was a Saturday evening that I was to catch my return train to Salisbury / Harare at 9: 00 p.m. sharp. It was a pre-booked date. I had packed my Kit bag and placed it in the boot of Vincent's car without him knowing, a bright red immaculate zephyr zodiac Mk 3, that he was so proud of. We went, as usual, to our favourite drinking den, The Skittle Inn on thirteenth avenue to play darts and enjoy the usual alcoholic binge prior to attending the Saturday night Dance session. You see, I had a close circle of friends namely Winston Gallagher and his brother Burns, Billy Armstrong and his brother Patrick, Vincent Manuel, Lewis Rhodes, Reginald Francis and Hubert Lees. At around 8:30 pm I asked Patrick to drive me to the Train Station which was really a stone's throw away from the pub. They all tried to persuade me to stay and party with them, but I was determined to go as I had to report back to the Military on the following Monday. We said our goodbyes, not knowing that that would be the last time I would see both Winston and Vincent alive. The terrible accident occurred that night around 2:30 a.m. after the end of the Barham Green Dance session which usually ended at 2 a.m. most weekends. The precise spot was at a 'Y' junction at the beginning of the Bulawayo city centre coming from Barham Green direction. It appeared that Winston, who happened to be the driver that night, failed to negotiate the junction at high speed and the car smashed into traffic lights or embankment or some other obstruction killing both himself and Vincent. The other passengers, Billy Armstrong and Reginald Francis survived, Billy with a fractured hand and Reginald with a severe head injury of which he was never the same again. The rumour had spread to Salisbury / Harare the very next morning, which was a Sunday. My girlfriend at the time thought it was me having heard the name Francis mentioned however that was referring to Reginald Francis who had been injured not killed. It could have been me though, without any doubt, on that occasion as I would have been seated at the front next to Vincent which was usually my seating position whenever we drove somewhere. The car back then did not have a separate front passenger seat, it was just one elongated seat, seat belts were not part of the necessary vehicle safety equipment either during those days. The full impact of the death of my two friends only hit home when I had completed my national Service and returned to civilian life. It took me a long time to overcome the emotional impact of this tragedy, for these were my brothers. We lived together, ate together, drank together and went everywhere together. We were inseparable. That bond was suddenly broken, taken away from me on that occasion. This tragedy happened sometime in March of 1975 as I later learned, that the car, a red Zephyr Zodiac MK 3, was on display at the Bulawayo Trade Fair Police stand as a deterrent, a warning to the public, against drunk driving. Their vehicle on display looked like a discarded squashed piece of newspaper, a terrible sight. I do not know right until this day how Billy and Reginald came out alive, apparently, they were flung out during the momentum of it all.

On completion of my Military National service I returned to civilian life, to my normal job at Morewear Industries Bulawayo. The war continued and I was drafted back, as all others were, into service on 60-day call-ups every three - six months. It was during these regular call-ups that a number of negative experiences occurred, two of which were of my own doing and the other three were unforeseen tragedies. The first one I shall relate involves my dear brother Clement. He was recruited soon after me to do his twelve months national service as part of Intake C4 Protection Company. The sad thing is that the military slapped his company with a six-month extension just days before they were to complete their service, pass-out as it was termed. This inconsiderate deplorable act by the military destroyed my brother and others for the rest of their lives. A number of them developed mental health issues almost immediately that's how badly they were affected. I came to that realisation when I completed a sixty-day call-up and was at Cranborne Barracks in Salisbury / Harare to be discharged. As soon as we were discharged, I heard a rumour amongst fellow soldiers that there was a prisoner that was handcuffed and in leg irons ready to be despatched to detention barracks on insubordination charges. We searched for the prisoner out of curiosity and found him secured to a tree just outside the office of our resident Sergeant Major named Thomas. To my horror I soon discovered that the prisoner was my own brother Clement. I was perplexed not knowing what to make of it. I walked up to him to enquire about his situation only to be met with a blank expressionless unrecognising stare. It seemed that he did not recognise who I was. He had this fearful countenance as if he was experiencing some hallucinogenic episode. I immediately knew that something had gone wrong with my brother, he had literally lost his mind. No one seemed to be aware of his condition; just me, they just could not see beyond the external countenance that this was a soldier, a man, in distress and crying out for help. I decided to have a word with Sergeant Major Thomas who fortunately was at his desk at the time. He allowed me an audience and listened attentively as I described what I was observing and I knew my brother and at that moment that was not him, the brother I knew, a gentle soul, soft spoken and unassuming. I went on to explain my interpretation of the situation and requested that he be seen by a doctor to ascertain his mental status prior to their decision to send him to detention barracks. Sergeant Major Thomas, to his credit, agreed to immediately look into the matter. I left it at that, trusting that he would carry out his word and left, once again back to civilian life. I soon learned that the Army had subsequently given him a dishonourable discharge after diagnosing that he had developed a mental disorder, schizophrenia. They discharged him without any care nor support for his condition which, in my view and that of others, as there were a number of other young men who had suffered the same fate, was the most uncaring callus move, the insensitivity of it all to use and dump humans like literal bags of garbage.

The end result was that my brother caused havoc in and amongst the residences around Saint Martins, Arcadia and Vietnam 'Coloured folk' suburbs in Salisbury / Harare. My other brother Billy who resided in Saint Martins at the time organised for Clement to be taken by the Police and despatched to a mental hospital in Bulawayo. My girlfriend Mary told me at the time that he had also smashed one of their windows to their property in Vietnam. That is how we discovered what had happened to him after being discharged. Sometime later I contacted Mr Greenland, a representative of the Coloured community in Bulawayo including my ex primary school headmaster Mr Levi Mayers to see whether we had a case against the military. To their credit they raised the issue with the Army and we received a response practically 'a washing of the hands' a refusal to acknowledge their responsibility. The fact that the additional inconsiderate increase of my brother's National service time from 12 months to 18 months given just two days before they were due to be discharged, resulted in his, including some of his fellow colleagues, terrible mental breakdown from which they never fully recovered. The Army concluded that his schizophrenia was 'hereditary' and not as a result of their action. A claim that had no basis as there was no evidence of such an occurrence in my family line. Mr Mayers advised that pursuing a lawsuit against the Government would be a no win expensive fruitless endeavour. That was the final blow, no justice for my brother and for others who had suffered the same. Their lives were ruined forever. All these unfortunate young men, although they experienced bouts of improvement from time to time, always relapsed and returned to the hospital, the mental asylum Ingutsheni Hospital as it was called back then. My brother's life was destroyed by his military experience. He was never the same again. The burden was left on his family, on us, to care for him right up until his death in 2002 at the young age of 47. Life continued as I had to cope with my brother's condition through to my next mishap episode. Mary moved to Bulawayo around 1977 and we shared a Flat in Denham Court at the corner of Fife Street and First Avenue. The first risky, thoughtless incident was when I was deployed in the Nkayi District some one hundred and sixty kilometres north of Bulawayo. I missed Mary so much that when an opportunity came to see her I took it without considering the risk. I was based with a chap called Dale Porter who somehow had managed to bring along his car, a peugeot 404 Sedan. He invited me to come along with him to Bulawayo on a weekend 'awol' (absent without leave) from our location in the

Nkayi district. This was a risky stance as the road to Bulawayo was usually mined with anti-vehicle explosive devices. It was a dirt / untarred gravel road. Anything could have happened to us! We were undeterred. Seeing our women was worth the risk we thought. We arrived safely in Bulawayo on a Friday evening and I knocked on my girlfriend's door to surprise her. I really don't know how she felt, but her response was just a smile of surprise. Here I was standing at her door with a full military kit, camouflage, hardwear webbing and a loaded weapon. She no doubt thought I was crazy or stupid or both. Fortunately, we enjoyed our weekend together and Dale drove us back on Sunday without incident, arriving back at our location safe and sound to join our other colleagues who had covered for us. It was like we had never left.

The next risky incident occurred when My Brother George visited during his two week R and R (Rest and recuperation) during his eighteen month service, you see, the military had increased the National Service time frame from twelve months to eighteen not long after our intake. At that time my mother had been moved from Sable Vale to Gwanda town. The Rhodesian Government forcefully acquired our land and that of all the land owners, some twenty homesteads for unclear reasons and provided inadequate compensation for the acquisition. I later understood this was for developing a gold mine as there was always a rumour that there were gold deposits in that area and the fact that we used to play on an old gold dump which probably was the original location for Bar Twenty gold mine. The government had then constructed some substandard housing. Unplastered, tiny, two bedroomed dwellings similar to those in New Thorngrove; a 'Coloured' suburb in Bulawayo at the time. The door frames and doors were made from metal and the corrugated roof sheets were of Asbestos cement. That was the apartheid system of substandard housing for all Black indigenous people including people of colour. The money that was paid out, in compensation, by the government was then put in a Trust fund for us five children. Mother was left without any source of income. Her livelihood now depended on our support right to this time of writing as father had passed away in April of 1975. I was still in the military but deployed in Rutenga at that time. We were assigned to protect the railway line by carrying out nightly patrols looking out for any unusual activity, such as placement of explosive devices on the line, whilst at the same time being alert to the 'Hell-run' , an armed vehicle that also patrolled the same line at random times during the night with orders to shoot anything that moved. This was like a death trap. We were like 'cannon fodder' sent against not only our own friendly forces but also against our 'enemy' the guerilla forces. It was shortly thereafter that I received a telegram stating that my father was gravely ill in hospital and that I was urgently required to which the Army favourably responded and I was discharged from that assignment on compassionate grounds to go home for a short leave of absence. It was only many years later in 2018 at our family reunion in Bulawayo that I learned how I had escaped a showdown with the guerilla forces who attacked our section the very next night. Yes, it sounds unbelievable. I couldn't believe it either. The fact that I had escaped yet another close encounter with death once again.

I met up with my brother George as planned and we decided to hire a car to visit mother on his first weekend of his R and R. We took a change of clothing and bought a bottle of 100 pipers whisky to indulge in when we arrived. We were excited about the visit, so we set off promptly on a Saturday morning. George, Brian Edwards, a cousin of ours, and I. I was really an inexperienced Driver at the time having just acquired my driver's licence around November of 1975 but not owning any vehicle, so basically this was my first real driving experience. I remember the car very well, it was a blue Alfasud, Alfa Romeo model.

We arrived safely and spent the day with mother, conversing and enjoying each other's company whilst we boys indulged in our alcoholic drink. It was during this occasion that George told us how he had had a close shave with death by literally an inch. They had been ambushed in Honde Valley along the eastern border of Zimbabwe into Mozambique. The incident happened just when their truck negotiated a bridge across the riverbed then 'all hell broke loose' with an exchange of gunfire. Fortunately, they all escaped unscathed and lived to tell the story and to show me the evidence, a bullet hole at the front of his GI cap just an inch above his head which he proudly wore as if it was some souvenir. By the time evening came we were a little tipsy having had a few so we decided to drive back to Bulawayo to attend a dance session. This was the stupidest and callous idea ever! We were going to risk our lives for song and dance knowing full well that 6.pm to 6.am curfews were in place outside all city centres, and to add to the stupidity of it all there was a military base in Balla Balla now called Mbalabala, a village 66 km south east of Bulawayo. The original name Mbalabala is derived from the Ndebele word for Kudu, a robust well-built antelope type animal grey in colour with menacing vertically twisted horns. The area is known for such animal crossings, but we were not at all afraid. We said goodbye to our mother and drove away excitedly only to crash the car on a bend just twenty kilometres or so from Balla Balla. I can still vividly picture it, George sitting on my left and fiddling with the radio station, it was at this moment in time that I lost concentration, as I was busy worrying about the radio station he was searching for rather than concentrating on my driving and I could have sworn that a dark flash of 'something' crossed the road in front of us, so I swerved the car to avoid hitting that imagined 'something' only to lose complete control of the vehicle. It spun out of control several times and eventually rolled over countless times and ended up some way away from the embankment, ripping the fencing into farmland until it ran out of momentum and finally came to a halt right side up. I recall that at the moment of realisation that we were done for, George and I locked eyes without a word. I literally somehow fitted my body between the steering wheel and the floor pedals whilst George did the same on his passenger side stretching out his hand to the windscreen to prevent being catapulted out of the vehicle. Brian on the other hand lay between the rear seat and the two front seats. When it all ended, we eventually climbed out of the vehicle through the smashed front and rear windscreens. It was sheer good fortune, a miracle if you like, that we survived to tell the story. On leaving the vehicle we walked some twenty kilometres to Balla Balla Police station to report the accident. As we were walking and laughing about the whole callous episode and the fact that Brian searched for his lip-ice, a kind of moisturising vaseline type gel applied to the lips, before asking us how we were, whether we were injured or not. We suddenly heard a military vehicle heading our way towards Gwanda. Our Military training kicked in and we dived for cover on the roadside embankment and lay flat on our bellies with our heads down which saved the day as we were not spotted. I hate to imagine what could have happened had the soldiers spotted us.

We arrived at the police station, reported the incident and were given the necessary paperwork which we completed for insurance purposes. The Constable in charge drove us back to the scene to investigate the details we had provided. On inspection of the car he took one long look at us, shook his head and muttered " how on earth did you blokes get out of this one?" We just shrugged our shoulders. It was frightening: we couldn't believe it ourselves on observation of the irreparable damage done to the car which was eventually written off. The policemen drove us back to Balla Balla to complete his report and let us go. We hitched a ride from there, on the back of a 5-tonne truck, back to Bulawayo and arrived sometime around 9am that Sunday morning battered and bruised covered in dust. Brian and George went their way and once again I knocked on girlfriend Mary's door. Yes, you can imagine the look on her face and all she said was "what happened?" To be honest she only heard the true story many years later. I did suffer, though, from chest pains for some time after that accident and had to go into Mater-Dei hospital for an internal investigation as my ribs had taken a thorough bashing but eventually healed with time. The Doctors found nothing untoward, so I was discharged. The incident was soon forgotten, it was just another story, another experience in my life's journey. Sometime after this incident I moved my mother and siblings from Gwanda to a flat in main street Bulawayo, Derby House until the Land Tenure Act was repealed in 1977. The timing was perfect because we had just qualified to receive our inheritance that had been saved in a Trust Fund when the Government moved our mother from Sable Vale to Gwanda town. This money was paid to us individually on turning twenty one years of age. We used it to purchase our first family home, a home for our well deserving mother, in the suburb of Saurestown not far from the city centre. It was a pretty three bedroomed property with a well lawned front garden but constructed from substandard materials during the second world war. So when the right opportunity arose we sold it and moved mother nearer to Bulawayo city centre where we purchased the final family property namely number 1 Mcintyre Avenue where mother still resides at this time of writing. It was a lovely home, immaculate then. A typical colonial style house well-constructed of normal brick and mortar and situated at the end of the street. A double stand with ample yard space and a swimming pool. We actually purchased it in 1983 from one of my work colleagues at Morewear Industries, a Mr Derby who later immigrated back to England. Mother was thrilled, this was her home where she could put her final stamp and a stamp she did by planting some thirteen, yes! thirteen fruit trees, multiple lemon and mango trees, guava, avocado, apple, orange, peach, paw-paw, narchie / clementines, even banana. It was her paradise and still is although a little run down now due to lack of maintenance. A sad affair brought-on by limited finances, the high cost of living and the decline of the Zimbabwean economy.

My final military stint was sometime early in 1979, I remember that well as it was the time when I contracted malaria on my return to Bulawayo. My girlfriend and I were renting a flat in a block named Alasco directly opposite Ramjis, an upmarket men's clothing store. I am grateful to Doctor Johnson, our family doctor who is now late at this writing, who treated me to full recovery together with my girlfriend who cared for me. It was a frightening experience. We were just immature kids just starting off in life, I lay in bed for three weeks experiencing the most uncontrollable vile body trembles, sweats ever including severe headaches. Fortunately, I recovered in time and did not experience any hallucinations as many have done. Sometime after my recovery I received a final call-up in 1980 just prior to the end of the war that resulted in the Independence of Zimbabwe. I was fortunate to receive an exemption which my employer had applied for on strategic business grounds. I was elated, eventually the war came to an end, it was finally over, everyone celebrated. Many lives had been lost including that of some of my High school friends and sadly that of my brother Philip too who was killed by guerilla forces in October of 1976 whilst working as a Road Supervisor for the Ministry of Roads in Kamativi. An innocent man killed at a young age of 45 years; the tragedy of war. New doors of opportunity were opening, the Colour bar system of apartheid was finally legally, by legislation, dismantled for good but sadly not in the hearts of the hard-wired racists who continued for some time to prevent equal opportunity and made various attempts to stifle integration - by statements such as 'The job advertisement has been filled' or 'the advertised vacant accommodation has been taken'. These scenarios soon dissipated as the economy and political situation progressed. Doors were eventually truly opened.

Base Camp Pub Night 1975

At Miliary Base Camp 1975

My friend Bernard Bell and me 1975

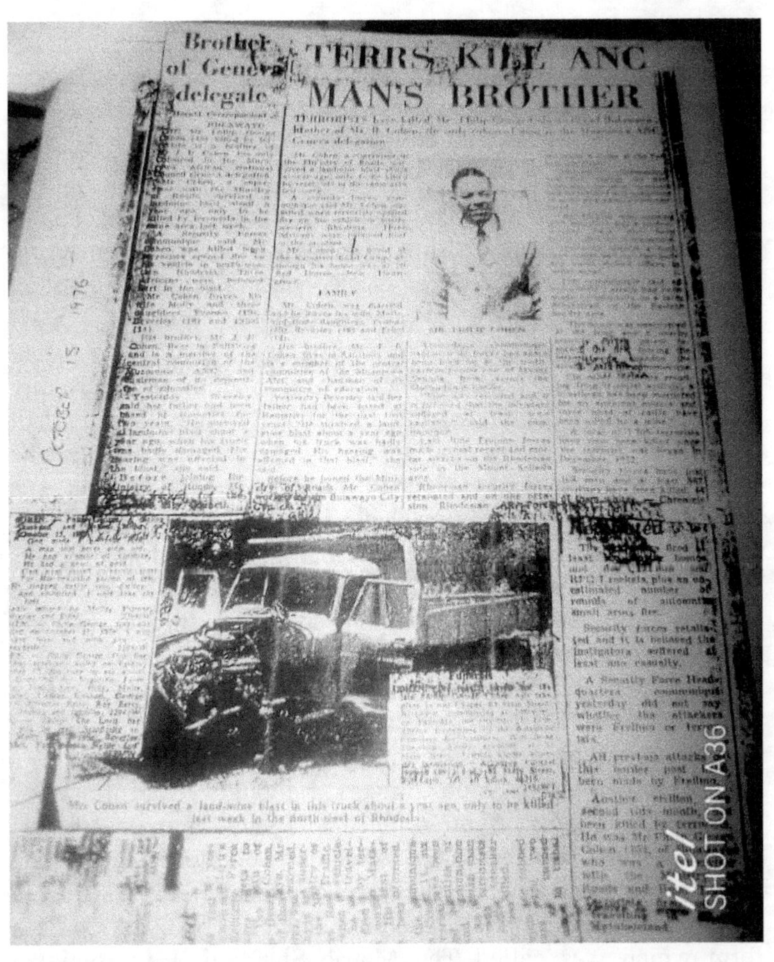

Bulawayo Chronical Philip incident and Joshua report 1976

DOORS OF OPPORTUNITY

When did my first door open? As I have already stated in chapter 5 that first door was finding employment in an engineering establishment called R.E.S.C.CO. (Rhodesian Engineering Steel Construction Company) followed by employment as a Steel Profile cutting Operator at another Engineering company called Morewear Industries in Bulawayo. The third door of opportunity occurred after I completed my National Service at the end of August in 1975. I returned to my employer to find that the colleague I had trained to operate the three headed profiler was still in that position meaning that I had now been permanently replaced. What was I to do? I decided to approach my Works Foreman, Alan Smith, through my friend Stanley Woodend who by then had proved to the company to be a highly skilled and efficient Boilermaker outclassing the rest by far. I asked Stanley to speak with our Works Foreman on my behalf to request an apprenticeship. Stanley proved to be a very highly skilled tradesman and an asset to the business. So, for him to put in a word for me was a good strategy I thought. When Stanley conveyed my request Alan Smith called me in for an interview. I don't recall all the questions he asked me, but I do remember one in particular. He asked me what level of education I had achieved to which I responded that I had completed the first year of sixth form which was called The Matric Standard. He exclaimed "standard six!!" Standard six in those days was the first year of secondary schooling he obviously misheard so I reiterated "No! Form six" He was alarmed "what!" he said and I proudly responded "Yes form six." which was six years of secondary schooling. His surprised response was no doubt due to the fact that most, if not all, apprenticeships back then were white kids who had achieved either a Form two, leaving certificate level, which was the second year of secondary school education, form three being the third year etc. I had now done my best at that interview and patiently awaited the outcome. I think it was some days later that Alan Smith called me into his office. I knocked at his office door and nervously entered head downcast and said a greeting which was the norm "Good morning Mr Smith". He looked up at me and extended his hand in a handshake greeting and congratulated me stating that the company had decided to offer me an apprenticeship as a Boilermaker. This job role terminology was used in Rhodesia, and in Zimbabwe for a time, in South Africa, Australia, Canada and in the United States of America as far as I am aware, however Zimbabwe changed the terminology a number of years later to 'Plater Welder' or Steel Fabricator Welder. This is a more accurate term rather than Boilermaker which appears to just mean one who manufactures Boilers! That was not the case. The role refers to a skilled man who fabricates / builds, from blueprints and sometimes also welds the fabricated steel components and structures and may also at times carry out the installation of such structures. The company would organise my College attendance and training, and guess who they decided would be my best mentor! Yes, my friend Stanley. There are no words to describe how I felt at that moment. I was to be the first non-white apprentice to be signed up to an apprenticeship scheme / program for the first time in the history of Morewear Industries in Bulawayo way back in time in early 1976. It was termed a 'Major Apprenticeship' because I had passed the normal sixteen- to-seventeen-year age group for apprenticeships. I was twenty-three years old then, mature and appreciative. The normal time frame for apprenticeships in those years was five years which included one-year National Service so was effectively a four-year program. There was a provision in the scheme to do a competency practical test termed a Trade Test on completion of three years if one deemed themselves to be capable. These tests were stringent and at times included fabricating complex shapes 'Developments of sheet metal products' although the industry was a Heavy Metal fabrication business. I took the plunge and successfully completed a trade test early in 1979. I was now a qualified Journeyman as the term went, a Boilermaker in late January 1979. Alan Smith had supported me all the way and displayed confidence in me as he observed the complex structures Stanley and I manufactured.

There was no challenge we could not meet, my artistic gift played a major role in my abilities. To me Steel Fabrication was and still is an art which brought me great satisfaction and pride. It was a competitive industry between ourselves on the shop floor to achieve the best results possible; to produce dimensionally accurate components and structures in the shortest time frame. Alan Smith once told me that the apprenticeship officer had conveyed to him that I would make a good Artisan because of my artistic talent. I did not expect such recognition especially from white folks, you see, we had this thing that we were no good and that we were to remain ever Second-Class citizens in every respect. We had to accept our place, and that we would never be viewed as equals. The clear reminders were always in our faces, the ablution block within the company, for example, was signposted 'Whites only,' 'Coloureds' and 'Africans' meaning the black people. I found this term 'African' which was applied only to black people quite odd, after all were we not all Africans!, white, brown and black? Born in Africa and citizens of the continent!! It was just a senseless description in my view.

College attendance was like going back to school but only this time, I meant business. I was determined to achieve the best. To prove that our grey matter,(no matter what colour of skin we have on the outside, we are the same on the inside), part of one human race. Our blood is red too. I passed with flying colours as the saying goes, credits in all subjects and was invited back to do an advanced heavy metal fabrication course on completion of the basic Boilermaker Fabrication Craft Course. Unfortunately, I was not awarded the Fabrication Apprenticeship of the year award for my intake. It was awarded to Vernon, a white boy from Kwe Kwe, he was a friend. He and I had become close and got on well as friends do during our college days. Whenever he faced a challenge or struggled in Technical drawing or whether it was a maths question I helped him as friends do. At one point he even whispered a maths question he was struggling with during our exam to which I provided him the answer without the examiner spotting us. We both passed our Craft course with credits to our common joy. The end result is that he received the Craft Course apprenticeship of the year award. I was happy for him and there were no ill feelings between us. I guess it was expected. After all there was not a single award ever given to non-whites at that time. I think he did not expect to receive the award, because he appeared troubled by his being selected for it. I drew this conclusion from what he said to me. "Francis, you deserved this award more than me". I was humbled and appreciative of his candid and unsolicited remark. It was the ' all white' Examiners and Lecturers that made the decision. I really don't know to this day whether that decision was based on genuine achievement or whether it was a racial bias or both. We parted ways when we completed the college Craft Course in 1977 and I never saw him again. The strange thing was that I was later invited to do the advanced Craft Heavy Metal course which I passed once again with credits. Vernon did not attend this Advanced Course, whether he was invited and declined or not remains an unanswered question till this day. Nevertheless my Employer was pleased with my results and that achievement seemed to set a precedent and opened the doors to other non-white kids including my brother George to join the apprenticeship scheme at Morewear Industries Bulawayo. This was the beginning of a long lasting companionship with my brother George. We were inseparable from that time onwards, we lived together in a rented property for a time, we worked together for many years in Zimbabwe, then in Botswana following that when I returned to Zimbabwe in 1994/5 until we parted ways sometime in 1996 when he moved back to Botswana where he established his expatriate Fabrication Business.

In time some of our black friends, who were initially tradesman's assistants, labourers or 'skill hands' also joined the Boilermaker ranks by being upgraded and trained accordingly. I recall giving two of them, Themba Jubane and Wiggen, who were our work mates, lectures on weekends teaching them the technical drawing skills applicable to the trade for a fee. The two of them were, in time, able to successfully complete Trade Tests and thereafter also qualified as Boilermakers - they became the first Black Boilermakers at Morewear sometime in the early 1980's. I was so pleased for them and overjoyed for having played a part. Life was certainly evolving in a positive way, but we soon realised that the pay structure was not a level field. We were paid less based on racial lines. You see, white folks were always paid higher salaries than everyone else no matter whether one did the same job or whether we were higher skilled or better qualified. I did wonder though, whether such pay structures were determined by the assumed differences in our standards of living. A kind of standard of living index or some sort. That was the unfairness of it all. A revolving door secular reasoning scenario where one lives in substandard accommodation because that is all one can afford while the opposite argument is one is paid less because one lives in such an environment.

Within a month of being qualified in January of 1979 I was promoted to shop floor Chargehand, which was a supervisory role, another milestone in my journey. My promotion, as a non-white came as a total surprise. It was a first, considering that segregation and apartheid laws were in force. This role was no small task because the company employed some one hundred and fifty to two hundred, at least, personnel on the shop floor comprising Boilermakers, Welders, Fitters and Turners, Grinders, Press Brake, Guillotine, Rolls and Drilling Machine Operators, profile cutters, overhead crane Drivers, sandblasters, Spray Painters and general Labourers / Trade hands. Turnover was in the hundreds of tonnes per calendar month of fabricated steel structures and components mainly for the Mining and railway rolling stock sectors. We manufactured hoppers, flue ducts, conveyor systems, steel support structures, steel framed buildings and railway goods wagons. The shop floor was a noisy environment always abuzz with activity. There was money to be made as overtime working was without limits for those that were industrious. Employment opportunities were at their peak during those years. The country was booming as the expression went, life was good. As I have already stated 'The Colour bar' was legally, by legislation finally dismantled at independence on 18th July 1980 when Rhodesia, Zimbabwe-Rhodesia more correctly, became Independent Zimbabwe. Mr Robert Gabriel Mugabe became our first black Prime Minister and thereafter President.

It was then that Mr Mugabe's government declared an amnesty to all white people, they were encouraged to remain to build the country, to thrive along with all other racial groups on an equal footing. There were to be no repercussions for the past wrongs, all was forgiven and to be forgotten it seemed. However, white folks did not see things that way as many 'packed their bags' sold out and left the country in droves making their way mainly to South Africa, Australia and the United Kingdom. Their reasons for doing so were never really clear but we assumed that they were afraid of retribution for their 'sin', a self-developed doctrine of white superiority / supremacy. They unfortunately misjudged or did not believe the true forgiveness that the black majority would extend, as a whole, the welcoming spirit to work together and rebuild, whether their refusal to believe this was due to the propaganda machine of the Rhodesian government was never clear. Nevertheless, they left in droves leaving behind many open doors, beautiful homes. It was like the exodus of the Jews from Egypt. A mixed blessing. Industry had to function and we and those folks that opted to remain picked up the pieces.

The doors included the opportunity to buy property at rock bottom prices, as a direct result of the housing market crash. We could now buy property and live where one could afford by choice, to go for meals at any restaurant, to school our children wherever one could afford, to have the freedom of employment in any skill set or professional field without prejudice. To have the freedom of movement anywhere and anytime without restriction. It's true to say that this began slowly with the repeal of the Land Tenure Act during the Muzorewa, Zimbabwe-Rhodesia, coalition government of 1979 but was not fully implemented as there was still much resistance. We felt like adopted and abused children who now for the first time in their lives came of age and were given the freedom to fend for themselves in an open opportunity environment where only sheer hard work and determination would be the criteria to success and not their background nor the colour of their skin. Just to give one example of the effect this had on us is an occasion early in the 80's. I took my family, my wife and our daughter, as we had only one child then, to the Selborne Hotel in Bulawayo for lunch. We went to the back garden area which was the preferred ideal tranquil environment. It was a lawned space with patron tables and chairs surrounding a common central swimming pool. The poolside pub was located at the rear end. It was a comfortable, welcoming and attractive setting. My first thought was, this is what the 'Colour-bar' system of apartheid kept away from us. It was such a selfish act driven by a white supremacist ideology. This was a typical example of places that were once upon a time reserved for whites only. We were glad of course to be there, to have this opportunity opened to us as and when we wished. We never had such facilities, ours were substandard drinking dens you could say comprising a bar area, a darts area for those keen to play the game and a general seating area. We were debarred from all restaurants. If you wanted a meal, you made sure you ate at home before going out or you bought fish and chips or 'russian' sausages from a cafe on the way. After a night out, during the early hours of the morning we would pass at Dibella Bakery to enjoy freshly baked hot succulent pies. That was our typical weekend situation. I kind of wonder how white folks thought about it all. Did they even consider the selfishness of the apartheid act? Did they ever think of how the deprived majority felt? Did they put themselves in our shoes to try to even understand? What did they think about our black people who were required to carry identity cards / certificates (isitupa in ndebele) and had city area curfews imposed on them after 6pm, namely being prohibited from the city centre and in and around the white only suburbs? Did they think about the inhumanity of it all? I doubt if such thoughts occurred to them. As their deep-seated viewpoint or ideology was no doubt instilled from their childhood, a system of entitlement and white supremacy, indoctrination to the core. A fact I discovered much later as explained to me by an English friend later in my life. Even in the supermarkets and stores and other business services, they were always given first preference, first in the queue, some would cut-in to be served by their own kith and kin ahead of the rest of us who had to just wait our turn. White folks were too aloof, it was beneath them to even permit a black person, their own domestic employees for that matter, to sit in the front seat of their vehicles. This was a rare sight. They would either be designated the back seat or rear end of their pickup trucks. The same scenario that was evident during the colour bar years in the United States when black people were designated seats at the back of the buses. What a life! It was heaven on earth for them as they seemed oblivious to our struggles, both physical and psychological, they had the best schools for their children, the best houses, swimming pools, exclusive clubs and it seemed that the Almighty had even 'blessed them' with the best weather cycle in the world constant sunshine for weekend Braai-vleis / BBQ's. I am not here painting the whole white society with the same brush nor am I angry about it all. I am just saddened by man's inhumanity to man and the fact that we, the deprived at the other end of the spectrum, had no choice but to accept the status quo with quiet dignity or fight for our rights for equal status. The fight did materialise eventually, in a guerilla civil war that took place from 1967 through to 1980 orchestrated by the leaders of the black majority who felt that that was the only way to bring about their self dignity as a people through political change. My late brother Joshua became involved in that struggle but the rest of us remained neutral. We just continued with our lives the best way we could. I wish to point out here that Apartheid also affected some, though few in numbers, in the white community in the sense that they were ostracised, abused or even excommunicated from their own race for having friendships or relationships across the racial divide. How many white fathers would have yearned for the children they fathered but could not live with them for fear of rejection. The system affected everyone; it was like a virus of the mind.

The independence of Zimbabwe on July 18 1980 ended all that. It was a time of celebration and the celebration did indeed come at Harare international Stadium with a capacity crowd of some 70,000 people of which my brother Clement was one of them. They enjoyed the music of the late Bob Marley and the Wailers who were engaged by special Government invitation to entertain the masses. The crowd's favourite songs were titled 'Songs of Freedom' including that of my late brother George's favourite 'The Redemption Song' which seemed to touch the hearts of many on that day and for years to come and rightly so. I wish to conclude this part by stating that many of the white folks who chose to remain in the country after 1980 reaped the benefits and enjoyed the hand of true forgiveness and reconciliation, a hand that was extended to them not only at government level but in our hearts, the non-white majority, the black and brown Zimbabweans. It may be a strange thing to many that we didn't hold any resentment nor feelings of hatred for that matter, we were just glad that it was over. We were in a new era, a time of equal opportunities and open relationships and friendships. There were, though, pockets of resistance at first in the housing and job markets where efforts were made to prevent non white 'infiltration' one could say, but sheer economics eventually directed the countries business future as job vacancies had to be filled and properties occupied hence in time the resistance eased and the fisted hands were slowly unfolded. It was a time for self-determination for individuals to choose their own path in life's journey, their own destiny. For that I became foremost, a pioneer in my field. I believe in the non-white community in Bulawayo as I shall show next.

That opportunity came early in 1980. The manufacturing Inspector of Mashaba and Shabani Mines approached me during one of his visits to Morewear Industries, the engineering establishment I was working for, and advised me that another company that he visits regularly had a vacancy for a Works Foreman and asked whether I was interested. Being a shop floor Chargehand and Inspector at the time, I was his front-end man as it were during his inspection visits. I was rather taken aback as I was not aware of any non-white Works Foreman at any heavy engineering company in Bulawayo in those years and so I thought I would have no chance of being employed as such, but he had confidence that I would. So, I agreed for him to put in his recommendation to which I was invited for an interview almost immediately. The remuneration was attractive, I could not resist as it was literally almost double my salary at the time, a salary that afforded me to buy my first car, a yellow AlfaSud which I was so proud of. It was one of those 'boy toys' which was cleaned and polished everyday to the annoyance of my wife. The company was named General Steel and Construction and the owners were George and Edith Clarkson, a pleasant Scottish couple. The company carried out work for the National Brewery in Bulawayo and the general mining sector. Its main products were various tubular fabrications for the breweries, hot and cold pipe bending, bitumen lined induction bent pipes of 4" to 6" diameter, various Tube Flange manufacture, screw conveyors for the mining industry and other light to medium fabrications. It was interesting technically challenging work considering that we had no computer aided design capability in those days. Everything was manually produced. Complex shapes were drawn, marked out, profile cut and formed by conventional rolling and bending machines. I loved the challenge and I proved to be a vital asset to the business so much so that the company obtained military service exemptions for me throughout that year until the war ended in mid-1980 at the declaration of independence. George was a generous and fair boss and initially treated me with respect, recognizing my skills, skills that he defended to his white business associates who questioned why he had employed me, a non-white, to run his shop floor business. You see, I was the first non-white in that capacity in his company so that seemed to trouble his business partners. His defence was basically that 'the proof is in the pudding'; that I was the right man for the job and well qualified and furthermore the products we produced were of high quality complex components that required great skill and accuracy that met their standards. His opponents had to acknowledge those facts and eventually came round to accepting me. The racial divide was difficult to fathom. The psyche of the racist was a hard one to deal with, as they just would not accept a non-white as being their equal. At first, direct communication with me was taboo in their mindset. George became the middleman to convey their technical requirements to me at shop floor level. Their viewpoint, fortunately, did mellow in time and things became less awkward. George and Edith were certainly non-racist and would invite my family and I to their house each year end, during the December shutdowns, to celebrate the company's achievement, a celebration that included dinner and drinks served around his garden swimming pool. It was a beautiful setting. They lived a life of luxury indeed, which I witnessed first-hand. This was my introduction to the lives that white folks enjoyed. I unfortunately worked for George for only two years as we had a fall out one day over his micromanagement style which I could not handle any longer. I had a different way of doing things than he did and the fact that he was a qualified CopperSmith whilst I was a Boilermaker / Steel Fabricator better suited for the industry. So it was the clash of the Titans you could say as I was firm and confident in my abilities. I always produced products that were dimensionally correct and of good quality so his insistence on his way of doing things was unnecessary I felt. At the end I had had enough. We amicably parted ways and I returned to work for Morewear Industries once again in 1982, going back to basics, as a shop floor tradesman.

The shop floor chargehand at that time was a chap by the name of Crawford; a Farmer and Boilermaker by trade. We knew each other and worked together from when I was an apprentice back in 1976/7. He was a down to earth bloke, his uncle, a Mr Van Vuuren a well-built Afrikaner, Farmer and Boilermaker was the Works Foreman. We got on well and respected each other. They had an unusually good relationship with all the shop floor workers and spoke fluent Ndebele which ability put them in good stead with all the Ndebele speaking black workers thus commanding their great respect. I guess this was typical of the farming communities around the country, as a whole. Its true to say, though that at times the 'K' word (Kaffir, derived from the arabic word kafir meaning - unbeliever or infidel) like the 'N' word (Nigger) both very derogatory terms were readily used in anger against their employees or in general expression of annoyance against black folks. It is ironic for that word ' kaffir' to be applied to black people, who by nature are highly spiritual religious people in general. It's interesting to note too that the probiotic, fermented drink, kefir, note the different spelling, is not commercially sold in South Africa and Zimbabwe, could the similar spelling perhaps be the reason I wonder? Perhaps not, because both South Africa and Zimbabwe have their own in house produced probiotic fermented yoghurt called Amasi. What

I have described so far dear reader may sound unbelievable because we now live in different times, but that was our life, the raw details of our experience. The Inhumanity of it all which has affected many of us deeply, for life:in one way or the other, with some having deep seated feelings of inferiority, the chip on the shoulder scenario, or feelings of superiority depending on which side of the colour spectrum one is, whilst others contend with inbuilt anger and resentment that occasionally surfaces in one way or the other. A case in point that shows just how deeply ingrained racism is. I met a Scottish man who was a fellow Christian 'brother' in France around 2019 who had grown up in Rhodesia and had served in the Rhodesian Army prior to his conversion. We met him and his wife when my wife and I visited her childhood friend who had relocated to Brittany. I mention his nationality because it was uncommon for people of Scottish descent to be racist after all my late uncle Jock Dorward, Uncle George Edwards and one of my ex-employers, the Clarkson's, were Scottish and these individuals did not display any racial bias whatsoever as far as my observation went. However, this fellow Christian related to me how he had grown up and was influenced by the racist attitudes of the apartheid era and how this bias had rubbed off on him but thought he had overcome it during the many years in our Christian Faith; only to have it resurface suddenly on one occasion in France. He went on to relate to me that he had gone to a supermarket to buy some groceries and for some reason the Checker at the till, a black woman, addressed him rather rudely to which he said he immediately uttered the 'K' word in his head without any deliberate prior thought. He said to me "Francis, I couldn't believe what I had just said to myself, the wicked thought that flashed in my head, It nearly came out of my mouth, I had to bite my tongue." Yes, dear reader, that is how deeply all of us were affected by apartheid both the perpetrator and the recipients alike. It is an ongoing inner struggle with oneself.

The country was heading in the right direction after independence until Gukurahundi occurred between the rival national parties, Robert Mugabe's Zimbabwe National Union (ZANU) and Joshua Nkomo's Zimbabwe African peoples Union

(ZAPU) which had originally merged to fight the Rhodesian Front Government of Ian Smith. It seemed that the government of independence in 1980 was threatened by 'dissidents', disgruntled former guerilla forces of ZAPU. This clash occurred from 1982 until 1987 ending when a unity accord and an agreed coalition government was signed between the two rival parties which appeared based on tribal lines, between the Ndebeles and Shona tribes. It's reported that some 20,000 black folks mainly in the rural areas of Matabeleland lost their lives during this time. I became aware of this as it was reported not only in the press but also first hand from individual accounts of fellow workers as one after another took time off to bury their dead relatives. Ironically both the guerilla war of Liberation also referred to as the Second Chimurenga a Shona name which translates as "collective fight" or "Liberation war" and the war against the 'Dissidents' did not affect city life. There was no spillover in the streets. It was as if nothing was going on. It was business as usual for many of us. The ethnic minority including the young were mostly oblivious to it. To them the news reports were just like, ugh! Another passing story; however for the rural folk at the receiving end it was a 'genocide'. Fortunately to the relief of many this period came to an end and once again peace was restored.

I was happy to have returned to the company that afforded me my first opportunity, Morewear Industries. During my first week on returning to work I recall that Mac approached me and made a rather surprising comment. He said "Francis, I hear that you have now become a devout Christian!" I was amazed as to how quickly the rumour had spread. "Yes I have" I said. Of course I was always 'Christian' but in name only having been baptised and confirmed as Catholic in my childhood. I stopped attending church when I left school. I felt that it was irrelevant, unstimulating, and too ritualistic. I had now walked on a new path having been converted and become one of Jehovah's Witnesses in June of 1980 which I proudly declared to him. Mac had noticed the change in me. I was now a different man to the one he knew way back in the mid to late 70's. I think it may have been my quiet countenance, respectful clean speech, a better grasp of the spoken word compared to my previous mostly slang and four letter expressions which was the norm back then, the street and military language of the day. Mac respectfully listened and proceeded to relate to me the persecution and murder of Jehovah's witnesses in Malawi orchestrated by the first president Hastings Kamuzu Banda early in the 1970's. Mac had lived in Malawi during that time in the 1960's to early 70's so had first-hand knowledge about that history. I shall discuss the details of my conversion in a later chapter: the reasons and my dramatic 'calling' experience as the saying goes.

I worked at Morewear Industries until 1987. Within six months of my return, I was promoted to Section Foreman along with Mr Crawford. His uncle Mr Vanvuuren was now production Manager. The arrangement worked well as the business was a buzz with major contracts which included the upgrading of Hwange / Wankie (old Colonial name) Power Station comprising some 1500 Tonnes, at least, of steel Flues, Ducts, Hoppers, and structural steel support frames designed by Babcock Africa; a subsidiary of Babcock International a UK based Engineering business. My main focus was on the technical supervision and inspection of all the manufactured steelwork to ensure dimensional accuracy and quality. It was during this employment that I decided to do a correspondence course in Structural Engineering with a London based home study college. I felt I was now a little stagnant as the trade was becoming saturated so I wanted to further my engineering knowledge and scope. My great appreciation goes to Mr Van Vuuren, my Production Manager at the time who supported me throughout and permitted me to do the course whilst at work as long as it did not jeopardise the quality of and the delivery timeframes of the project in hand. I was over the moon as this would not interfere with my family life. The course took me six years to complete to obtain a Diploma in Structural Steel and reinforced concrete engineering.

The next surprising door opened to me in 1985. I was suddenly called into the office by the then General Manager Graham Bryce and the Contracts Manager Rusty Hatton and offered the position of Contracts assistant. I was in shock and it came as a complete surprise. I later discovered that Rusty was moving to greener pastures to a company in Gaborone in Botswana. I accepted the offer and the challenge as I was literally thrown in the deep end. I received on hand training from the General Manager, after Rusty had departed. The role included producing Project Cost Estimates, assistance with the drafting office tasks and general Contract Management reporting directly to the General manager. This was a daunting role and major milestone in my life, a first for a non-white to be employed in such a senior position at Morewear Industries Bulawayo. The role became more of a challenge when the general Manager, resigned and moved to R.E.S.C.Co another engineering company, a competitor, for some six months leaving me to solely run the Technical Contracts department, basically the whole Contract Management of the business reporting to the Group Technical Manager who was based in Salisbury / Harare. Did I experience any racially motivated incidents because of this unexpected promotion you may be thinking, the answer is, yes,of course, which I shall relate briefly. It is an issue that raises its head every now and again in my life, a real ball of contention.

Firstly, prior to my promotion to Contracts assistant / manager we had daily shop floor management meetings in the production Manager's office where both Crawford and I attended. Discussions were candid and amicable mainly focusing on the daily tasks but occasionally various topics of interest would come up. I recall that one morning the topic of racial inequality came up, Van Vuuren and Crawford clearly displayed a level of bias claiming that black people were somewhat less intelligent by design. I argued on the contrary in defence of my black kith and kin. The issue I argued was that all humans are created equal in the eyes of God Almighty in accordance with Christian belief but that the issue was education not the colour of one's skin. The apartheid ideological view was that the darker one is the more unintelligent one is. It was clear that that was the view they expounded. I believe that I eloquently explained my position on this matter to which they surprisingly acknowledged my practical reasoning. Returning to your probable question dear reader, namely: Did I experience any racially motivated incidents because of this unexpected promotion, yes indeed and it caught me off guard to be honest. Suddenly both my Production Manager and Works Foreman stopped talking to me, they would walk past my office each day to a meeting with the General manager and would ignore my cordial "good morning" greeting. This went on for approximately two years, I felt intimidated and isolated. I believe that the main reason for their stance was that they perhaps found it rather difficult to accept the fact that I was now, by job role in a position, senior to them. What was I to do and how was I going to deal with this emotional pressure. My response may surprise you dear reader because I did not resign as they would have preferred nor retaliate in any way. I opted to be peaceable and respectful and continued my daily good morning greetings although these were met with silence. The following biblical principles helped me throughout this period: "A mild answer turns away rage" (Proverbs 15:1) "If your enemy is hungry, give him bread to eat; if he is thirsty, give him water to drink, by doing this you will be heaping fiery coals on his head and Jehovah will reward you" (Proverbs 25: 21,22. Romans 12: 20.) meaning the action will soften the person and melt his hardness, like a refining process that will , in time, bring out the best in them. Another principle that came to mind was Romans 12:18 and 21 which state "as far as it depends on you, be peaceable with all men" and "Do not let yourself be conquered by the evil, but keep conquering the evil with the good" Applying these biblical principles proved true as both Van Vuuren and Crawford changed their position towards me in time and once again we were on friendly talking terms. These principles dear reader I have religiously endeavoured to apply from that time onward and throughout the rest of my life. They have proved to be a guiding light and strength right to this present time of writing.

The next milestone took place around the end of 1987 when a Mr Howes, who worked as Manager of Kabot Brothers, offered me a position as Production Manager. He said to me "Francis the company is looking for a production Manager and I have advertised for that position but without success, I believe you are the right person for the job" My first reaction was "Ralph! You really think I have a chance, that company has never had a coloured in such a position!" His response was, "send me your application and I will recommend you", which I promptly did. Once again to my surprise I was offered the position early 1988. I handed in my resignation at Morewear, to the surprise of some, and I began my next new challenge at Kabot Brothers. Kabot Brothers was a thriving family-owned engineering business, part of the group of Halsted Brothers, builders merchants, Wynns Engineering machine shop and United Spring and Forging. Ralph was transferred to United Spring and Forging in a new position as Engineering Group Manager with overall control of the three companies Kabot Brothers, Wynns engineering and United Spring and Forging. He became my immediate Boss for a time. Kabots manufactured light to medium steel components, bakery equipment such as ovens and bread moulds amongst other sheet metal products. Their main line of business, though, was the manufacture of Mazda and Nissan pick-up vans rear body pans for Willowvale Motor Industries in Harare and various Trailers for the heavy haulage transport sector, Dumpers and Tippers for the construction Industry. It was interesting work and varied as it involved elements of structural and mechanical design. Later in time I convinced the new Manger, a Mr Stamp, who was brought in from Halsted in KweKwe to relieve Ralph of the oversight of Kabots to expand and include the manufacture of Steel Structures such as warehouses for the Construction Industry. Mr Stamp confidently agreed and we created an extended concrete slab adjacent to the main factory to enable such manufacture. The end result was a positive one. I increased the turnover of the business by thirty five percent during the first year of my employment with net profits of fifteen percent per month. Was I rewarded for this, yes, I was with an attractive remuneration package. It was during this time in 1988 that I employed my young friend Tommy Cannesius as an apprentice Boilermaker / Fabricator. I met Tommy around 1983/4 when my wife and I were residing in Parklands, a reasonably affluent suburb in Bulawayo. We had only two children then Francine and Benjamin who were just 3 and 1 plus years old respectively. Tommy was at senior school then and used to visit our family as he lived in Kumalo a suburb close by and I was his Bible Teacher. We developed such a strong friendship from that time onwards right to this day of writing. Our friendship has proved to be like that of David and King Saul's son Jonathan who was twice his age as recorded in the Bible book of 1 Samuel. Tommy and my brother George were my companions and confidants, the only two persons I trusted completely who proved to be my trusted work colleagues for many years in different companies and countries having worked together in Zimbabwe and Botswana. We parted ways early 1997 and met up again, this time in Bristol England in 2002. More info later about that seemingly miraculous encounter.

Life was good for us as a family back then, we lived comfortably having bought our first property, number 35 Lancaster Avenue in Hillcrest in 1985/6. It was then that another door of opportunity opened, two companies offered me senior management positions, one in Bulawayo Lantric Engineering and another Pars-wana (a name combination derived from the name of the founder Mr Parsons and the location Botswana) Engineering in Gaborone Botswana. This was an expatriate business that offered me directorship and an opportunity to have a percentage ownership. It's true to say that when these doors and others opened for some of us, we became driven by ambition to be the best and to achieve the possible utmost. The rungs on the corporate ladder of progress seemed endless. We were like children who were brought up in a strict protective environment and who had now suddenly been let loose; free to satisfy their wildest dreams. Yes, it was like a dream come true. Both remuneration packages were enticing to say the least, company transport, free fuel and maintenance, a domestic employee and Gardener plus as an added bonus private education for my children all at the company's expense. Who in their right mind could refuse such offers I thought. I thought about my current situation at Kabots. Yes I had a good salary, yes I had free company transport but that was it, I could never progress any further, I was talented and ambitious. What really prompted my next move was in late 1991, the manager at Kabot Brothers, Mr

Stamp, had moved on and was replaced by an Englishman called Steve Shea. He was my manager for a few months. One morning we were having a general discussion about the business when Steve dropped one on me, he said "Francis I am thinking of moving on, I don't have much to do here except to sign cheques, you control everything and I have recommended that you be promoted to be the next overall Manager of the business" I was like "what!" Then he continued and said "But Halsteds won't have it because they are of the view that it would be bad for business' ' meaning they were afraid that they would lose the white owned and managed business customers. What could I do but just shake my head in disappointment. Mr Halsted and his Financial Director, Mr Holborn were really nice gentlemen, they always treated me with respect and acknowledged very often with a handshake and a cordial "well done Francis for your excellent turnover." I was always pleased to be acknowledged and often thanked them for their recognition. So unfortunately for them, when my Manager Mr Shea was compelled to let the 'cat out of the bag' I made my decision to move on if an opportunity arose, and yes it did arise. I discussed the two offers with my wife and she opted for us to move to Botswana. We were excited, a new life in a new country, new adventures and opportunities for our growing family, little did I know the challenges and stress I would face. We had three children then Francine, Ewan and Michael. Francine was eleven years old, Ewan five and Michael three years old. My wife is an adventurous woman always keen for a new experience, a new environment, another move. When I met her they always seemed to live in different places in Harare and when she moved in with me in 1977 we continued the trend. By December 1991 we had lived in a number of different flats in Bulawayo, a trend I will expand on in my next chapter. Once I received the formal offer of employment from the Managing Director of Parswana Engineering, a Mr Parsons from Harare, I handed in my notice to my manager Mr Shea who was not at all surprised. I served a month's notice and at the end, on the last day, I was called into the office of Mr Holborn at Halsteds. I thought 'ok it's goodbye time now' ' as the previous day I had had a formal leaving get together at Kabot Brothers where I was presented with a gift I still have today as of this writing, a silver Letter knife and jug with the engraved letters; Kabot Brothers 1987 to 1991. Sadly, the implements have turned grey for lack of polishing lustre. Mr Holborn welcomed me into his palatial office and offered me tea and biscuits. We had an open discussion about my move and since I was moving to Botswana, another country, and not another competitor in Bulawayo my decision was welcomed and accepted with much regret. Mr Holborn later handed me an envelope, shook my hand in a gesture of appreciation for my service and said to me "Francis, on behalf of Halsted's managing Director, if things don't work out in Botswana there will always be room for you here, you will be welcomed back any day." I was speechless, I thanked him and left with the envelope tucked away deep in my trouser pocket.

I opened the envelope when I arrived home that evening, I nearly fell off my chair as the expression goes, The envelope contained a letter of appreciation and a cheque for the taxed sum of twenty thousand Zimbabwean dollars. Remember dear reader that this was in 1991 when the zimbabwe currency was Z$4.8 = £1. I was in a state of shock, I do not know of any such occurrence to any person of colour in those days. The previous incumbent on the other hand had been awarded fifty thousand dollars when he was promoted to overall Engineering Manager and moved to United Spring and Forging in 1988, how did I know that? Because he informed me at the time. That however did not worry me at the least, as he was a specially gifted individual and deserved it as he had proved to be a successful efficient manager. I was just so appreciative; we now had the financial means to begin a new life in Botswana. So, what was I to conclude about the statement that my promotion to Manager at Kabot Brothers, if it had materialised, would have been bad for business? Their final remuneration to me made me honestly conclude that if I was in their shoes, I would have most probably made the same decision based on business criteria and not racial bias as I had initially thought.

Before I accepted the offer at Parswana Engineering, the managing director flew us both to Gaborone where we had a meeting and physically inspected his business premises. The company had such great potential I thought, it had the space, and an attractive office block. The shop floor had adequate equipment to carry out the business manufacturing functions, however, they did not appear to be busy at the time. I concluded that, perhaps it was due to the fact that it was nearer to year end shut downs. I did request to see the balance sheet at the time just as a reassuring gesture to ascertain the financial situation of the business. This was promised but the promise never materialised. After a while I said to my wife, " I think the business is in trouble financially, do you still want to go?" She nodded and I thought, well let's give it a go and we did.

We moved to Gaborone early January 1992, and discovered to our dismay that Parswana could only afford to house my family in a single bedroomed flat in the suburb of Marua-Pula. Yes you guessed it, I was both shocked and disappointed. To make matters worse the company was in the red, with a negative balance of some three hundred thousand Botswana Pula and to cap it all the company's order book was zero. When I walked into the office that first Monday morning, the workforce looked at me with "hungry mouths," as the expression goes, what were they to do? as it seemed there was no future work. Robert Calder whom I had known from Bulawayo was employed as the shop floor foreman. I recall having a meeting with Robert who proceeded to explain to me the goings on and that basically the Botswana municipality and Botswana Defence Force, their main customers, had lost faith in the company due to late delivery, poor quality and service. The company's bank overdraft had been maxed. I was in real trouble, what was I to do? The shop floor was soon swept clean and all outstanding deliveries were soon completed. I had to confront everything head on and I did with vigour and determination to succeed. I had to put on several 'hats' as it were, that of Sales and Marketing manager, Project estimating Manager, production and Project management roles, all in one.

A colossal task indeed, never did I foresee what the resulting stress would do to me. Not only did I have the business pressure to contend with but also, more importantly, how was I to care for my family and how well would we be able to serve God and be happy members of the congregation? I prayed like never before and worked in accordance with those prayers. Eventually after many marketing visits to the previous customers and letters of appeasement to creditors on the basis of 'new management scenario' the light appeared at the end of the dark tunnel. I was given a chance, another stab at business. I re-registered the company with the Botswana Government Tender Board and was subsequently awarded a number of contracts throughout 1992 into 1993. I manufactured Truck Dropside Bodies, trailers, water bowsers and tractor drawn dumpers for the municipality of Gaborone and for private customers. We were back on track, the bank reopened the company's overdraft facility, times were changing and the company was moving in the right direction. I had now moved my family into an attractive three bedroomed house close to the city centre. We were comfortable, my daughter was attending Broadhurst, a private Primary school and the boys eventually attended another private junior school, Khyber International. The balance sheet was good at the end of 1992 so much so that we awarded the whole workforce a bonus at the mid of December for the usual shut down period. I too took my family on a grand holiday down the 'garden route' of South Africa. A scenic route down the east coast of South Africa from East London to Port Elizabeth all the way down to Cape Town via Johannesburg, Ladysmith, Pietermaritzburg and Umtata, a two-day drive. It was a breathtaking experience never to be repeated, driving on a magnificent dual carriageway that meandered down the east coast like a giant serpent that occasionally afforded one a glimpse of the mighty Indian ocean. The return drive after a two-week holiday took us through the Northern cape back to Lobatse and finally home to Gaborone. I concluded that God Almighty had indeed answered my prayers after months of strife and uncertainty. I took my family on excursions to the wine farms and to the animal sanctuary where we, for the first time, came face to face with a two-hundred-year old tortoise nearly 60 cm tall. It was such an awesome experience. We capped our visit with a day out on Table Mountain via the cable car to enjoy the aerial view of Cape town, finally we spent some days enjoying a swim in the Indian Ocean a distance of some twenty-five kilometres from the city back up the east coast as the Atlantic Ocean is rather cold. The visit to the Cape of Good Hope at the extreme point of Africa where the Atlantic meets the Indian oceans was and I guess still is a view to die for, to see the merging oceans in their spectacular colour as they seem to clash and withdraw to each other's corner in a kind of tug of war. My love for Africa and the wonders of God's creative masterpieces was indeed fulfilled, there and then I was in awe. My wife and kids have never forgotten that holiday till this day.

1993 proved to be a challenging year, for some unknown reason the Botswana Tender Board suddenly shut down for that year. Rumour was that the Government was cleaning up the internal corruption activities that had been taking place for a while in various departments. The situation was serious and as a result of the clampdown many manufacturing companies shut their doors and left, Companies that were our competitors in the same line of business. We, fortunately survived for a time as I had secured close to a million Pula contract with 'Spie Batignole' a French civil engineering construction company based in Mapharengwane, a new site for the Botswana Defence Force. It was a major contract and a positive milestone for the business. It was at this time that I invited my brother George to come work for me as an On-Site Foreman. I needed someone I could trust that was not only a good Boilermaker / Fabricator and Steel Erector but also an individual with intuition, orderly and passionate about the job. That person was my brother George. A gifted talented Tradesman. My friend Tommy too had already been working for me, in 1993, as a Draughtsman, based at the workshop in Gaborone. He produced all the working manufacturing drawings / Blueprints / sketches for the shop floor staff. We were a Team. We were thriving, my employees were in good spirits and secure until the next hiccup, end 1994, which proved to be not a hiccup but the final straw that broke the Camel's back, a blow we could not recover from. The bank pulled the plug on us, so we were unable to administer the contract due to cash flow constraints. We were still struggling to catch up with previous creditor payments. I think the bank was not convinced that we could get ourselves out of the mud as it were as the business climate was dire during that year. We were well established by then with a workforce of some thirty-two personnel with the majority being housed at the Maparengwane site. I had two foreman, one installation / erection site foreman, my late brother George and the other Robert Calder running the workshop. The stress was immense, as I had to be all things to everyone, all hats on board, one manager / director to administer the complete contract, something had to give way. One day my body told me in uncertain terms, it was as if it said "Francis, enough is enough you are heading for a heart attack" I was driving from a site visit to Maparengwane Botswana Defence Force base some seventy five kilometres from Gaborone via Molepolole. I suddenly had a hypoglycemic episode, it came from nowhere, I had never had any symptoms whatsoever prior to that day. I didn't even know what it was until I was diagnosed with the condition at the end of 1994. I was feeling faint, whilst I was driving, like I was going to pass out at any moment. In this part of Africa, the road is sparsely occupied. Very often one can be driving along a long stretch without encountering another vehicle, this day was no different. I prayed for strength to get to Mapolole, a small village about fifty kilometres from Gaborone. Fortunately, I managed to arrive there and parked at a fuel station. I purchased a drink and chips from a nearby kiosk to satisfy my thirst. I felt much better, in fact, back to normal after consuming that meal, so I then continued my journey home and went back to my normal activities as if nothing had happened. I did though have bouts of dizzy spells from that time on but just brushed them off as my body's hiccups. We eventually had to unfortunately liquidate the business as it became unviable. The main contractor, Spie Batignolles, took control of my workforce and all our site assets as a result. Final notice was given, and we shut shop at the end of December 1994 handing over to the administrators and the liquidator. I was permitted to keep the company car until March 1995   to afford me time to re-organise my family's future.

The next window was not an easy one. I knew that the 'writing was on the wall' sometime around September of that year so I applied for employment in South Africa. A vacancy had come up in a medium engineering company outside Johannesburg to which I forwarded my C.V. The company was looking for a workshop foreman to manage the shop floor, of course I had the credentials, and I was soon invited for an interview. My wife was excited as she wanted to join some of her family who were already residing in Pretoria in South Africa. She thought this would be the best move for us rather than to return to Zimbabwe so, I was willing to make a go of it. We were both adventurous, young, and full of energy. Her siblings seemed to be living comfortably in South Africa, so we thought it would be a nice fresh start. My interview went without any hiccups. I thought I came across confident and proved my skills and experience but when we were about to drive away, I noticed that the workforce was predominantly white folks as they walked out of the workshop to the canteen area. Straight away I became apprehensive, doubt set in, South Africa had just become independent in April of 1994, Apartheid was still rife. I had no chance, I thought. These folks were not ready to accept a nonwhite fellow to be their immediate boss, I prepared for the worst. We returned home to Gaborone , Botswana and awaited a response which came a couple of months later. Of course I was 'unsuccessful' ; they eventually 'found someone else' more suitable and better skilled I guess. I'll leave you to draw your own conclusion dear reader.

The time finally came when we had to move house. We stored our furniture in a friend's warehouse until further notice as we did not know exactly where we were going to end up. We packed the car to the limit and moved to Pretoria and boarded with my sister in law Desiree and her husband Ernest who were renting a lovely spacious house which had sufficient room to accommodate my family. My wife and children lived with them for a couple of months whilst I had to travel back and forth to Gaborone to take care of business. It was then that another opportunity arose:

Morewear Industries in Bulawayo had advertised a position for a production Manager required to set up a complete, new production line for manufacturing heavy haulage super-link semi-trailers, a massive contract they had recently secured. I felt that this was the ideal opportunity, so I promptly faxed my C.V. and application letter to which I was offered the job without even an interview. It seemed that Morewear's quick response was based on my previous legacy with the company over the many years I had worked for them. I was over the moon, signed the letter of acceptance without batting an eyelid, I thought it was a no brainer to go back home to an environment I was comfortable in. I drove back to Pretoria after finalising all business and arranging a removals company to deliver our furniture to an address to be advised. When I arrived back in Pretoria my wife told me that she had found a school for the boys, but an incident had occurred that displeased her. The head Teacher was basically a bully who traumatised our boys. That did it for me, South Africa was not the place for my family, apartheid was still deep seated within society, it just seemed to be a more aggressive environment. I had also left my C.V. with an employment agency but without any success, perhaps I was naive to apply for a senior management position in a country that was so segregated. I really felt justified in my decision to return my family to Zimbabwe. I told my wife about my decision and to my surprise she was rather unhappy at first as she had preferred to settle in South Africa. I was a little presumptuous I suppose. Immigrating to South Africa was not a problem as my wife had South African ancestry and so our residence application would be on that basis, an application that was already in progress. After some discussion and cohesion on my side she reluctantly agreed to support my decision and move back. Once again, we were on the move back to Bulawayo. We rented a house in North end for some six months, sold our property in Hillcrest which we had rented out during our stay in Botswana, and bought another property in Riverside. It was an attractive house with a large terraced garden and domestic quarters overlooking the Joburg road. The address was Number twenty Brentwood road, Riverside, Bulawayo. The boy's schooling was literally just up the road, Masiyephambili (meaning let us move forward in the Ndebele language) Primary, a private school with a good reputation. Private schooling was one of the perks of my new Job Title. My eldest daughter, Francine, went to Townsend High, a senior school with a great reputation, a legacy from the Rhodesian days. Zimbabwe as a whole had at that time achieved one of the highest literacy rates in the world which was around 80% back then and 89% as reported for 2021. It was known to have produced a highly skilled population, skills that were well sought after not only in South Africa but also as far as Australia particularly at the Trades level. My own experience proves that to be true and was especially apparent when we settled in England in 1997, an experience I shall discuss in my later chapter. We now had four children, the fourth being a daughter Melanie who was born in Botswana in April of 1994.

Life back in Zimbabwe in 1995 was still of a high standard. My wife never had to work after we had our first child Francine in 1980 until the day we immigrated to the United Kingdom in 1997. I still, to date, believe that we had one of the highest standards of living in the world all the way from the 1960's through to the 2000's, sadly today there is no middle class anymore as the economy has been devastated, there is only the rich and the poor and I have been eyewitness to that fact during my visits to the country. It brought me great sadness whenever I visited to witness the meltdown. I last visited in December of 2022 and was a little encouraged to see evidence of improvement. Let me not digress, I shall expand on my experience a little later, for now let's go back to 1995.

We are now back in Zimbabwe, I am Production Manager at Morewear Industries, my task in hand was to set up a production line to manufacture two hundred Super link heavy haulage semi-trailers for Wheels of Africa, a company based in Harare with its headquarters and South African Branch in Johannesburg. Its founder and director was an affluent Zimbabwean businessman who was now based in South Africa. This was a colossal undertaking. Did I have the technical tools to administer such a task considering that my past experience was always in a job shop environment manufacturing one offs and bespoke components? The only mini production line I ever managed was the manufacture of pick-up truck rear bodies for Willowvale Motor Industries at Kabots in 1987 through to December 1991. Fortunately, this time, I had begun a correspondence Associate Mechanical Engineering Degree course, with a college based in London, which provided me with the necessary understanding of the workings of production Lines. My wife would complain at times about my never ending studying. She would say "where is all this learning going to get you?" and I would reply "one day it will all prove worthwhile" and it did; not only at this time but in later years as I will discuss in a later chapter. This course was just perfect timing, an in-situ application of knowledge and an 'apply as you go' scenario. Not only did I have to design the production line but had to set up the complete infrastructure, the floor space had to be concreted, jigs and fixtures had to be designed and manufactured, the right skilled workers had to be employed in the correct numbers, welding equipment had to be purchased. I had to also source the right Shop Floor Manager with the necessary skills and discipline to undertake the shop floor management. The only individual I was comfortable with and had total confidence in was my brother George. I had tried someone else who seemed qualified who had responded to our advertisement but proved to be unsuitable. I was stuck with no other takers but my brother George, how would I appoint him to such a position without being accused of nepotism?

I decided that the only way was to refer him to the General Manager and C.E.O, who would then independently interview him together with the HR Manager. The C.E.O. was himself a well-qualified Mechanical Engineer and I was sure that he would make the right decision recognising my brother's skills; and he did. George was then offered employment as Works Foreman. My brother delivered in every way, my floor plan, a double line flow with six working stations. The target was to produce a complete super link, a tri-axle front trailer coupled to a rear tandem axle trailer set in two days. Yes! Two days, I had envisaged a preparation time frame of three months. George designed and manufactured the physical Jigs and Fixtures during that time frame. Manufacture had to adhere to just-in-time principles which proved extremely challenging as most of the materials had to be sourced from South Africa. Zimbabwe is a land locked country so the flow of goods was always going to be problematic and then there was the challenge of unforeseen occurrences and other issues like import licences, cash flow interruptions etc. I requested that the company purchase buffer stock of one month's delivery, namely twenty sets, to alleviate such problems but unfortunately my request was rejected by the head office in Harare. Did we meet the challenge, yes, we did to the satisfaction of all parties. Did the head office eventually agree to fund a buffer stock? Yes they did but only after we experienced a major supply chain breakdown at the Firestone tyre factory in Johannesburg. Trailers were piled up in the yard as a result, awaiting tyres for delivery. This incident proved the short-sightedness of our head office. They first tried to point fingers at me, but the evidence convinced them otherwise particularly after they examined my flow chart and detailed correspondence with the supply chain. Peter and I had made numerous visits to each South African supplier where delivery requirements were discussed and schedules agreed. At the end of it all, the contract was a success story, we achieved the target and George and I were promoted with attractive packages which included monthly production bonuses, George to Production Manager and I to Project Manager. We had earned the respect of all, we were in our element you could say, we had carried out the largest heavy haulage trailer production line ever in Zimbabwe at the time. These trailers were designed for a combined payload of fifty metric tonnes and operated literally from Cape to Cairo by Wheels of Africa.

George and I both worked for Morewear until mid 1996 when we were both suddenly fired for reasons I shall now explain. This was a traumatic experience for both of us, it was like a mighty crash, all the way down from the top rung of a ladder right to the bottom to lick the dust. We did not stay down though, it was time to make 'A Plan' a next plan as the Zimbabwean expression goes. In Zimbabwe, I guess in Africa as a whole, if you don't make a plan you starve. Morewear Bulawayo, under my watch, had (in the same year in 1995, whilst the trailer production line was still in progress) secured a massive contract from Bateman South Africa for the supply and manufacture of approximately two thousand tonnes of fabricated steelwork. That steelwork comprised thirty five conveyor systems complete with discharge hoppers and chutes designed to deliver iron ore from recently discovered deposits located twenty five kilometres from the main mine at Z.I.S.CO (Zimbabwe Iron and Steel Company) located in Kwe Kwe. The conveyors would be situated above ground, travelling along the land topography, with gantries over the Kwe Kwe river and into the main mine. This was another major project on my shoulders. Hard to believe isn't it dear reader. It seemed like I was a slave to punishment, but I welcomed the challenge. We were confident in the capabilities of the labour force however the contract demanded beefing up the 'Drawing / Drafting office.' Technical drawing was a manual task those days and only a few engineering companies that I knew of in Bulawayo had begun to implement Autocad, computer generated drafting. We were learners in this area, so we had to source subcontract Draughtsman to assist. Once again I turned to my friend Tommy and suggested he apply to our HR department who were struggling to find an Autocad or manual Draughtsman. Many had taken the opportunity, due to demand, to subcontract their services. I had by now managed to source a number including Andrew Hann, who was the only one qualified in Autocad, who I employed as Chief Draftsman. The others including my nephew, Johnathan Ncube, were manual draughtsmen. We were a team once more, George, Tommy and I. That was early in 1995. The problems materialised a short time after. The initial plan was that the trailer contract had been scheduled to have been completed by the time the company engaged the Bateman Project which of course did not happen as planned. The unfortunate breakdown at the Firestone tyre factory in Johannesburg and the fact that head office in Harare gave a late go-ahead to implement buffer stock caused a major delay in the completion of that contract which then impacted on the administering of the Bateman Project. Cash flow too became a big problem causing material delivery delays both locally and externally. I could see it coming, the writing was on the wall, I proposed that subcontract companies be used to meet the manufacturing demand. I was running around like a headless chicken visiting various companies in Kwe Kwe, Bulawayo including our main branch in Harare. Batemen management applied the pressure on us, it was relentless, so much so that our skills both George and mine were being questioned. Batman had employed an expediter, a retired mechanical Engineer in Bulawayo to scrutinise our company's performance and he actually asked me one day, during one of his visits, whether I was a qualified Engineer. He had the audacity I thought but then again, I would have probably asked the same question if I was in his position.

Meetings with the Bateman Project Manager proved to be extremely uncomfortable as I could not divulge the whole truth, the reasons for the Project Slippage mainly cash flow and supply chain issues. You see, the head office knew it so to save face and to save the contract George, Peter Wyss our C.E.O. and I became the scapegoats. We were blamed for being incompetent and promptly fired without notice. George thereafter left Zimbabwe to work in Francistown in Botswana. It was a case of necessity being the mother of invention as he later started his Fabrication expatriate Business which functioned right until his death in 2022. Peter 'jumped ship' as the saying goes and moved to work for Radar Industries in Bulawayo. I on the other hand managed to stall my departure for a month as I proposed to work a handover period of one month which I stated would be the right practical thing to do for the best interest of the company including for the new incumbent. The company accepted my sensible proposal. I moved to Hogarths after I left Morewear. The manager of Hogarths, an Englishman, a chartered Structural Engineer, had plans for me, he initially employed me as a Production Planner with a view of later moving me to manage the whole shop floor as Works Manager. He was informed of my technical and managerial capabilities by the previous Chief Executive of Morewear Industries Bulawayo. It just so happened that Hogarths was a subsidiary of Radar industries at the time. What a coincidence. I felt as if Almighty God was supervising and directing my life, I was convinced that he was responding to my needs. My wife and children could never understand the stress I was under, so I never burdened them with knowledge of my inner turmoil. I had an interesting time at Hogarths, I worked along with Kresta Hague management consultants who were brought in to set up a quality control management system, a first in Bulawayo, an ISO 9000 quality control system. My role was to impart my manufacturing hands on knowledge and experience which would be the basis for a production control system on the shop floor. This was a new door of experience for me that would prove crucial in later years when I moved to England.

The time soon came for that move in mid-March in 1997. My wife expressed her desire to move to England towards the end of 1996. Her mother had sadly passed away early that year. My wife was distraught and traumatised by the whole experience and could not overcome her grief. Bulawayo had too many negative experiences in her life and she wanted a change, a new opportunity, a new beginning to start afresh. She had, in the past, tried to find her father, an Irishman, who had long been deported from Rhodesia, when she was only a six-year-old child. Her father was deported because of his political views at the time as he was an active supporter of the liberation struggle hence was in direct conflict with the Rhodesian government. I think that his Irish ancestry may have contributed to his strong feelings of the injustice he witnessed. He loved his children, my wife and her brother, and had promised to take them to England someday. A promise that never materialised, so I understood my wife's desire to find him. I was not over the moon but cautiously agreed for us to move, the details of our move will be discussed in a later chapter. Moving house and or country is classed as one of the most stressful experiences in life, next to a death, and indeed it has been for me and my family as I will explain later. My Manager was rather disappointed when I handed in my notice early in February 1997 but he understood. He warned me though, with questions like "How are you going to cope with the extreme cold and snow etc etc." Yes! One negative statement after another. He loved Zimbabwe, he was living a life of luxury, a house with a swimming pool and a tennis court in his yard, a life that only millionaires live in the UK. Hence he had no plans of ever leaving. Zimbabwe was paradise for him. He thought that I was naive and foolish to leave, well! He did have a point and he proved partly to be correct as I shall explain in a later chapter. However, I could see that 'the writing was on the wall' for the country as I observed the declining exchange rate which showed the volatility of the economy. It was slow, but definitely a steady downhill trend.

CONVERSION

Where do I begin, firstly I believe it's true to say that Rhodesia and the Zimbabwe I lived in was and still is a predominantly christian country. Christianity has fragmented, of late, into countless denominations in the country; so much so that the late President Mr Robert Mugabe once referred to them as 'Briefcase Churches' no doubt describing the nature of such fragmentation, the business-like effect. However, I was born in a different era when christianity was basically only mainstream, meaning that it was made up of mainly the well-established Colonial religions such as Catholicism, Presbyterian, Lutheran, Baptists, Anglican, Methodists and such-like including of course Judaism, Hinduism and Islam. Mother was a staunch Catholic and had us all baptised as such in our infancy hence my name Francis I guess named after 'Saint' Francis of Assisi. Father was a non-practising Jew from what we could tell, I don't know whether he ever attended a synagogue in Gwanda after all he was based in the rural areas. The only thing he practised religiously was refraining from eating pork. Mother had us all confirmed as Catholics at a young age and we attended the Catholic Church in Gwanda for many years which include all the years in Primary School. I attended Founders High School boarding at Saint Elizabeth Hostel in Barham Green Bulawayo from 1967 through to 1971. I attended church regularly there every Sunday together with other boys. It was routine and was the right thing to do during those years. The form of worship was basic, uncomplicated and gave us a basic moral compass, I guess. The deep questions regarding the meaning of life were never taught nor did we consider such questions. We just went with the flow, the pomp and ceremony and routine form of worship. We were never encouraged to read the bible nor was it made available on the pews. Mother expected my attendance plus it was compulsory. I was quite committed then, even to the point of requesting a Bible as my prize choice at the end of my first year in High School. The school would award book prizes to all the children who achieved outstanding results for the year and I was one of them, and my choice of a book; was the Bible. Why did I make that choice, well! I don't really remember, for one thing I was never a reader. The only books I read were comic books because I was interested in their artwork. We never carried a Bible into church back then, it was taboo, not permitted nor encouraged as far as I could tell and so we never read it. All we learned, as Catholics back then, was Catechism, a compilation of Catholic doctrine. Church liturgy and services were in Latin back then and mainly ritualistic. As time went on, English was included later in the form of printed tracts with repetition type liturgy. I felt so 'holy' as a child when I was appointed to serve as an Alter Boy during my primary school days. I even used to play the part of a 'Priest' when we boarded with Mrs Oswald in Gwanda offering my siblings and boarders 'X' mints, as the 'holy bread / host. I was about eight years old then, of course in high school it was a different story as I have already stated in my previous chapter.

I received my prize at the end of my first year in high school, an attractive illustrated Bible which contained amazing artwork of various biblical scenes of well-known stories such as that of the Flood, Daniel in the Lion's Den, Jesus' healing scenes etc. The only reason I can think of for requesting a bible may have been because Mother had started a Bible study program with Jehovah's Witnesses in and around that time 1966/7. That was her first time ever to read the bible. A chap called Ngoma visited her on a weekly basis for a period of time. I recall joining in on one of those lessons, conducted in Ndebele, during my school holidays. Mother eventually was moved, no doubt by what she was learning, to legalise her union with Father in marriage on January 6 1972. Surprisingly, my mother told me that it was my Father that initiated the marriage proposal after reading an article, in one of Jehovah's Witnesses publications, about God's view of cohabitation. Both my father and mother were receiving these magazines by subscription. No doubt father was moved by the biblical references regarding marriage and courageously proposed. He actually showed mother the particular article. This was really a bold stand on his part due to concerns of not only Apartheid - the colour bar system but also due to his Jewish ethnic background. Nevertheless, it did happen and we were at last legitimate children in the eyes of the law and in the eyes of God. Later on in time mother got baptised in the Mtshabezi river and thereafter arranged for us children to have bible lessons with an english gentleman, one of Jehovah's Witnesses, named Mr Levings. I remember him well, a short stocky man with thick eyebrows. He was very active in and around Gwanda concentrating his preaching in the English-speaking territory including our suburb Sable Vale / Bar twenty. He had limited success, I guess due to opposition and the fact that most folks belonged to the mainstream churches and did not feel a need to change. However, there were some, my mother included, who had open minds to welcome a different approach to Christianity. So, Mr Levings did have some success amongst such individuals which included the conversion of my primary school teacher late Mrs June Noach, once a devout Catholic too, and also my father's change of heart. Mother did confirm that in time my Father acknowledged and accepted the fact that Jesus had indeed come and was indeed the Messiah - the Christ. I have no doubt that Mr Levings and mother had an influence on his change of heart. For a Jew to accept that fact was and is still anathema. My father was special in that sense it proved his sincerity and reasonableness when presented with the facts. He had gone through his own crisis of faith at a young age when he was earmarked to succeed his father who was a Rabbi. Father was the oldest son in his family so was next in line to the priesthood, unfortunately my father had his own ideas and did not want to go in that direction so he left home together with his cousin Jack Klein. Ours was similar in a way. The rest of us did not respond in kind, we just went through the motions I guess to please our mother. I can still vividly remember, as I write my story, me standing on our front veranda of the house in Sable Vale during school holidays and observing Mr Levings yellow and white topped Consul (vehicle) progressing from one house to another across the valley. I would watch anxiously expecting our turn. When our turn came, I was nowhere to be seen as I would escape and 'conveniently' visit my friends. I did at times, on a few occasions listen in, when Mr Levings conducted bible studies with my siblings. Father did not oppose the arrangement but seemed indifferent to it all.

Little did we know that our father would pass away suddenly in April 1975. Mother never really told us anything about his health issues other than him struggling with his legs, probably from poor blood circulation, arthritis or diabetes, I guess she didn't really understand it all. Father was buried in a typical Jewish ceremony within the time frame prescribed by the Jewish faith. The funeral was arranged by his two daughters and son, from his first marriage, without our knowledge. I recall going to visit my father in his hospital bed at Bulawayo Central after being granted leave of absence, on a compassionate basis by the military. Unfortunately, I found him in a comatose state and unresponsive. Father may have developed diabetes and hence circulation problems that affected his legs. Whether that was the cause of his death, I do not know having not seen his death certificate. I returned a few days later only to find the bed vacated and I was informed that he had passed away. I was devastated. We started making funeral arrangements to bury father only to discover that he had already been buried in the allocated Jewish cemetery. We were shocked and upset by the fact that we were not formally informed although we were father's legitimate family. We presumed that either the Jewish community or his Jewish white children by his first marriage had taken it upon themselves to carry out the burial without our knowledge. We would have respected Jewish customs and practice and would have contributed in some way. What upset me most was that my father's grave was left as a bare mound of sand without a tombstone for some months. I was livid by this act of disrespect for him, I knew of no other reason. I took it upon myself, as the oldest child of the family, with the support of my late brother George to do justice for father to do the right thing, the respectful thing by organising a gravestone of polished marble, a stone of the same quality befitting the rest of the grave stones in that cemetery to be erected for father in order to dignify his burial. We carefully chose the engraved wording to be all inclusive as in "Sadly missed by his children and grandchildren." We were so proud of it when it was finally set up, it provided the opportunity for our whole family and future generations to witness, and I must say at this point of writing that it is still immaculately maintained by the Jewish community in Bulawayo as I last visited in December 2022.

With regards to my spiritual journey, mother sowed the seed in me during my high school days. She would write me letters, quoting and referencing bible verses to which I felt obliged to read as she would ask me if I did whenever I returned home on school holidays. I do not recall, though, what those verses said but what I do remember is having these repetitive vivid dreams of 'God's' finger pointing at me out of the clouds. Dreams that continued on and off for some years and particularly post schooling years. It was often a frightening nightmare experience for me, a tiny dot on a brow of a hill, staring at the huge finger of 'God' pointing in my direction from within a cloudy, colourful sky accompanied by lightning and thunder. Perhaps it was my sense of guilt for my sinful ways, a bad conscience and perhaps exaggerated by my artistic vivid imagination. So, how did it all start?

A turning point occurred when my girlfriend and I were living together. It was taboo those days to live together without being married; the moral climate was very much influenced by religion, we just ignored it, suppressing our consciences. Passion overtook morality, I begged her to come live with me as I could not stand being apart from her. She too felt the same, we were madly in love. We finally did, 'the deed,' moved-in together in 1977 against our parent's wishes. Did I change my ways after that? Well! Not at first. I still continued in my drinking habits often coming home late and intoxicated to face girlfriends indignation. We were heading for a breakup and it would have been all my fault. We however later discussed our relationship as we both loved each other and wanted to make it work, so we decided to attend the nearest church in our area, a cry for help I guess, but we were not satisfied, it just didn't do it for us, there was something missing. I think we expected to receive or hear some form of direct council and direction for our lives to save us from ourselves, so we gave up. We didn't give it sufficient time I suppose. We were back to square one. She put up with me and I tried to behave as I loved her in my own twisted way. It was not always doom and gloom as we were a couple as any other couple experiencing ups and downs and also enjoying one another's company. We went out on weekends to the dance halls for music, dance and fun as all young people did back then. We called them the roaring 70's. It was during those days sometime in 1978 that I inadvertently came across an advertisement for a free subscription to a magazine called "The Plain Truth." I think it was in a Readers Digest book in our works office. I used to glance at it now and again and read a snippet here and there but that advert on that issue of Reader's Digest drew my attention. I thereafter subscribed to that magazine which I religiously read, at work, without my girlfriend's knowledge. The topics were intriguing and varied. I was spellbound like nothing I had ever read or heard before. You may call this a coincidence or God's calling, but she too had had her own similar experience on the quiet during the same period. We didn't tell each other what we were doing, it was our personal secret at the time. She was working for the fuel rationing office in Bulawayo during that time. It was a time when Rhodesia was subject to economic sanctions from the western governments, particularly the United Kingdom for having declared unilateral independence from Britain. Fuel was scarce although the government of the day had very cleverly devised a solution creating blended fuel, a mix of petrol and ethanol derived from cane sugar. It was an amazing innovation in the 70's. So her job involved dispensing fuel coupons to the public. It was during this time that she was given a bible, a 1938 translation of the King James Bible, by an English gentleman she worked with. Then one day as she was reading it under her desk she was approached by a certain gentleman, an individual who had converted and had become one of Jehovah's witnesses, a zealous preacher well known in the coloured community, who asked her what she was reading. The following day he gave her a publication produced and published by Jehovah's Witnesses publishing establishment the WatchTower Bible and Tract Society entitled "The Truth that leads to eternal life" and said to her that it would help her understand her Bible. She gladly accepted it and read it in one night. He returned to her at the fuel rationing office after some days and offered to pick her up for church together with his family on one Sunday to which she agreed. That Sunday morning she dropped the bombshell on me and said "Francis, someone is coming to pick me up to attend church this afternoon, would you like to come?" It came as a complete surprise, I was a little hungover that day and had no plans so I thought "why not". After all, I too was searching for some enlightenment. The man came promptly, he may have been surprised that Mary had brought her boyfriend as well. I was very casually dressed in typical 1970's fashion, blue denim levi jeans and jacket, high platform shoes and a well-groomed 'massive' afro. I had no idea what to expect. It proved to be an occasion I would never forget, a turning point in both our lives. I cannot tell you what the sermon was about as we don't remember it but what I do remember was the warm welcome we received, the handshake greetings and warm friendly smiling faces from the attendees, from across the racial divide both white and coloured folks. I watched and observed their interaction across the ethnic divide. This was a first, we were welcomed without prejudice, the whole atmosphere was the opposite of the colour-bar practised outside that environment. The man offered us a free one to one Bible study program when we got home. This was unheard of. We were going to be given personal one to one attention, just as my mother had, an offer we gladly accepted. That was our turning point, it was as if the Almighty had found us. The format was a topical study format, the book being used as a curriculum and a study guide. It covered many basic topics that, put together, explained the whole essence of the bible's message including the detailed explanation of the first half of the Lord's Prayer, a prayer that we had said so often so ritually but without understanding all through our lives up to that point. It was an awesome revelation for me, as it included scripture proof texts on every subject and for every point made. We learned too that that same publication had made it into the Guinness book of records in 1975 after reaching a record publication of over one hundred million copies. Our study program went on for one and a half years and resulted in both of us getting baptised on June 28 1980. That book was the instrument that changed our lives. In my view God used it to open our eyes and heart to understand his word. How did I feel about it all? Why did it take so long? What would my family and friends think? What would I experience from the general public? Would I be received kindly and welcomed?

The things that I learned affected me profoundly. I was like Jeremiah the prophet: unstoppable! The whole world had to know about the precious pearl I had found;the knowledge of the Almighty. I had discovered, for the first time in my life, the complete explanation about the meaning of life and the history of humanity. It was as if the scales of ignorance were being removed from my eyes and I could for the first time 'see' the whole essence of the entire word of God and to view the world scene from a fresh perspective. Even my spoken language began to change from that of slang and uncouth words to the proper written English. It changed for the better. I finally too appreciated the meaning of the logo and words on my Founders High school blazer badge, namely "Truth is ever simple." That realisation has proved to be re confirmed as true even in my later years right to the present time of writing, true in every aspect whether with regards to religion, science, politics or even in my interactions with fellow humans. Truth is ever simple, the opposite: untruth, is always complicated, nonsensical, and sadly often defended by violence and slander. There is no need for truth to be defended by violence because it is self-evident. If something does not make sense; it is nonsense in my view. My new adage is I have also learnt later in life the fact that truth is historically first violently opposed - vehemently rejected, then it is tolerated and finally accepted through evidence, and this applies in every facet of learning.

Why did I take so long to accept God's 'calling'?Simply put I needed that time to change my ways, my thinking, to be humbled in the true sense of the word, total repentance, a complete one hundred and eighty degree turn around in my conduct and thinking. I needed to have answers to many of my basic questions including that of the true meaning of life. I challenged my bible teacher and sought independent historical proofs for the things I was now learning. To confirm the 'facts' I visited the Bulawayo

Library on several occasions to satisfy my curiosity that what I was now being taught was historically correct. I investigated these profound facts, regarding the developments of some of the major doctrines of Christendom, as I sifted through the pages in the renowned and trusted volumes of Encyclopaedia Britannica. We had no internet in those days so great effort was required to source trustworthy information, and the library was the only place for such inquiry. I was stunned to discover that what I was being taught was indeed confirmed by history. I never realised until that point that I had such an inquisitive mind, a mindset that has carried me through until now. Remember dear reader that I made a statement in my previous chapter about my military national service that there was one religion that refused to get involved in the Rhodesian racial war, its members chose imprisonment rather than war, this was it. I finally understood the reasons for my troubled conscience during my military days. Many of us had the same view at that time, a view based on consciences, that our involvement in that conflict was wrong because it was a conflict based on upholding the status quo, of white supremacy and partiality, both tenets which are the opposite of God's love and impartiality. I was finally convinced that this was the religion for me, a religion that believed in the tenets of non-violence and political neutrality. My live-in girlfriend was of the same mind. We had made spiritual progress to the point of legalising our relationship by getting married on June 29 1979 and thereafter made the ultimate choice to serve God forever and symbolised our dedication to him by water baptism on June 28 1980.

Mother was over the moon; her wayward son had finally done what she had always hoped and prayed for. I was united with her both by blood and in Faith. My wife and I shared our truth with family members. Sadly, most were indifferent, they were just not ready, perhaps they were satisfied with their lives. We soon realised that "faith is not the possession of all people " including my close friends who faded away as we now had different interests, I guess different lifestyles and paths in life. When we learnt that preaching was a Christian requirement as Christ commanded I was apprehensive at first feeling that I could never accomplish such a task especially because I had a speech impediment from a young age. I had a terrible stammer, certain words were difficult for me and caused me great anxiety. It was a daunting assignment I thought. I felt like the prophet Moses, who when appointed by God to lead the Nation of Israel out of Egypt, fearfully expressed his anxiety when he said *"pardon me LORD (Jehovah) but I have never been a fluent speaker, neither in the past nor since you have spoken to your servant, for I am slow of speech and slow of tongue"* (Exodus 4:10). My stammer was so bad in school that I would ask my classmate to speak on my behalf whenever the teacher asked me a question. Preaching to strangers in the door-to-door ministry was a massive challenge which took me many years to get used to. I, with God's strength and support, was able to overcome my stammer, my impediment, and qualified as a public speaker in and around the congregations in Bulawayo and later in Botswana. It was a wonderful privilege. I felt that the Almighty had moulded me to carry out his will. Making disciples is a command from our Lord Jesus for every individual who claims to be Christian as far as my understanding of scripture and I took this assignment seriously helping others to do the same. It brought me great joy to see different people throughout the years who have taken the same steps including my late mother-in-law, my youngest sister, my late granny, some of my cousins, and two of my childhood friends amongst others. It is an indescribable joy to see people who were once strangers and how the power of God's word slowly changes their personality, improves their family relationships and moulds them to serve him more fully. It is like observing the cycle of metamorphosis from caterpillar to butterfly scenario and how wonderful it is to be a part of that cycle. Balancing the preaching activities with my family responsibilities was not always easy. I needed to be reined in and Church Elders did notice and did bring this matter to my attention. They helped me see the importance of balance and that charity begins at home, family first.

I believe that Christianity is a way of life, "The Way" as it is referred to in some passages of scripture and my family and I strive to live it, everyday, everywhere and in every circumstance whether adverse or otherwise. My preaching resulted in a mixed bag of reactions, from downright opposition to sincere welcomes and acceptance of the message. How often I would encounter signposts on the front gates of people's houses which read "Beware of Dogs and No Jehovah's Witnesses or vice versa." I kind of viewed them with mixed feelings of amusement and pity, I thought well! It's their choice after all, a choice based often on lack of knowledge, prejudice and misinformation. Jesus must have felt the same when he was rebuffed by his own people against their own interests. I understood what our Lord went through. At times we would be rudely shouted at or we would be threatened with dogs or have doors shut in our faces. On one occasion we were accused, by one white lady, of being cowards for not engaging in the war. She told us that she had lost her son who was in the Rhodesian Light Infantry and unfortunately had been killed by the guerilla forces. I politely tried to reason with her that our stand was based on Christ's commands in scripture and that the war had proved to be a fruitless exercise, as the country was now ruled by the same former guerilla forces and that, basically, her son and those of others including some friends of mine had sadly died in vain. In this instance I felt that her comment was a personal unjustified attack and I had to respond based on my own personal experience in the Rhodesian army. To me this was an example of the folly of humanities misdirected ideology. However, in most cases people were just indifferent and prejudiced. We were always encouraged though never to take opposition personally. It was not us as individuals that they were rejecting but it was the message in our hand - the Bible, God's message. A message with such power to reveal the real intentions of the heart, the inner person. (Hebrews 4:12). This is what I have experienced throughout the past forty-three years, as of this writing, and continue to experience in my entire Christian life that has included life in Rhodesia, to Zimbabwe Rhodesia, to Zimbabwe, to Botswana, to South Africa, then back to Zimbabwe and finally to England where we have resided since 1997.

The journey has been a profound one, cultures are different and they bring about different challenges but God has empowered me and my family to face them all. I have grown in faith, in understanding of scripture and am more convinced now than ever that mainstream Christianity has lost its way as it continues to fragment into thousands of sects, denominations as they search for truth and sadly in some cases that 'search' has been distorted by greed, human ego and self-promotion. As of this writing there are a staggering 45000 different denominations globally according to the Centre for the study of global Christianity. I believe that Christianity should be measured by its adherence to first century practice and belief and should not be tainted by the political climate nor infiltrated by human philosophy and ideologies.

When I look back through my spiritual journey: the more I have conversed with people of different faiths, backgrounds, walks of life, the more convinced I have become of God's truth as I understand it. Every man or woman has his or her own 'truth' but for me this is my truth. What more could I ask for? God has fulfilled my spiritual needs and has totally satisfied my spiritual journey to his praise. No longer do I envision his finger of judgement pointing in my direction but have experienced his warm embrace and outstretched arm and finger pointing me in the right direction as he whispers in my ear "This is the way - walk in it". (Isaiah 30:21)

Founders_High_School. Badge

My warning nightmares

Wife and I Ministry early 2020

Family at JW Convention 2019

MY FAMILY

As I have already discussed in my previous chapters, my life from leaving school right through to my early twenties was normal like everyone else, I suppose. Perhaps a little extreme at times: we worked hard, drank hard, smoked like chimneys, partied hard and chased the girls. That was the vicious circle of our lives back then. I had only one serious girlfriend prior to meeting my wife. We dated for some months when I was doing my national service in 1974 to 1975 but eventually broke up. She was too adventurous for me, if you get my meaning. How did I meet my beloved wife? It was in December of 1975. I was visiting my late brother Billy and other family members in Harare. I was accustomed to having a change of scenery every Christmas season as engineering factories would shut down for two weeks during this holiday period. So December of 1975 was no different. I loved visiting Harare because entertainment was more diverse and inclusive and there was more choice of venues. The music scene was awesome with bands like Soul and Blues, a ten-piece band. They were just great musicians. What we enjoyed most during those years was the competition between the groups from Harare and Bulawayo bands such as Eye of Liberty, The Invaders, Cassims and others. So Christmas Eve and New Years Eve were special occasions of wild abandonment. So, December of 1975 was no different. Folks in Harare were different to us in Bulawayo, they were more entertaining and hospitable. On that day a childhood friend of mine who was based in Harare whilst attending university picked me up to spend the day together. We cruised around for some entertainment visiting the usual hotspots enjoying drinks with other acquaintances. He told me that he had a date later that evening and would pick me up first so we could all go to the dance together. I had no car back then so was pleased to have him around and that he enjoyed my company. We had known each other for many years, having gone to the same schools and boarded at the same hostel during our secondary schooling days. He was a real gentleman and had gone about it the right way and had asked her mum and step father if he could take her out. So off we went, smartly dressed, afro combed out, well-groomed and my friend knocked at the door. Her stepfather opened the door to receive us but seemed displeased to see me. I'm not sure who he thought I was. Perhaps I appeared like some menacing character, so he vented his displeasure at me. I was kind of shocked and thought this must be a case of mistaken identity and just ignored the rant and he soon calmed down. She came out and my friend introduced her to me. She was a natural beauty, no make up, of slim build, with brown hair which was well styled with a flicked back fringe. She had these eyes, warm hazel in colour with a greenish tint and dimples on her chin and cheek. She was really cute and came across so innocent, fresh out of school as I learned later. Her skin tone was light and tanned. I just admired her beauty but had no intentions after all she was my friend's date for that evening. We went to the dance and sat all together, but as the night wore on and after some drinks we really got on well together and I found myself being attracted to her. By the end of that night I think the feeling was mutual. I am not sure whether my friend noticed it as he did not display any signs of annoyance for the fact that I was 'moving in' rather fast. We had a great time that night and my friend took her home as he had promised and made a date to pick her up the following day. The arrangement was that he would pick her up together with me from my brother Billy's house in Saint Martins, perhaps he thought to save a trip as she lived in a suburb called Vietnam some distance from Saint Martins. I must say that I was rather surprised to see her and her brother that day. She however told me that my friend had arranged to pick both of us up at my brother Billy's house and hence the reason she was there. I think it was at that moment as we waited for my friend to arrive that the spark occurred. She was so beautiful I just couldn't help myself. The attraction was just too great so I boldly said to her and her brother "Let's not wait for my friend, let's just go ahead alone." To my surprise she agreed and that was the day, it was love at first sight and so off we went. I never saw my friend again until some months later. I think he saw the writing on the wall as he didn't turn up. Perhaps he did turn up but we had already left so he may have thought, well that's it I've been snookered. Some 'friend' I was, but then again, she was not his girlfriend, she was free. I had not even considered his feelings; how I had upset him. Somehow he got over it and we remain friends to this day.

For my girlfriend and I this was the beginning of a long-lasting relationship. She was just sixteen years old, fresh out of school and I had just turned twenty-two worldly wise, hardened by my military experience, carefree, self-confident with a huge responsibility towards my mother and siblings hanging over me, a responsibility I have borne right to this day. She too had her own responsibilities together with her siblings as they were not a well-off family, so life was difficult. She was so innocent, a blank page, but came across very mature for her age I thought, caring with a quiet personality. I loved her deeply, this was really love at first sight. It was rather difficult at first since we lived apart so we could not see each other as often as we liked. We were four hundred and forty kilometres apart; she in Harare and I in Bulawayo. Our relationship blossomed and grew as we continued to maintain very close contact in the form of letter writing and weekly telephone conversations. A visit to a phone box every Friday afternoon became my regular routine for months on end as I did not have access to a telephone where I was living. We exchanged visits every so often. I would travel by train to Harare for weekends and she did likewise to Bulawayo when we would spend weekends together. At first she would spend those weekends with her granny in Barham Green. That became our rendezvous where we would meet. Later on she stopped going there and came to spend weekends with me in QueensPark where I was renting a friend's house. This went on for months and I think it was sometime around the end of 1976 or early 1977 that I asked her to move in with me and to my surprise she agreed. This was taboo in those days, she was too young as the age of consent was twenty one back then and she was just turning eighteen at that time. Her mother and family were displeased but they could not stop her. I was independent and had no one to answer to. My mother only found out after the act. To us, it seemed like it was the natural progression of our relationship. Please note dear Reader that I have chosen not to mention my girlfriend, who later became my wife, by name out of respect for her. She chose to remain anonymous as she is a very private person and wishes to remain so.

I was now sharing a flat in Bertha Court, Connaught avenue in Bulawayo with my young brother George and a friend Stanley O'Brian when she moved in with me. She didn't seem bothered at first I guess she was happy to be with me and I with her and that's all that mattered. At some point Stanley moved back to his family leaving just the three of us. I was happy that he moved out but George stayed with us. I didn't have a choice then as I had the responsibility to look after him, so she understood my situation. So all three of us then moved to rent another flat opposite Ramjis in Grey Street as it was nearer to my job. It was a better location, nearer to the city centre and amenities. It was at this flat that an unexpected turn of events occurred. We accommodated my friend Stanley Woodend who was struggling with mental health issues at that time. He had no one to turn to but me as we were home-boys and close friends. It was Stanley that had put in a word for me for an apprenticeship back in 1975 so I felt obligated to help him in his time of need. We were after all working together at Morewear Industries. My girlfriend did not object so I thought it was the right thing to do. In addition to Stanley, my brother Clement lived with us too whenever he was discharged from the mental hospital. So here we were living with two mentally unstable men together with my young brother George. It was a real volatile situation as both Clement and Stanley would experience relapses now and again and be referred back to the hospital. How my girlfriend coped in silence I do not know.

One day we faced an unexpected frightening encounter with my brother Clement who was having a hallucination episode as he had relapsed. My girlfriend and I were conversing in the lounge when suddenly Clement lunged at me with a knife directed to my chest and stabbed me, fortunately the knife he chose was home made from flimsy metal and long-bladed so it bent on impact. He had accused us just prior of claiming to be Mary and Joseph, the biblical characters. It was a frightening experience from nowhere, sudden and without warning. I noticed, in just that split second, that he was really zoned out and hallucinating as he said to me "So you think you are Joseph" and to my girlfriend he said "so you think you are Mary" and the next thing he lunged at me with the knife stabbing me in the chest. We all ran out of the flat to the streets to call the police who later apprehended him and admitted him to the mental hospital. Life was proving to be topsy-turvy, how my dear beloved girlfriend coped with that situation having to share a home with four men I really don't know. I was just oblivious of her feelings and thoughtless. I just thought everything was ok until she had had enough and moved out to her own flat in Denim Court, a block of apartments. We were all traumatised by that experience, so I understood that she had reached her tether breaking point. That was the last straw for her as she couldn't take it anymore. I wondered how she managed to rent a bachelor flat at Denham Court as this block of flats was segregated for white folks only. It just so happened that they thought she was obviously white although with some reservation and only agreed to let the flat to her when she said that her father was white and he was prepared to prove it, of course her real father was in England so one of her work colleagues, an older English gentleman, was going to stand in for her. That worked to dodge the apartheid system which was still prevalent. Coincidentally it was at this time too that both George and I were called up to serve a stint in the military. George for his National Service and for me it was another sixty-day call up, this time in the Nkayi District, a rural area outside Bulawayo. So conveniently, my girlfriend accommodated my furniture, which wasn't much, and I went to do my stint. It was during this time that some risky incidents I was involved in took place as I have already described in a previous chapter. When I finished my military call-up at Nkayi I returned to civilian life and my girlfriend and I had made up and we moved to a one bedroom flat in the same block at Denham Court. It was then that Jehovah's Witnesses began a weekly bible study program with us. I did not immediately change my conduct, I was still misbehaving until she 'kicked' me out together with my furniture one night after I went on a binge drinking night out. She locked me out until the next morning, forcing me to spend the night at my mothers house in Sauerstown. I awakened that morning only to see a van pulling into the yard with all my furniture. I think that incident really shook me to the core and brought me back to my senses. I redirected the driver to go back to Denham Court and I humbled myself before my girlfriend who once again took me back. We again made up, kissed, and cuddled. It was soon after that that I gave serious thought to our relationship and the biblical truths I was learning and began to make changes in my life. Slowly at first but gradually things got better and our relationship improved. I was still smoking and drinking though but moderately. It was then I went down with malaria for a few weeks. I may have contracted it from my military service in the rurals, malaria really knocked me for six. I was absent off work for nearly three weeks: ill in bed with uncontrollable shakes and serious headaches. My Doctor and my dear girlfriend nursed me back to health. It was then that I made a decision to give up smoking and cut down on my drinking. The only way I could do this was to refrain from going to pubs because I would always relapse when I did. That worked for me as I eventually gave up smoking for good in 1979. Our bible study program continued and in time we decided to get married as it was the right thing to do in God's eyes. We did this on June 29 1979 after obtaining an age waiver by consent through her mother as my wife had just turned twenty this still was under the age of consent which was twenty one in those years. We got married in a civil ceremony at the magistrate's registrar office at the High Court building and as we came out to be greeted by family and friends we were surprised to see our bible teacher who was coincidentally attending a different wedding ceremony. I guess he was pleased to see us taking a stand for morality. Our reception was a simple one conducted in my mothers garden in Sauerstown in a huge temporary canvas gazebo. Stanley Woodend was my best man and he and I celebrated with a bottle of one hundred pipers whisky and that was the last time I ever overindulged. I made a promise to God and to my mother-in-law on that day that they would never see me intoxicated ever again, and I have kept that promise to date. My mother in law booked us a suite for the night at the holiday Inn. My wife looked stunningly beautiful and as we entered the Holiday Inn some white chaps were dining and drinking in the main Foyer and they all suddenly turned in our direction and one of them said to me "you lucky man you!" which I took as a compliment. Back then no white person would engage in friendly conversation with any of us, non whites I mean, it just didn't happen for fear of being ostracised, so this commendation was rare. It felt like I was receiving some sort of approval from them.

Our bible study program was really a Godsend. It helped us navigate through our relationship as we learnt to apply the true standards necessary for a happy family: the God ordained standard of conduct between husbands and wives, parenting standards and child and parent relationships. It was during this time that Jehovah's Witnesses published a bible study aid entitled "Making your family life happy." I remember that publication so well. It was a thirty-two page book, green in colour and was published in late 1978. It was used during the Church's weekly bible study arrangement in smaller family groups conducted in a home setting. It was the 'perfect' study aid, the whole breadth of God's standards with regards to a successful family unit, all condensed in this publication. I learnt how to be a father and a husband and my wife a mother and wife in accordance with God's word. We learnt about what God expects of us as parents, how to bring up our children and how to discipline them in love. It was just the perfect gift and a perfectly timed one. Without it we were going to fumble our way through, treating each other as we saw fit, either in accordance with our own standards or perhaps in accordance with the conduct we observed from our own parents or otherwise. I can't remember the number of months it took to go through that book but at the end we were ready to start a family, which we did with our first child, Francine, who was born in January of 1980. We were now convinced that we had found a religion that satisfied all our needs, a form of worship that would be a way of life and we both dedicated our lives to God and symbolised that dedication by water baptism on June 28, 1980.

When Francine was born, we were living in an attractive flat in Kings Court Kings Avenue in Bulawayo. Materially, we were doing well too. We were fully furnished and I had bought our first car, a yellow Alfa Romeo Alfasud. I was proud of it, and cleaned it 'every day.' My wife eventually stopped working, by mutual agreement, as we felt it was the right thing to do in order to give our children the full attention that they would need in God's eyes. I could afford to take care of my family so I agreed for my wife to be a fully fledged housewife and mother which she did for the next seventeen years. Fran was a lovely child who did not give us any stress at all. We bedded her in her own cot and she used to sleep soundly most nights. She proved to be a real pleasure to us parents. As time went on she developed into a pleasant, well behaved, mature and bright child in terms of intellect. Her caring, motherly personality came to our aid in later years as I will explain a little later. Our second child Benjamin was born August 14, 1983. We both thought at the time that God had given us the perfect 'pigeon pair' and that our family was now complete, we had a son and a daughter. We named him Benjamin after my father. He was a handsome boy with bright blue eyes and a cute, dimpled smile. I now had two beautiful children including a beautiful wife. What else could I ask for? I felt fulfilled in every way. When Benjamin was born we moved to a house in Parklands, one of the eastern suburbs in Bulawayo, a property that would provide the space and grounds for our children to enjoy. Life was good, the country enjoyed one of the highest standards of living in the world, and I was fortunate to have a job that enabled me to provide well for my family to the extent that my wife would never have to work again. We had a gardener and domestic employee, a maid, to help out with chores. During those years in Rhodesia many parents opted to have their children looked after by their maids whilst they worked. Whilst this option proved economically advantageous for such families my wife and I and many other parents of like mind felt the opposite that such an arrangement would be detrimental to the child-parent relationship. As the saying goes, "the proof is in the pudding" and both my wife and I have celebrated the fact that the decision we made has proved to be the correct one as we continue to have close contact and a close relationship with our children. Life was really good back then, we enjoyed probably one of the highest standards of living in the world. Added to that was the perfect climate and holidays to South Africa each year. Also holidays in our home country included trips to Kariba, Victoria Falls, weekend picnics and BBQ's at Matopos Hills. It was a wonderful way of life. That was the average Zimbabwean lifestyle back then which I have treasured to this day. It was after one such holiday to South Africa in December of 1985 that tragedy struck my family. It was the worst of nightmares that I would never wish on anyone, not even my worst enemy.

We went on holiday to South Africa and on our way back we visited one of my mother-in laws friends in Johannesburg. We all visited the branch office and printery of Jehovah's Witnesses in Krugersdorp, a suburb just outside Johannesburg. We spent the afternoon there and enjoyed a brief guided tour of the facilities. Benjamin seemed rather boisterous that day and during the whole holiday, a bit of unusual behaviour. He had disappeared from us for a few minutes in a clothing store at one point, but we eventually found him amongst some ladies clothing. For him it just seemed like play time: for us it was a scary moment. The second incident occurred when we were leaving my mother in law's friend's house. The car was packed and we were saying our niceties and goodbyes only to realise that Benjamin was missing. We were frantic, my sister Gwen was also with us on that occasion, we looked everywhere inside the house and in every possible hiding place to no avail. The child was gone, disappeared, then my wife ran down the driveway into the next-door neighbour's property and found him there wondering about in his own little world. He had made his way down the hill, as the house was on an upward incline, out the main gate and around the corner into the neighbours. We were relieved and overjoyed. We completed our goodbyes and off we went on the long journey back to Bulawayo. The third incident occurred on the road. Those days our cars had no seat belts, Benjamin was seated on my sister

Gwen's lap in the rear seat, fortunately Gwen was holding him around the waist but somehow he managed to open the door of the car whilst we were travelling at high speed. A quick reaction from her prevented a disaster, and Gwen shut the door on impulse. We eventually arrived home safely, stressed and exhausted and thought Satan was after our child or was it just a case of the 'terrible twos syndrome'. I went back to work the first Monday in January after the usual two-week holiday season. That was the week that changed our lives forever.

My wife decided to visit her sister that Wednesday. They had a lovely house in Morningside complete with a gated swimming pool. It was during school holidays and the kids were playing and running around in the yard whilst enjoying a swim. She had ensured that the front door leading to the pool area was locked and that the children were safe inside. My wife was always very conscious of where the children were at each moment in time and that day was no different. She was enjoying conversation with her sister in the kitchen whilst Benjamin was inside playing with one of the girls. At lunch time her sister's husband came home for lunch and during their conversations he stated that he had a strange feeling that something was going to happen that day. Apparently in that week someone had died each day in a different property in succession leading up to theirs, so he thought that he was going to be the next statistic on that day. This may sound a little weird dear reader but that is the plain truth of what occurred in that week, it was as if Satan literally walked that street, in that week, to cause harm but instead of my wife's brother-in-law being the next victim in his imagined scenario it was our son Benjamin.

The front door that faced the swimming pool area was inadvertently left ajar. It was a busy day with children running around swimming and playing, and our son Benjamin somehow made his way, without being noticed, out the door and into the swimming pool where he fell in and drowned. All my wife could hear was a scream from her niece who was with him, in one of the bedrooms, a few minutes earlier "Benjamin is in the pool!" My wife was frantic as she ran out to the pool area. By then one of the older boys had jumped in and got him out and laid him on the cemented pool area where she tried to resuscitate him by mouth-to-mouth resuscitation to no avail. The ambulance was called, and they rushed our son together with my wife to Central hospital. She was distraught. I cannot imagine the emotional turmoil she went through at that moment. This was a mother's worst nightmare! A nightmare she would never awaken from.

I was at work on that day. It was a busy day at the office. The phone rang constantly for business, from customers and suppliers: it was never ending until the next caller ended it all for me. This time it was my sister-in-law at the other end of the line. All she said was "Francis, Benjamin drowned, my sister has gone to the Central hospital with him." It felt as if I had been struck by a ten-tonne truck! I was dumbfounded in shock. Did I hear correctly I questioned? I rushed out of my office and told my Manager the bad news I had just received. I frantically drove like a maniac to hospital, almost causing an accident on the way. I arrived at the hospital and was directed to where my wife and Benjamin were. The ambulance crew and the hospital had tried everything possible without success. My son was dead. They had laid him outstretched on a bed in a private room. He was still in his water drenched clothes, handsome as ever and appeared to be asleep. He was just two years and three months old. I hugged my wife and we sobbed uncontrollably together as we observed his lifeless body which appeared so tranquil, so at peace as if in a deep sleep. We eventually composed ourselves and just stared at Benjamin in silence. It seemed like we could not fathom what had just happened. It was like a bad dream that wasn't real, a dream that we would awaken from. We eventually had to leave him but returned over and over again as if to confirm the reality of the situation. The nursing staff on hand were most sympathetic; they were saddened too and seemed to understand the trauma of losing a child. We went back home devastated by it all. We prayed to God in tears and asked him a simple question "Why Us?" My faith was rocked and so was that of my wife. This was five years down the line of our conversion. We felt like the man Job in the bible account: we finally understood his and his wife's trauma. We couldn't think, we had no clue what to do next. Everyone soon rallied to our aid, family and friends. The Elders in our congregation took the reins and organised everything for us, all the funeral arrangements including the church service. It was a time of unimaginable emotion and overwhelming support from not only our congregation members but others from elsewhere, from friends and family, a multitude of people. We laid our son to rest in a white coffin draped with a beautiful bouquet of flowers and had the following words engraved on his headstone of grey marble "In Loving memory of our beloved son and brother Benjamin, we hope in the resurrection of the dead when we will see you again, Daddy Mummy and Fran" and included a reference from the bible 1Thesselonians 4:13,14. We received such support for weeks on end, we were never left alone until we were strong enough to stand alone. I felt like the Almighty was holding my hand all the way, like a parent holding the hand of his child whilst they learn to walk, until we were able to stand up alone once again to carry on with our lives. We had our daughter Francine to care for and each other. Satan had indeed succeeded. We were convinced that he had struck us a devastating blow just like he had done in Jobs' case but we were not going to give up nor blame God for what had happened. We slowly settled back into our routine; my employer had given me one month's fully paid compassionate leave to enable me to recover sufficiently to get back to work once again which I did. Life had to go on. Full recovery was long and painful. We mourned our son in silence for months. I prayed incessantly for God in his mercy and begged him to recuperate us like he did with Job. Months passed: we had to change the environment as the house in Parklands had too many memories of Benjamin. So I eventually managed to buy our first house in Hillcrest Bulawayo in early 1986. The move contributed to the healing process as it was a fresh start, a new home for my family and future family.

Soon my wife got pregnant and gave birth to another son Ewan who was born in 1986 and following that our third son Michael came along in 1988. God had indeed answered our prayers by blessing us not only with one more son but two in succession. God had truly healed us because the pain of loss subsided in time, and we were able to continue living concentrating now on our new family. I was later appointed as an Elder in my congregation, a ministry that I fulfilled with diligence until 1997 when we moved to England. It kept me and my family spiritually focused and engaged. Time passed, and we later on, at the end of 1991, moved to Gaborone in Botswana as I have already discussed in my previous chapter. My sisters Betty and Gwen, with the help of our cousin Lionel, organised a farewell get together for the family that December prior to our leaving. I borrowed a video camera from a friend to record this moment together with other moments of our home activities and play time as a remembrance for the future. My nephew Late Roy Cohen was sitting on the pool steps with my son Ewan on his lap, Francine was happily swimming along. It was then that we noticed my son Michael and my sister's son Brett playing a little tug of war with a snorkel. Michael had his back to the pool, it suddenly dawned on us that if Brett let go of the snorkel Michael would end up in the pool and no one would be close enough to get him out in time. He would drown, we thought, he was only three years old. We would have had another tragedy on our hands, perhaps our feelings were exaggerated but we could not take that chance, so we reacted automatically by shouting warnings directed at him which he and Brett fortunately heeded, and they moved away from the pool area. We still have this video and have viewed it a couple of times after our move to England. We cannot bear to watch it any more as this particular incident comes across as if my son was being reprimanded rather than being warned of the danger. My mother let the pool naturally dry up after that occasion and it remains so until this day, as she was in fear of another accidental drowning. The cost of maintaining it was becoming prohibitive too. The rest of the day proved to be an enjoyable relaxing time, the kids were having fun, and the adults ate and drank and conversed until the evening.

Soon we were on the road to Botswana, our new home for the next four years. We loved Botswana, it was a politically stable country with a low crime rate, and a free people. We lived in Botswana until the end of 1994. Melanie, our youngest, was born in Botswana in April 1994. We decided then that our family was now complete, four living children, two boys and two girls, a perfect balance. Life in Botswana, though, was a mixed bag of joy, hardship with the stress and strains of life. Many challenges to keep the business afloat whilst trying to maintain a balance in my Christian duties and care for my family. In the end things did not work out so we moved on as I have already mentioned previously. The stress had taken its toll on my health as I was diagnosed with Hypoglycemia when we returned to Bulawayo Zimbabwe in 1995. We had done the full circle and were back where we started. Once again we settled down, sold our property in Hillcrest and purchased another in Riverside. It was a lovely spacious home with domestic quarters and a large, terraced garden overlooking the Joburg road. We would often sit on the verandah just reminiscing watching the traffic whilst enjoying a cold glass of beer. It was a tranquil environment. I thought we were done. I had a good well-paying Job, my sons were in private school a stone's throw from where we lived, my eldest in a good secondary school, my wife did not need to work, we had a Gardener and Domestic employee / Maid to assist with chores. What more could I ask for; life was good we were back on track. I lived like 'King George' as my wife often reiterated so many times after we moved to England, and she was right as I shall explain in my next chapter.

Another tragic occurrence took place in 1995 with my mother in law's death. We just hadn't realised just how ill she was until the end. My wife took it very hard as they had a very close relationship. She was a lovely person and often spent some time with us. I too had a good relationship with her. I witnessed the changes she had made in her life including her religious journey and conversion as she too became one of Jehovah's Witnesses. We were now united, not only as family but also in faith. It was after her death that my wife expressed her desire to move to England, she had been traumatised and unhappy. I thought about it long and hard as a husband and father of my children. I thought about our future, the future in particular for my children, so I eventually agreed for her to go to England and investigate the possibility of our move. She went alone early in December of 1995 for a couple of weeks and returned with such a positive view of England. She looked refreshed and happy. I was pleased to see her uplifted and so positive but I was cautious. Perhaps a little too cautious as I contemplated all the 'what ifs' the negatives. What if the children didn't like it? Was I going to be happy? How would I handle the change? What if things went wrong? What if, what if this and what if that.! My wife asked me to sell the house so we could have sufficient financial backing. How I wish I had listened to her, this was one of my greatest regrets as I shall explain in a later chapter. She had made up her mind that it would be in our best interest. I wasn't so sure, I felt threatened and frightened for my family, so I decided to compromise. Okay, "we'll go," I said, "but let's rent out the house first until we are settled and then we can sell up." She agreed, and so we began our move.

Me taken Jan 1979

my wife when we met 1975

when we were single 1977

My wife on our wedding day 1979

our wedding day June 1979

Francine and Benjamin 1984

Our son Benjamin November 1985

Benjamin Painting 2017

My son benjamin resting place 2023

Family in Botswana 1992

my family 1995

My families home Bulawayo 1996

MIGRATING TO ENGLAND

My decision to move to England was the most troublesome decision for me as there were too many unknowns. My wife was sure that it was the best decision for us as a family. She had such a positive attitude that I had to recognise, for one thing she had travelled alone for the first time in her life to a foreign country determined to find her father and to obtain all the necessary documentation we would need to effect our move. She travelled as far as Liverpool to obtain her grandparents' birth, death and marriage certification in order to prove her ancestral lineage. The next step was to sell our furniture and most of our belongings with the exception of some sentimental stuff like gifts and 'necessary' items that we thought we were going to need to add to the little savings we had and to rent out the house. Items like linen, bedding, cutlery, her favourite cast iron frying pan, pots, pans, dinner sets, our favourite oval shaped mirror with gold painted cast framing including a pap stick. That was a must have. Where could we buy a pap stick in England we thought. We were typical Zimbabweans at that. This stick dear reader is an essential item in every household in Zimbabwe. It is a specially shaped wooden stick with a flat oval shaped end the same length as a long arm cooking spoon but designed to cook maize meal into a thickened porridge similar to mash potatoes but with a much denser viscosity. A favourite indigenous food in southern Africa. All the items were packed away and shipped to Southampton England by Glens Removals. We didn't even have the money to cover the cost of shipping so we had to borrow Z$5000 (£350.00) from the family. Little did we know that we would have to pay an additional £200 just to deliver these same goods from the port of Southampton to our first place of abode in the East London Borough of Barking. Following that we travelled to the British High Commission in Harare to submit our application for residency in the United Kingdom. We were briefly interviewed during the submission process and were advised that the High Commission would respond to our application at a later date. My wife had decided that she was going to apply for herself and the girls in London and hence soon after left with them late December 1996. I remained with the boys to finalise things and organise the letting of our house. Following that I moved with them temporarily to my mothers. The next three months were awful. I put the boys to school at Milton Junior until we were ready to move. That proved to be not a wise move when my son Michael revealed to me that he was being bullied by his teacher. I later took them out of school closer to the time of our departure. Next was the long waiting game for our visas. I was rather disappointed as I had expected to receive them on the same day after all we had all the necessary papers. To add to the stress, I had very presumptuously booked our Blue Arrow coach trip for 1pm 16 March 1997 including our flight from Johannesburg airport for that same evening at 8 pm. It suddenly dawned on me that I had taken a massive risk as there was no guarantee that we would receive our visas on time. The clock ticked on. February came and went, March arrived, then the weeks then it was days and still no passports no visas.! We were packed and ready. The stress was unbearable. My boys did not have a clue of what I was going through. Finances were tight. I had expended resources and only exchanged the maximum I could which was equal to a meagre £400. It was ironic that if one was going on holiday one could take out as much as fifty thousand Zimbabwean dollars per person as foreign exchange was plentiful and not an issue in those days however if one was immigrating the allowance was reduced to only a thousand dollars per person. This realisation came to haunt me in 1998 when I eventually sold our property. I would learn a hard lesson, a lesson of colossal proportions. A massive misjudgement of events. I will explain that a little later. The Zimbabwe dollar to British pound exchange rate back in 1997 was favourable at about fifteen dollars to the British pound but I had noticed already at that time that there were signs of a slow economic downturn. It seemed like 'the writing was on the wall', the markets were fluctuating. To think that at one point The Rhodesian dollar, which was later changed to the Zimbabwean dollar in 1980, was equal to the British pound between the years 1970 - 1980 and now the situation was so volatile. Perhaps my wife was correct, after all, it was the right time to jump ship as it were, although the rate of fifteen to one was reasonable in 1997 considering the time lapse of seventeen years from 1980. Never did I contemplate just how serious the economic downturn would prove to be in the 12 months that followed.

Our passports eventually arrived early morning on March 16 by DHL. I was exhausted after all the daily phone calls to enquire about the whereabouts of our passports. I soon discovered that the British High Commission office had misplaced our application and the passports, so after a frantic investigation and search they were eventually discovered, approved and shipped to us at the eleventh hour. I don't recall ever explaining this saga to my two boys as I didn't want to cause them unnecessary anxiety at the time. We were happy to receive them and at last, finally, ready to board our coach and make our way. We said our goodbyes with hugs and many tears. It was a painful departure for me. It was like my heart was being ripped apart, my love for my wife and kids on one side and that of my mother and my siblings on the other. My boys seemed excited and oblivious of my internal strife. They were always happy kids like twins, close, always together, slept in the same bedroom together, played together, they were inseparable. They had each other for company and I on the other hand felt so alone wallowing in my own pain. I was reminded of the biblical proverb which rang so true for me during that time "even in laughter the heart may be in pain" I could not be consoled. En route I heard my son Michael whisper to his brother "Dad is not talking to us Ewan" if only he knew what was going through my mind. The sadness I felt at the same time looking forward to being with my wife and daughters, my emotions were all over the place. We had never been apart as a family before this time, ever, so three months was like a lifetime. A very long time and it took its toll as it affected all of us, me, my wife and my children. Till this day of writing we have never really discussed our feelings in detail. We have kind of buried them with the view of letting bygones remain bygones, water under the bridge scenario. I just could not bring myself to converse with my boys in my usual manner and my son sensed it but did not understand my trauma. I also did not consider how they felt being away from their mother for so long, what were they thinking? I was silent with my own thoughts on that journey until suddenly the coach stopped in the middle of nowhere en-route to Johannesburg. We were long past Messina, a border town along the South African side, when the breakdown occurred. My first thought was "what now?" as we were racing against time, the clock was ticking, and we just could not afford a breakdown. I started thinking that this trip was never meant to be. This was a bad omen. All that was left was for the plane to crash. Fortunately the coach Driver and his co-driver managed to carry out the repair in good time, whatever it was I didn't want to know. We arrived in Johannesburg that evening and we were met by my brother in law Jacob who drove us to the airport arriving by the skin of our teeth as the saying goes. We had made it, now finally the last lap. My boys were excited; it was their first time on a plane. I perked up a bit too, we were nearly there. I had no clue though what awaited us. I do not sleep well on flights so was up most of the night whilst my boys appeared content and slept through. I had no idea what life in the United Kingdom was like. I had of course seen pictures in magazines but that was always a casual glance as I had no interest whatsoever about moving to England. Zimbabwe was my home. I loved the people and still do, to this day, the culture, the weather and most of all the quality of life, a standard of living we took so much for granted. I had never imagined life elsewhere. I soon was going to experience an awakening of such huge proportions; an awakening of such magnitude in so many ways. This was going to be my test, a test of who I was, a test of my spirituality and that of my family, a test of the strength of one's character both emotional and physical. The plane glided through space silent as if in harmony with my emotions until dawn broke. It was a beautiful morning. I looked out the aeroplane window and stared with awe just how beautiful England is from the air. This was God's artistic master brush stroke I thought I had never seen in my life. So many shades of green. The countryside is of such beauty in contrast to the many shades of brown and greys with some patches of green over some parts of the African continent. We landed safely the following morning, and were cleared without incident. Immigration called my wife on the intercom to meet us. We were welcomed with the words "welcome to the United Kingdom", so far so good I thought. The realisation had not yet set in. I was still rather detached in la la land as it were. This was the time of new beginnings, March 17 1997, a fresh start, a wife, four children and only £400 in my pocket.

NEW BEGINNINGS

My wife's determination came through loud and clear on that day, she was our guide. I was going to follow her lead as she had three months upfront experience. She had made the journey to Croydon to the Home Office and had successfully obtained her 'Indefinite Stay, a right to abode' visa including our girls. She had gotten a job in Derbyshire in the county of Lancashire, the northern part of England. She had found temporary accommodation as a friend's mother who was residing in that part of the country had invited her to stay with her for a time. We had met her mother during one of her visits to Zimbabwe some months earlier in 1996. We all had one thing in common, our Faith, being members of the same religion so we kind of felt comfortable with one another. What I had come to witness and appreciate throughout our lives to that point was that Jehovah's witnesses are a united Faith both in terms of belief, practice and Brotherly love, a unity that is rare but recognised all over the world. We had travelled in the past and met people we never knew beforehand in Durban, in Johannesburg, in Pretoria, in Botswana, in Bulawayo and in Harare and we were always welcomed and received kindly by reason of our common Faith. This was a true brotherhood experience. So, this was no different. My wife had been received kindly and accommodated hospitably by her friend's mother whom we had just briefly met. We left the airport and headed to the Coach Station to catch National Express to Lancashire. It was a scary moment, people everywhere, I had never seen so many people in my life, crowds on the pavements, crowds at the station all heading somewhere. We held each other's hands and those of our children including our baggage and fearing the unknown. We spent some days in Lancashire and then headed back to London and spent a few days with my sister in law's step daughter who kindly accommodated us in her tiny flat. She soon arranged for us to rent accommodation with one of her friends in Barking, a suburb in East London. Why did we end up in London and not elsewhere? Simply put it was because my sister in law's step daughter was the only person we knew in the whole of England, so it was normal to end up where one had some support. Most migrants to the UK end up living in the same areas with family or friends unless one is an asylum seeker where you can be placed anywhere. We had not done any research. We had no access to the internet, nor did we know whether there was information we could have obtained from books or magazines about life in England. We just failed to make any inquiries nor research. We were literally starting on a blank page: completely naive. The house we rented belonged, we thought, to a black family from the Congo. It was a three bedroomed property furnished but unkempt. It was a strange set up. The conditions they made with us was that one room would be out of bounds for us as it contained some of their belongings, the second condition was that they would from time to time visit unannounced to spend a few hours at the property. We accepted the conditions because we had no choice and also the rental was cheap, only £50 a week. My wife and I found jobs within the first three weeks of arrival in the west end of London through an Employment Agency. These were just labouring jobs, so we accepted what we got. We would leave the house early in the morning each day to start work at 7:30 a.m. in the west end of London and return each evening around 6pm. Why the west end of London? Could we not have got jobs in Barking? Yes, we could have but we didn't know any agencies in that area neither did we know that there were places such as Job Centres, so we just plodded on 'blindly' and later just got accustomed to the routine and didn't bother to search for jobs nearer to where we were living. Our eldest daughter was seventeen years old then and so she was able to look after her siblings when we went to work. Our youngest daughter was just three years old; and our two sons were ten and nine years old respectively. We owe our gratitude to our eldest daughter who took such great responsibility head on and carried it out without a single complaint. The new school term in the United Kingdom fortunately begins in September so our children had time off from school until then and it gave us sufficient time to re-organise ourselves and to find the appropriate schools for them. One thing we resolved to do as a family was never to miss our Church meetings so we found one as soon as we arrived in England in West Ham which we regularly attended. Our Christian brothers and sisters welcomed us with open arms; they were now our new and immediate extended family. We never let up on our preaching activities either which helped us to get to know one another and to familiarise ourselves with the surroundings and general attitudes of people. Our unity as a religious organisation which we had experienced in Africa was evident in England too. We were not alone anymore, our beliefs and practices and our form of worship were the same. We had a common goal united in purpose, a unity that is unique and rare in today's world. My letter of recommendation as an Elder came through and I was to be reappointed in my new congregation, however this time I chose to stand down as I felt that my family would require my full undivided attention because of the challenges that lay ahead. Emotionally I was not up to it. It's a wonderful privilege to serve the flock of God as an appointed man, to shepherd them and care for their spiritual needs but this time, I was not in the right frame of mind. This time I too would need the help and so I felt I could not in good conscience do justice to my 'brothers and sisters' and so I decided to step down.

During our first few weekends we tidied up the garden of the house we were living in. It was overgrown with weeds and once we had done that it revealed a neatly paved patio beneath. Our neighbours were so impressed and would greet us or comment as they passed by, a well kept garden is a big thing in England. The neighbours are always unimpressed with an unkempt one as it spoils the neighbourhood, so many were appreciative for what we had done including the 'owners' who then brought us a colour television as a thank you gesture. We soon discovered that this was a Council property and that the people we were renting from were actually breaking the law by subletting the property and that was the reason why they would show up unannounced to give the false impression of residing there. Thereafter we soon moved out to our own rented property in the Barking town centre close to the train (Tube) station. It was a large three bedroomed Flat above a shop. We were comfortable and our children were happy. We organised their schooling and our life became settled and orderly. Our jobs were mainly warehouse Operatives at the start, we would be sent anywhere to work in production lines or warehouses to do 'picking' of goods, loading, and unloading delivery trucks. It was back breaking work. I finally appreciated what labouring was all about. I went back in time in my mindset and reflected on the hard work that black people were subjected to during the apartheid years in Rhodesia, the abuse that they experienced from unappreciative employers. It was slavery in a different form than how they were underpaid and often overworked as Gardeners and Maids. This was an awakening for me after twelve years of sitting in an office in a managerial role back home. My wife and I eventually found decent permanent employment in the west-end of London, she at the Hilton Hotel as a Housekeeper and me in a shoe distribution warehouse of Faith Shoes in the west end of London. We just about managed with our combined salaries to take care of our family. Life was stressful but had started to improve for us. My wife was happy and felt fulfilled with a measure of independence. On the other hand, I was hurting inside. I was unhappy and depressed. I was in 'zombie' mode most of the time going to work, silent in my own thoughts whilst listening to the warehouse radio blasting out Robbie Williams' signature song "Angels". I felt like the Jews when they left Egypt: how they longed for the 'onions and the leeks and the garlic' they had left behind. I longed for my life in Africa, the comforts, the culture, and the people. I needed something different, I needed to get out of the warehouse environment and back to my profession to have my mind challenged. I trolled the newspaper adverts for jobs in my profession and eventually landed a job as a Project Estimator in a town called Wolverhampton in the Midlands of England. I began work at the company called Doncasters Paralloy Fabrications in January of 1998. My accommodation at first was a Bedsit, a single room in a shared facilities building. I soon became accustomed to my new routine, the usual Monday to Friday work, church group meetings on Tuesday evenings and weekends in London with my family. My train journey to London each Friday was always pleasing as I was looking forward to being with my wife and children, however the return trips were upsetting to say the least. It felt like I was returning to my dark and dingy prison cell. Living apart from my family was a very depressing time for me. This was now the second time in my life being apart for a period of time.

My job was interesting though it kept me focused and provided respite from my sadness. It was a new field in the petrochemical industry. It included the manufacture of Convection Heaters, various Pipe Spools in exotic materials, high grade stainless steels, in different configurations. I did the cost estimates and occasionally designed the support frames for transporting the Tube bundles. Our competitors were companies not only in the United Kingdom but also in the Middle East, Saudi Arabia, and India. It was during this time that my wife and children had to move to a smaller affordable place, a one bedroomed flat, which proved too small to accommodate all four children. We were now in a dilemma as our eldest daughter was now in secondary school doing her A levels. The two boys attended a primary school close by. We were surprised to discover that the education curriculum in junior school in England was really substandard in comparison to what our boys had learned in private education in Zimbabwe. This fact may come as a surprise to you dear reader as it is not normally discussed in the media. The fact that Zimbabwe had and still has a very high standard of education, hence the high literacy rate. They were literally a year ahead so did not fall behind considering they had missed some school during the move. The boys later moved in with me in Wolverhampton for their secondary schooling which began in September of 1998 whilst my wife and girls remained in London. This was a challenging time for me and my boys. For one thing I couldn't cook so we literally ate out of tins from our regular supermarket Aldi. Eventually one of our church friends, an elderly Jamaican couple, found us a three bedroomed house next door to them, No 71 Owen Road. His wife proved to be a blessing for us as she provided us with a cooked meal every Tuesday evening. How we looked forward to it, a tasty dish of curried / Jerk Chicken with rice and peas / red beans. Church friends supported me by taking care of my boys after school until my return form work each week. We would travel on weekends to visit the other half of my family, so this was an exciting time for the boys. My wife and daughters later joined us in Wolverhampton. Our eldest daughter had now completed her G.C.E. A levels and we were once again a complete family. I have never really spoken to my children about this sad time in our lives, this separation and the effect it had on them. I was too frightened. I felt I wouldn't be able to deal with their trauma as I was barely coping with my own sadness. So we have parked this episode of our lives forever as life was beginning to be kind to us. We were comfortable in the three bedroomed rented property right next door to our friends, the Smiths in Wolverhampton and I had bought my first car, so we had transport. My wife found a job not too far from where we lived, so things worked out pretty well. We were adjusting to life in England, which was not easy. For one, we had to both work to make ends meet, we had to find Childminders for our young daughter Melanie; we had to do all household chores including garden maintenance. This was no walk in the park! At least we now had decent jobs with decent working hours. We had made new friends once again within our new church congregation who provided good association for our children and the needed moral support for us all.

Do you recall dear reader that I made a statement earlier when we migrated to England that I would learn a hard lesson, a lesson of colossal proportions. A massive misjudgement of events. Well! This occurred sometime in September / October of 1998 when I eventually decided it was time to sell our property in Zimbabwe. Unfortunately the tenant had absconded so we had not been receiving any rental income for some months thus my decision to sell became the obvious one. I had made up my mind that we were not going back. We had to make things work for us in England although personally I was not settled but I was going to sacrifice my feelings for the greater good of my family. I had come to appreciate that if one's wife is unhappy, the whole family would be affected so I chose to set aside my comforts in Zimbabwe for the betterment of my family as a whole. I sold our property for a reasonable sum which equated to £34000.00 at an exchange rate of Z$25:£1 only for the Zimbabwean dollar to crash and free fall within two weeks of the sale. It was a colossal crash, a cliff edge scenario, I literally watched my hard-earned cash disappear in smoke within weeks from 25:1 from the time of sale to 100:1 in a matter of a few months. At the end of it all the resultant Zimbabwean dollar value was worthless. My wife and I decided to leave every penny with my mother for her upkeep. That too proved to be futile as the dollar continued to free-fall to its lowest depths and further exacerbated by the financial market crash of 2008, to trillions to the American dollar. People were carrying 'sacks' of money to the Supermarkets. It was like the Great Depression of the 1930's only this time it was in my own country, Zimbabwe. It was a painful experience for us but no way near the experience of my countrymen and family we left behind who particularly took on, head-on, the consequences of the economic crash of 2008. Many were starving as food was scarce, supermarkets were empty, they scavenged for whatever they could find to eat. I have great respect for those that stayed behind to face the depression. Their stories of resilience touched me to the heart whenever I visited in later years and still do. I have witnessed, first hand, their resilience as they juggle finances in accordance with the ever changing exchange rates and use of multiple currencies.

Back to where I was; we were going to have to start once again from scratch, with nothing! My plan to move the money across was now water under the bridge. I poured my heart out in prayer for God to find us another way and left things in his hands. My wife fortunately reacted calmly, no finger pointing in an "I told you so" rant but all she said was "Francis I told you to sell the house before we left." Yes, she was right. I had made a costly grave error of judgement and now needed her forgiveness. She had done the Christian thing to respectfully acknowledge that I was human and had made an unintentional mistake. I was just too cautious. God almighty soon answered our prayers and compensated us in an amazing unexpected way. You can call it coincidence dear reader but to us it was an answer to many prayers. Whenever I told this story to my work colleagues they have always reacted with amazement and so I shall now relate it here.

My wife,as the one who always paid attention to the fine print, reading 'between the lines' you could say, picked up a newspaper that I had discarded after just reading the bad news headlines as I usually did. On this occasion she came across an advert in small print in the usual advertising columns which read "Looking for a house to rent / buy, struggling to get a mortgage, contact this number." We had recently applied for a 100% mortgage for a four bedroomed house in Birmingham which was turned down by the particular building society offering such mortgages at the time. Their reasoning was not because we couldn't afford the repayments nor did we have a negative credit rating; it was solely based on the misunderstanding of the ancestry visa stamp on our Zimbabwean passports which read "Right to remain until a period of four years without recourse to public funds". What that statement meant was that we had the legal right to live in the United Kingdom for a period of four years without any claims to public funds / benefits, but that on completion of the four-year period, in the fifth year, we would be entitled to claim at least some child benefits and also other benefits. The additional benefits, we discovered, were based on earnings within a certain threshold. We were grateful that we would now be entitled to receive child benefit payments and, thereafter, at the completion of five years could apply for British Citizenship. The Building Society misinterpreted this to mean that we were to then return to our home country at the end of the four-year period so hence declined our mortgage application. We were back to square one until my wife came across the advert. When she said to call the number, I was rather apprehensive at first, second time doubting Thomas' scenario, thinking this was some dodgy deal but I agreed with her. She called the number. A man of Indian descent was on the other side of the line. He explained to my wife who he was and what he did for a living and invited us to come and see him, which we did. He was a pleasant, well-spoken and well-dressed individual. He explained to us that he was a professional Quantity Surveyor in the construction industry and had set up his own real estate business as a property developer, buying and selling houses and his criteria was helping people like us who were struggling to get started in the property market. He understood our situation because he too had come from India to settle in the United Kingdom with nothing. He seemed genuine so we complied with his offer. He said to us "I have two properties from which you can choose to rent, you rent it from me for a period of six months and thereafter I will pay you back your rent in full so that you can use it as deposit for a mortgage which I will arrange for you." Yes! Dear reader, we were 'gobsmacked' as the expression goes. Did we hear right we thought? How can someone literally give us a property of our choice for free. I was convinced that God almighty had indeed answered our prayers and compensated us for our loss. We soon moved house to Birmingham in early 2000. We chose an attractive three bedroomed Town house with two floors and a garage not too far from the city centre and schools. It was a convenient location, not the best but affordable. The man fulfilled his promise. We were now proud owners of our own property. I had to renovate it though to bring it to a good standard, new double-glazed windows, front and rear doors, new kitchen, re-carpeting and landscaping the garden. We were truly revived and on our way, materially speaking. Our eldest daughter had already found employment in the city, my wife changed jobs and the children settled down in their new schools once again. We changed congregations too, met new ' Brothers and sisters' and settled down to a new routine until the next blow. I lost my job in Wolverhampton after three years. Competition was too great so the company eventually shut down and I was made redundant.

This began the next phase of our life. Once again, I trolled newspaper adverts for other engineering jobs. The year 2001 was really unsettling for me. I managed to get temporary employment in one small engineering concern which was short lived, but also managed to land an interview for a Production Manager post in a heavy haulage trailer manufacturing business. I was sure that I would be a suitable candidate especially after my experience in Zimbabwe. I was shortlisted and called in for an interview. I never imagined that I would face another racially biassed scenario. This was England after all, so far I had not experienced any racially motivated incidents. I thought I had left all that behind only to be reminded once again that racism was still alive and well in England too although undercover and subtle. Sometimes I think my surname gives people the wrong impression. Cohen is a very rare surname for a non-white. I think my Interviewer, the managing Director of the business, was a little surprised to see my brown face. What he did confirm though was that I was one of two he had shortlisted. His questioning proved to me that he was concerned by the fact that I was non-white and was worried how his employees who were predominantly white English would accept me. It was like a repeat scene from 1994 when I was invited for an interview in a fabrication business just outside Johannesburg in South Africa. He asked me what my thoughts were with regards to managing a mainly white workforce. My reply was, "I judge people for what they are, by their skills and characters not by the colour of their skin" and that I had managed a multicultural workforce in Zimbabwe. That type of questioning and concerns left me with no doubt that that was the end of the road and that I would once again be 'unsuccessful' and I was. I had to find another Job and eventually registered with a number of agencies for general vacancies. I landed an interesting job with a company called Space4 in Aston Birmingham which specialised in 'Flat Pack' housing manufacture. It was a newly set up German based business with an up-to-date state of the art production line with modern CNC operated equipment. They basically manufactured houses in 'Kit' form. My job task was to assemble the inner partition panels and to ensure their dimensional accuracy. At last I felt this was a decent role especially having worked as a Meter Reader for a time after my redundancy, a job I disliked, and there was now a possibility of an upgrade into the Drawing / Cad office. I worked for Space4 for around six months until the next door of opportunity opened early in 2002.

A few things happened during late 2001 which caused us some distress. Our boys were being bullied by unscrupulous individuals who would wait for them after school to rob them of their meagre pocket money and sometimes even their casual jackets. My boys were traumatised so much so that our youngest son suffered from what we later learned were stomach migraines induced by stress. This was an unheard-of diagnosis and it came by after several visits to different doctors. It was at that point that we decided we had to get out somehow, sell up and move elsewhere to a different area or city. Birmingham was proving to be an unsafe environment. I started to troll the internet after purchasing my first computer and prayed for some guidance in finding a decent job elsewhere in order to move my family to somewhere safe. Two opportunities soon came up with employment agencies based in the city of Bristol, southwest of England, who advertised for a Manufacturing Engineer with a Fabrication and welding experience. The timing was perfect, we had just put our house up for sale with intent to move out of the area into somewhere safer for our children's well-being to which we received a positive offer within days of going to market. I had emailed my job application and c.v. during the same period and I received a positive response to attend an interview within days of submission. My interview took place in the first week in January 2002. Soon after that I was invited to a second interview which included a workshop tour. I just felt comfortable on that tour and seemed to have resonated with the Manufacturing Engineering Manager who conducted the tour. He later turned out to be my future Boss. I returned home to Birmingham feeling that I had done my best and would now await my 'fate' as it were. The reply to my interview came in my mailbox within days. I was offered employment with an attractive package and benefits incumbent to a professional business. The company was called Strachan and Henshaw based just on the outskirts of Bristol city centre. I relocated to a Bedsit type accommodation and started work 3rd January 2002. It was during this time, once again that by some miracle, you may call it a coincidence, dear Reader, but for me it was more than a coincidence it seemed as if it was planned and not by me. Tommy and I last met up in Bulawayo at my late brother Clement's funeral in mid February 2002. Tommy told me then that he was soon going to join his sister in Bristol England. The same city where I had just begun employment on the 3rd January 2002. How do you explain such an event, where you meet up with your old friend, out of the blue, in a foreign land amongst a population of some 60 million in the same year and in the same place? It's just a mind boggling event. We reconnected after some six years as I had no idea what had happened to him since our previous parting in 1996/7. We probably exchanged telephone numbers at my brother's funeral that permitted our re-connection in Bristol. The rest is history, one can say. Tommy applied for a job where I worked on my recommendation and was offered a shop floor post as a Fabricator in 2005. So, here we are today, our friendship rekindled and thriving to this very day. He is now well established and happy with a wife and two children of 18 and 11 years of age and all live a 'stone's throw' from my wife and I and my children. We speak almost every week and are constantly in comms via WhatsApp. He has been part of my family since a young age of 14 years old and remains such at this day of writing. The company changed hands twice and was finally taken over by a International Engineering conglomerate of the United Kingdom with branches in Scotland, Australia and Canada. This was the ultimate in Engineering and the best engineering environment I have ever worked in. Unfortunately I cannot divulge its name and details due to a Non-disclosure-agreement. I later discovered that my Job Role had been advertised for some eight months prior without success hence I proved to be the ideal candidate they were looking for. The main feature of my success was my skills set, I believe, having acquired multi-skilled practical qualification in Africa, from shop floor to middle and senior management roles including the understanding of design and project management principles. I soon realised the difficulty the company found itself in as the individual I was replacing was soon to retire having worked in the business from apprenticeship level. They had acquired a multitude of practical hands-on skills which proved extremely difficult to fill in the United Kingdom as most skill sets are specialist and not very often multi-faceted. So, here I was on my first day. How would I cope? How would I fit in amongst the predominantly all white staff? Would I be able to adjust quickly? Would I be able to shake off this racial 'chip on the shoulder' as some call it, the legacy from the apartheid system in Rhodesia, a system that was ingrained in us from childhood and that I awakened to in 1967? Would I face the same in this company? Would I be able to stand my ground if subjected to it? I will deal with these and other questions in my next chapter.

We eventually sold the property in Birmingham and purchased another in Bristol, so I was able to move my family down in June of 2002. My eldest daughter was now married and so remained in Birmingham for some years. They finally also joined us in Bristol. We were now re-established once more, new jobs and new schools for our three younger children. As I have already stated we moved about in England due to sheer necessity having lived in London, Wolverhampton, Birmingham and finally Bristol. What I did come to appreciate was the diverse cultures in these cities. It seemed ethnic minorities appeared to settle in certain areas perhaps due to previous ethnic ties however Bristol was and still is predominantly White English. My children thrived in their new peaceful environment so much so that my young son's stress induced stomach migraines he suffered in Birmingham finally ended. We were happy we re-settled in a new congregation and continued with our worship and spiritual life making new friendships once again. My wife and I determined to remain close to our Church environment from the day we set foot in England as we believed and still do that a spiritual based way of life would provide stability to our family and all the needed support both moral and physical. My Christian family in Bristol was no different. The congregation was made up of a number of nationalities which included English, Scottish, Polish, people from Ghana, Nigeria, Sierra Leone, Italian, Greeks and of course us from Zimbabwe. I had discovered rather quickly on arriving in England, to my dismay, that the moral climate in the United Kingdom had declined substantially in comparison to the one we were brought up in namely Colonial Rhodesia followed by Independent Zimbabwe. Much of the British values of yesteryear were maintained in Zimbabwe so I naively expected to experience the same moral climate. It's true to say though that Britain was a Christian country having based its Governmental structure and laws on Christian principles but as of this writing, and for some years now, has become more and more secular and religious influence has declined immensely. For me, I was shell shocked when I came to that realisation. The culture was very different from what I had expected. It depressed me, and I am not one who is inclined to depression but the whole environment affected me in a negative way. I was unhappy for some years and felt like I had lost faith in the British system. Being the inquisitive person that I am, I strove to investigate the reasons for such moral decline. I came to realise too, that generally people in the United Kingdom are curious too in wanting to know where you are from due to ethnicity which is a good thing as it destroys the stereotypes and provides dialogue. One day I met a Christian English Brother from our congregation and we just seemed to click because of similar interests and mindset so I asked the inevitable question that concerned me about the moral decline I was witnessing. He offered me a book to read written by Christopher Hitchens, a well-known Writer and Journalist in England titled "The moral decline of Great Britain." This book was an eye opener for me as it explained the multifaceted reasons of gradual decline particularly from the so called 'Flower Power' generation of the 1960's. The decline has been so profound in my view especially when I compared my life in Africa where censorship of media, literature, and unwholesome reading materials such as adult magazines in the public domain was so thorough that one was never exposed to any unwholesome entertainment or such materials. We had only one television station for many years, Zimbabwe Broadcasting Corporation, prior to the advent of Satellite television. The shocking contrast I noticed in the first years of our immigrating to England was the opposite. Exposure to sexual content and violence was everywhere from Escorts (Call Girl) advertisements in telephone boxes to top shelf / adult magazines, in every corner store / newsagent. We became aware when entering such an environment to walk-in with downcast eyes or eyes focused straight ahead so as to avoid the unhealthy exposure. I felt like Lot in Sodom and Gomorrah. In addition to the above there was the red light district in London called Soho. Lap dancing clubs are everywhere in the UK. I finally understood where we were in the stream of time. It was a massive awakening for me in the land of all sorts, Pagans, Goths and White Witches, Religious folk, Naturalists and Atheists. When one speaks of

Witches in Africa we speak of them with regards to Voodoo and the black arts but I soon discovered that the White Witches in England are of a different sort. The expression "Decadent West" finally made sense too. I had made the right decision to protect my family from such influences and to be resolved to stick close to our Church environment in order to maintain our moral christian values.

We settled down well in Bristol, an attractive city, picturesque with much history attached to it from that of the slave trade to the great Isambard Brunel an Engineering genius who built much of the British civil engineering and railway network projects including the famous Clifton suspension bridge in Bristol. My depression soon subsided, and I felt like Bristol had restored my faith in British culture. I have grown to love this city, its people and way of life. England is a beautiful island with breathtaking scenery, beaches, woodlands and with much history as I came to realise once more. Surprisingly too it has diverse accents conducive to their different regions and Bristolians are no different as they have certain linguistic anomalies which I found rather amusing at times but have grown to love their quirkiness. Our children did well in school as they experienced stability in their lives. They were amongst the rather few ethnic minority kids in our area. They made friendships with the white kids in their school including the diverse kids within our congregations. My wife and I soon realised the possible risk of unwholesome influence and the strong force of peer pressure so we decided on an open door policy whereby we allowed our children to enjoy the company of their friends within the safety of our home environment. That way we could assess their behaviours. One thing we did not permit was for our children to sleep over at their friends' houses which seemed to be the 'normal' thing in this part of the country. Neither did we provide them with televisions in their rooms, our policy was that we eat together and watch television together, our mindset was as the saying goes "families that eat together stay together". Kids were in and out of our house on weekends. This was the thing I grew to love, to see the intermingling across the racial divide, something I had not experienced when I was growing up. It improved my trust in humanity and that to children, colour was not a thing. It brought to mind an experience in the United States we had discussed at one of our church meetings of a parent who had come to the realisation that most children do not see colour amongst themselves. This parent's child had asked his mother whether he could bring his friend over to play to which she asked the question "what colour is he"? To her surprise the child said "I don't know, I didn't look / notice" to this child his friend was just another kid like him. This discussion in our church meeting drove home to me that racism is acquired. It is learned, it's taught, it's an indoctrination of the mind. A mindset that is extremely difficult to unlearn. For me it has always been in my subconscious, always aware that at some point in my life it would raise its ugly head. Did we experience it in England? Yes we did, my sons did and I did too as I shall discuss in my next chapter.

My children left school and entered the job market. My sons joined the ranks in the Engineering fields as apprentices and my youngest daughter did an Accounting apprenticeship. My eldest daughter had the desire to enter university to do a degree in Biology and Chemistry when she achieved her A Levels in 1998/9. She had been accepted to the university in Birmingham but unfortunately I could not afford it and our children were not entitled to university loans at that time. She settled for an Accounting qualification instead, attending night college whilst working. To me this was the right path to take rather than being in debt through university education. You see, during this time there was a drive, by the Government, for kids to enter university degree programs. This benefit, however, was for those families who had British Citizenship but unfortunately for my daughter we were not citizens as yet so she would have had to enter university as an external student at a cost of some £30,000-00 in 1999. England, I must admit, has the most prestigious universities and degree programs recognised the world over so it would have seemed to be the right thing to do, but we were of a different mindset. I would often have this discussion with my work colleagues who were ever so proud of their children attending university whilst I would also stress how proud I was of my children joining the technical apprenticeship schemes and

I would emphasise this point and; debt free. University loans would have to be paid back once the recipients earned above a certain threshold, and that, to many, is a lifetime debt. Today the country finds itself with a massive skills shortage which, in my humble view, is a direct result of the misguided mindsets back then of the drive for university education to the detriment of the much needed 'shop floor' technical skills. I had strong views on this perhaps due to my own experience so imparting this mindset in our children was a natural progression particularly to our two sons who didn't quite know which direction to go. Our two girls were more focused; they knew exactly what they wanted to do, well! Boys will be boys I guess following in the footsteps of their fathers, my engineering footsteps in this regard, footsteps that walked a challenging path full of stumbling blocks.

My employment in Bristol afforded my family much stability and security. We were able to take our children on touring caravan holidays from time to time, we also enjoyed holidays in France, Portugal and Spain. We were adventurous and so wanted to instil the same spirit in them. A spirit of adventure, of exploration, the sky was the limit. I have benefited immensely from working for a professional business in a highly prestigious field of high value engineering components projects, projects of world-wide scope in the nuclear, aerospace, and naval industries. It has been the most challenging field in my entire engineering career which would challenge my skills to the limit. I thrived in this environment and proved worthy of recognition. A recognition I had to 'fight' for as I will explain in my next chapters. I eventually retired in 2018, satisfied having achieved a legacy to this day amongst not only my fellow colleagues, which I am still in contact with, but also including that from one of our major customers based in the United States. Yes, it has proved to be a long satisfying seventeen years of security and uninterrupted employment. I did not have to retire. I chose to for reasons I shall explain later. The road to success has not been easy, it's been a challenging one throughout and which I believe I have navigated successfully as I shall now relate.

My family England 2007

My Family England 2016

My wife and I 2016

Son Michael and Gabi New Zealand 2020

Ellie. Francine Melanie 2019

My Friend Tom

Tom and I JHB 1997

NAVIGATING THROUGH NEW CHALLENGES

Moving to the United Kingdom brought new challenges, challenges that I had not contemplated nor anticipated. My reason for moving to England was for the betterment and opportunities for my children and for the sake of my wife's peace of mind. It was never about me. True to say that I eventually grew into it, adapted, and subsequently accepted my new life. I thought of the bible story of Jacob and his entourage of seventy plus people including his sons. How he had to move to a foreign land, Egypt, due to sheer difficulties brought on by a severe drought. Jacob, I wondered, may have had some mixed feelings at the time although he was invited to move by his son Joseph who had now become a key governmental figure, so, from a material point of view he was better positioned in Egypt, a world power at the time, with all the trappings of technological advancement and sophisticated order. Did he contemplate the challenges he and his family would face in terms of clash of cultures, religious differences and negative influences I wondered. Of course the Bible does not provide the detail of everyday life in Egypt but we have the pleasure to see in hindsight as archeology and history has revealed to us the sheer magnitude of Egyption advancement and religion. Biblical history tells us the end result of his sojourn into Egypt, how his descendants were eventually controlled and subjugated to slavery for centuries. slavery brought on by political influences. Was I, together with my family, going to face similar challenges and to what degree? I had no idea what to expect, you might be thinking dear reader, that had I not moved to Botswana? Yes we did but Botswana is Africa, Black culture is somewhat, to a large degree the same throughout the continent, so we easily adjusted, it felt like home but in a different city. My view with regards to England was that we share a basic common ground as we had lived under the English system brought to us by Colonialism in Rhodesia, same language, same education and same religious environment, same technological qualifications, however, I soon realised that things were different at ground level to my surprise. It is these differences that became the challenges. How would I navigate through them was the question. In order to address this question, I will categorise the areas as I experienced them as follows: culture, work ethics, racial prejudice, religious environment, and finally my adaptation.

During my life in Rhodesia and thereafter Zimbabwe I had become aware that English people, by this I mean those that I had interactions with, in my church environment and in the secular business environment were different, in a positive way, with regards to their interaction with us non-whites. They were somewhat at odds with most of the white Rhodesian counterparts who came across racist and upfront you knew exactly where you stood with them. You were not their equal in their eyes, but the English were more accepting and respectful as I observed within my circle of interaction. I grew up believing the 'English gentlemen' saying but at the same time I was also aware of the scepticism often repeated amongst Black Africans "not to trust the white man - they came with the Bible in one hand and the gun in the other" they would say, it was that 'two faced' contrast that bothered me. A contrast that I was to witness to some degree when I moved to England. The clash of culture became a major challenge for me. I soon learned that I was not the only one that felt that way. The more I conversed with ethnic minorities from different backgrounds and countries the more I learned that our experiences were shared across the board. One thing that this clash revealed for me, in addition, was the fact that we are all humans influenced by our upbringing and environment and that there are both good and bad aspects of our cultures. When the good aspects from each culture are brought together and combined both bring-about positive and attractive as a whole. I shall now try to clarify what I mean by this by way of some examples: beginning with cultural differences.

I believe that Africans in general are hospitable people in terms of the basic meaning of hospitality - the friendly and generous reception and entertainment of guests, or strangers. Its basic root meaning being 'a love of strangers.' So, our culture as

Zimbabweans is just that. I believe we are a friendly, peaceful people and the first thing we do is greet all we meet with a friendly handshake or slight bow with hands clasped or just a simple greeting as in 'hello, hi, good morning, afternoon or evening before we converse. I remember when I was a child how people passing by would just shout a greeting from down the road "Salibonani, linjani e kaya?" which in the Ndebele language means hello, how are you all at home? If a visitor arrived unexpectedly during lunch they would be invited to share the meal. It was viewed as rude to speak to someone, a visitor or stranger for that matter at the door without inviting them in to sit. This hospitable nature amongst indigenous black Zimbabweans in particular was common and evident. I occasionally experienced this during our door to door preaching activities where at times we would knock at a door and find the householder just about to have their lunch. They would automatically invite us to join them and would offer us a dish of water to wash our hands and a towel to dry them. This act to me was a typical patriarchal practice of past histories which appears to have been maintained in African societies. Refusal of such a gesture would be viewed as rude. In England it's a paradox because at government level for one, asylum seekers as an example are generally welcomed and recognised for their struggles and suffering but on the ground the opposite is sometimes true, depending where one lives. There is no general love of strangers but rather they seem to be viewed with suspicion and dare I say,fear. Perhaps due to a large degree of crime, I suppose, but also due to the general moral breakdown which the previous prime Minister of Britain, David Cameron, once labelled as "Broken Britain." Another point of difference, which I found rather difficult to understand, is that when you meet someone in African culture and you engage in a brief conversation and you meet them by chance the following day you would automatically acknowledge that stranger by way of a greeting which sometimes would lead to another conversation. In England, the reaction would be the opposite as the same person you conversed with yesterday would 'blank' you as the expression goes, completely ignoring you as if you never met.

This, I discovered, was often not out of malice, but just a cultural norm that appeared to be acceptable and hence not an issue to most. This aspect of culture is prevalent in UK society from my observation and is accepted as normal, just a different mindset, just another approach I suppose which I found rather difficult to understand. I saw it even with my own grandchildren, born in England, how often they had to be reminded to say a greeting to us, their grandparents. I guess, to them, it is their normal way of culture amongst their peers; perhaps they have a different code for acknowledging each other. My daughter and husband have had to work very hard to instil this cultural mindset in them. I have always imagined that acknowledging folks and demonstrating that with a formal greeting each time is a world-wide custom. Americans for one as an example displayed this same friendly hospitable custom which I experienced first-hand when we holidayed in Orlando Florida around 2005 particularly at the shopping malls. Their customer service was really exceptional as they would greet you as you walked in and offered you their service. Was it a practice only at restaurants and shopping malls or was it a general American thing I wondered? This kind of customer service is rare in England, another display of the different cultural norm. I eventually came to understand that this difference seemed to be a deep rooted one particularly amongst the younger generation in England and was normal to them. I tried very hard not to pass a right and wrong judgement on such behaviour but to view it as another way. A different cultural mindset neither superior nor inferior and not to take it personally. I, therefore, in addition, had to adjust my thinking so as not to view such incidents as issues for confrontation or of prejudice - because 'I am Black' kind of thinking but this was just their way, another way.

Another major cultural difference I came to realise is with regards to communication. In my southern African culture, we are kind of direct in our speech, we say what we mean with no hidden double meanings and that approach is accepted by all without any feelings of being offended. I came to appreciate this aspect also amongst the Americans and Scottish folks I had interactions with and kind of drew the conclusion that this was common amongst other cultures too around the globe. In most cases if one had a difference, we would address the problem directly rather than resorting to talking behind one's back. It's true to say though that backstabbing in the workplace is a common trait amongst all peoples. It's a negative human condition and is prevalent too in England. That is what I experienced, so it wasn't only me. Although in all fairness my personality was sometimes the cause due to my very direct language and quick reaction to statements by others. Statements that I often misinterpreted as direct challenges to my authority. This backstabbing, 'talk behind one's back,' attitude at my place of employment was toxic at shop floor level. I wondered whether this was due to jealousy or was it another clash of personalities, just part of the human psyche. These were questions that troubled me as I had not directly experienced such behaviour in the past or perhaps, I was just naive, and not aware of it. The double meaning style of communication in particular was another surprise for me and the constant humour, the 'taking the mickey' at everything were typical English traits. One that can be viewed in both negative and positive ways. I guess sometimes it's good for the soul to laugh at oneself. Newspaper Tabloids in England are good at that as they very often come up with really catchy, humorous phrases and headings on different topics or situations of concern, to catch the public's interest. An example in mind about double meaning in speech I recall, was relayed by a Black American comedian during a stand-up comedy 'Live at the Apollo' TV show where he went on to relate an incident of a conversation with an English 'friend' who had passed some remark directed at him in jest. His response was that of laughter at the time the remark was made only for him to re appraise the conversation when he got home and it suddenly dawned on him that his friend had just insulted him. It was so funny but typical, he had learned his lesson about the subtleties of British humour and culture.

The suspicion of strangers is another aspect I struggled with when I first came to England in 1997. We lived in London from early 1997 to mid-1998 and I observed in time that eye contact with strangers was viewed with raised eyebrows as it were, a greeting was often ignored, met with silence and a surprised glare. People kept their heads down, in the underground 'Tube' trains, hiding behind the pages of a newspaper. I wondered whether this was just the morning blues as people went to the jobs they hated or was it the culture? As time went on, I came to the realisation that different cities had their own culture, a different spirit one could say. Wolverhampton people as an example were a little laid back and friendly, Brummies, people from Birmingham, were similar in nature, friendly and with a rather peculiar accent. Then we moved to Bristol and found that the Bristolians have their own peculiarities and terminologies too, like adding the letter 'L' to some words such as tomatels instead of tomatoes plus having a kind of rolling 'R' accent sound. I began to appreciate that in all these different cities that my family and I had lived in, it was mostly the elderly folks who were friendly and would exchange greetings and often willing to converse in a relaxed setting. They came across as having a more positive disposition in comparison to the younger generation who came across aloof and set apart in my observation. Was this a generation thing I wondered?. For example, in my place of employment most of the young people tended to start a conversation without even saying a greeting. It would be straight into a subject of discussion as if the conversation was a continuation from where they left off the previous day. When I recently asked my granddaughter about this unusual behaviour in my eyes her reply was, "Ba-da, that's what my grandchildren call me; it's like a mispronunciation of Grandpa or Grandad for some strange reason, we have a code." I would sometimes politely say "don't you say good morning at least before speaking?" then I would get this surprised expression. To them their conversational style was just normal and perhaps they were taken aback at my response. My overall impression of the interaction between the young and old was a general chasm, the elderly are ignored most of the time, it was as if the young were living in their own bubble, their own zone and we, oldies, were like the 'aliens' from outer space from another day. I guess this was and still is part culture and part generational.

Another aspect or cultural difference was the matter of indirect speech. In Britain it is generally the norm that one has to cushion their words so as not to offend and at most, people will not tell you exactly how they feel because they do not want to offend. There is a saying in the UK that English folks 'go round the houses before they get to the point' but others, like me, take the shortcut, straight to the point. I found this aspect of culture challenging to be honest, completely opposite to my upbringing as we tend to say what we mean without really considering the other person's feelings. We just took it as gospel that straight talk is normal, it breaks no bones, as both parties would know exactly where they stood on a matter and any issues would be resolved likewise and both would have a good night's sleep at the end of the day. So, my English colleagues at work would not directly say what they really meant at most times, some rather prejudged me as not being one to listen to their viewpoint. When my Engineering manager conveyed this matter to me, I was rather puzzled because they chose to complain to him rather than to speak with me. My immediate response to him was "they are behaving like kids in the playground because I am always open to suggestions and willing to listen to constructive criticism, but they do not talk to me". They of course had a different view. Their reason which I later learned from a close friend was that they did not want to talk with me because I was unapproachable due to my predisposed defensive attitude. I used to question myself at times, as to the reason why, in general, people appeared to be 'afraid' to speak with me on issues of difference but would laugh and joke with me in normal general conversation. In my mind I've always felt like I was a reasonable person willing to listen to constructive criticism and suggestions but to onlookers I came across rather different perhaps, they felt the opposite, I guess it was due to my outward persona. People have this thing, perhaps it's the look, the moustache, the frown on one's face or some other glitch that one can be so misinterpreted. On some occasions, to the extent that the conversation would first go 'around the houses' before getting to the point, especially if the point of discussion was controversial or if they had a different viewpoint. That used to frustrate me, and I would at times interject and say "why don't you just get to the point just say what you really want to say". I think my sensitivities were partly due to the fact that I was the only non-white Engineer amongst some 700 to 800 white folks and always on the defensive and always imagining that I would be attacked or undermined at some point - hence my 'attack first' in self-defence mode. Was this view perhaps a hang-up from the apartheid legacy where we were always undermined, and our opinions viewed as less important or not even listened to by white folks. Was this the same reason why Jamaicans come across as having an 'aggressive' nature, an accusation made by white folks in England, whenever they stand up in self-defence during racist confrontations. The relationship between black people and the metropolitan Police Force is well documented in England hence the massive current restructuring to weed out the racial attitudes amongst them. I did feel a little intimidated at times like Daniel in the lion's den so perhaps my persona was that of a defensive countenance at most times that caused my colleagues to be apprehensive about approaching me on matters of difference. It took some time though to get used to this difference which was more about clash of personalities rather than cultural and to come to accept it for what it was. We are human and different with our own personalities shaped by environmental influences and upbringing. I resolved, though, not to follow the negative aspects of the crowd as the saying 'to do as the Romans do' even if I was in metaphorical Rome but would continue with the positive aspects of my culture whilst absorbing too the positive norms of British ways. At the end of it all I guess I developed a form of hybrid culture and maintained that disposition no matter the annoyance and behaviour of others.

My sons too experienced some challenging situations at their place of work during their apprenticeships to such a degree that I had to intervene by way of a written complaint to their managers. It seemed like they were being targeted just because of their ethnicity. The fact that they were the minority in their engineering employment seemed to me to play a major part in their treatment. People of colour were not commonly employed in such fields and Bristol at the time was predominantly white English with a few pockets of people of colour. In fact in the two suburbs we lived in it was rare to see a 'black face' so we being the only 'Black' people in our street made the effort to befriend our neighbours by always displaying a friendly courteous attitude. This bode well as we were accepted in the community without incident. Of course, the situation has now changed twenty years down the road as more and more people of colour have since moved into the city perhaps for the same reason we did in 2002. Jobs, a better environment and lifestyle. This has proved true especially since Bristol was voted "the Best City to live in in England" in 2014. One thing I came to realise after moving a number of times in England is that some folks, the ones that I engaged with such as work colleagues, church members and general acquaintances, seemed to have a very limited knowledge of the real Africa. I wondered why this was so, my initial conclusion was that the media and the education system had a part to play, for one, the Child-Aid advertisements although well intentioned always depicted scenes of mud huts in remote villages of Ethiopia and emancipated starving children with snotty noses and flies buzzing around their faces. I guess that is what the general public were accustomed to seeing which influenced their impressions of Africa. High rise modern buildings, super highways, city skylines and modern city life were never shown on television, so that aspect was out of sight and out of mind. At times I would have to show my colleagues or acquaintances a picture of our home in Bulawayo just to set the matter straight and correct the ignorance. As an example, I used to conduct a Bible Study with one elderly English gentleman, who is now late. He was truly a gentleman, one of the nicest and most humble people I have ever met. He lived to a ripe old age of 92. I used to visit him once a fortnight for some 7 years until his death. We used to talk about everything during our bible discussions, he told me about his life during the second world war when he was based in Gibraltar and I shared with him my life in Africa to which he had no clue or full comprehension. In 2012 I visited my family in Zimbabwe and made a 3 hour video recording of the places I visited in Bulawayo and Harare and on my return to England I visited my aged friend and played him a number of clips which depicted the city centres of both Bulawayo and Harare including the posh residential areas just to show him the real Africa. He was flabbergasted to say the least as he stared at the screen in sheer disbelief. You see, my old friend had never seen such scenes of Africa in his whole 92 years of life, he had only ventured out to Gibraltar during the war years, true, he was an exception though as many British people of modern times have proved to be ardent travellers although mainly to holiday destinations in Europe and Asia. I think it's fair to say that as of nowadays many British young people have become adventurous travellers and have greater knowledge of the world scene in general. True the world has now become a global village and even the school curriculum has had to be adjusted as I witnessed recently during my employment as an Examination Invigilator in a Bristol School, where the whole map of Africa was included as part of an examination geography question. So, I guess folks will no longer ask an African whether he or she knows someone in another country in Africa as if that country was just another village. The conversation would often go something like this: My English colleague or acquaintance would ask "I met someone by the name of so-and-so, from such and such like from Zambia or Malawi, do you know them?" I would respond by saying, "sorry Mate but Zambia or Malawi is another country probably the size of England or larger, and not another village" To drive the point home I would then ask the question such as "I have a work colleague in Scotland by the name of so-and so would you know them? Only then did they understand the nature of their original question. This was a common experience. My wife and other friends too related the same encounters which we found rather amusing.

I hope, dear reader, that I am not coming across as judgmental or painting all England with the same brush, but this was my experience and the general experience of many ethnic minorities I have conversed with during my residence in the UK. Other Zimbabweans and peoples from different countries in Africa and elsewhere have experienced the same or similar. How do I know? Because I have had such conversations within our own Church environment as our congregations in parts of England where we lived are diverse, comprising some 10 to 20 different nationalities. Britain has always prided itself for having based their constitution and governing laws on Christian Principles and in some aspects this is true but the situation on the ground can be somewhat different. It's true that our Lord Jesus once stated "let your Yes be Yes and your No No" and if one has a difference with someone, rather than talking behind their back he commanded "to go and lay the matter bare by discussing it between you and him/her alone." This to me indicates openness without hypocrisy. The Christian tenet is to be who you are without being hypocritical but also to be polite and to let one's speech be palatable, seasoned with salt. I guess this is what the government understood the Christian principles to be. I understood them too but struggled to follow through at times. My struggle was with regards to the right choice of words, so as not to offend my listener, the directness of my conversational style was not the issue but the choice of words and the tone of voice was. I am not referring to bad language here as I do not use such language. It is an offensive form of speech in my view and unchristian. I can appreciate this latter part and that our choice of words is important in conversation and that I had to learn to practise that quality as one can use different vocabulary to convey the same meaning; but how often I failed. I would be miserable when I got home on these occasions after a confrontation at work and my wife could tell. I would resolve however in my heart to go back the following morning and apologise to my work colleague for having offended them by my tone and wrong choice of words. I would then try to explain in a calmer tone what I was trying to convey. The good thing is we always resolved the matter and maintained good working relations as my apology was always accepted. I tried very hard to apply the bible principles I had learned such as "never to go to bed in a provoked state and to always resolve matters quickly". I believe this attitude kept me in good stead with my colleagues on many occasions. Right to this time of writing I keep in touch with some of them and we have a yearly get together for shop talk and catch up over lunch and a pint of beer.

On the positive side, there are many good aspects of British culture and Britain as a whole. The one thing that has stood out for me is the welcoming nature of Britain towards foreigners particularly towards asylum seekers, those less fortunate peoples around the globe who have sought refuge in the United Kingdom. There are other attractive aspects such as politeness, maintaining one's place in a queue and certain behaviours that are taught as part of the school curriculum such as the need for good manners. Teachers seem to have taken up a large share of the parenting role in order to manage their pupils, some of which are troubled kids from troubled homes. Queue jumping is not tolerated in England nor is it practised. People just seem to be conscious of their place. It brings order and good relations within the public domain in a civilised society even with regards to the driving experience on very congested and busy road systems. The majority of British motorists are polite and considerate drivers, if not the best drivers in the world in my view. Drivers do act in polite ways most of the time and let you in. Another perhaps 'small' but critical aspect in British culture and values is the matter of time keeping. There is no 'African time' as the expression goes. Time keeping is taken very seriously as a sign of respect and social order in order to maintain clock-work-like order thus avoiding frustration and annoyance. Integration and Multiculturalism is another positive aspect of British culture. It is encouraged in Britain and has enriched our society in so many ways. In addition to this there are certain ethics that are like second nature in practice. There are basically three words that are probably uttered the most in England, Please, Thank you and Sorry. We have become so apologetic about everything; I say "we" here because I too have grown to accept these positive qualities of UK culture. British people are the most generous folks I have ever known. A wonderful aspect of the culture, their generous spirit is evident through their giving to various charities for the support of the suffering of people throughout the world. There are probably more millionaires per capita in the United Kingdom than anywhere else in the world.

Another peculiar aspect in the United Kingdom is the constant talk about the weather. It is on everyone's lips every day. In Zimbabwe no one says it's going to be a warm day today because it's always warm most of the year. The seasons are blurred, it's as if there are only two seasons, summer for most of the 10 months and winter for the remaining 2. Even in spring the weather is comfortably warm displaying a wonderful array of shades of purple and blue jacaranda trees. In England the seasons are clearly demarcated, beginning with the wonderful assortment of colour as flowers and trees bloom in the spring, followed by the endless shades and carpet of green during summer following that the awesome golden, yellow, red, and orange spectrum of autumn shades as the leaves fall and ending with the tranquil white of snow-covered hills. The talk of the weather is because of its unpredictable and unexpected nature that can often be literally every 15 minutes. It can be blue skies one minute and rain the next. Perhaps that is one of the cycles that make people depressed and more reserved due to the 'winter blues' accompanied by dark days although it seems that summers are getting much hotter of late. I now believe very strongly that the weather plays a big part in our human psyche including here in England. Everyone has a bright and joyful disposition when the sun is shining bright, and the weather is warm. Whenever I visit Zimbabwe, I have always noticed that people seem to be much happier and with a pleasant disposition at most times. Kids dancing to music outside the shops of some of the outlying city streets despite the extreme poverty and a huge divide between the have nots and the have all's. I can only draw the conclusion that this is because of the good almost perfect year-round climate, warm weather, constant blue skies though occasionally accompanied by short-lived rain during the months of October to April. I recall in fact that Bulawayo was nicknamed "Skies" because of the weather pattern, constant blue skies. This reminds me of a 2010 documentary called 'Slumming It' I once watched when Kevin McCloud, the 'Grand Designs' presenter on British television, did a documentary about life in the slums of one of the largest cities in India. He was struck with the simple lifestyle and happy countenance of the people including their children despite their poverty. This was a mystery to him as he compared their outlook of life to that of folks in England who come across as complainers about their lot in life although having everything by way of material provisions. I understood the difference very clearly, namely that happiness is not a result of having material riches, it's a result of other factors such as spirituality, close family ties, love, togetherness, friendships and adherence to positive principles. True, sustenance and covering are a contributor too for one to be content in life.

The next cultural difference I soon discovered was the rather detached behaviour of young people, a kind of in their own world scenario, a seeming disregard of the older generation and a rather disturbing view of authority, that of parents and the law in general. This is probably a generational thing too as it seems to me that the law has bestowed upon the young generation a view of being untouchable and a sense of entitlement. They do not 'see' the adults; it's as if we don't exist, as if we live in a different dimension. I recall once how in 1997, when we were just a few months in England and living in one of London's eastern suburbs, I reprimanded some young boys, who were playing with my boys, for their misbehaviour only to be sworn at by a nine year old kid. Sworn in the most colourful tirade of expletives of language. He addressed me in the most disrespectful vile manner as if I was his peer. In Africa such a child would be reprimanded, and their behaviour reported to their parents for some form of discipline which would be meted out promptly in one way or the other, well at least in my days. They would receive a severe reprimand from their parents or even occasionally physical chastisement if deemed necessary. In England this would be a criminal offence. I was dumbfounded, never had I been spoken to in that manner and in such language and there was nothing I could do except to prohibit my boys from ever playing with them. The law regarding the chastisement of children was rather strict those days but was eventually readjusted some years later to allow parents to 'slap' their children for misbehaviour but only when absolutely necessary but without causing any injury or leaving a 'red' mark on their skin, a statement that was often viewed with amusement by the Black community because a black child would not exhibit a red mark due to their dark skin, perhaps a dark brown or blue-black mark perhaps.

The cultural divide was noticeable, the moral decline evident so much so that parenting laws were enacted under the social services act in order to provide some structure for the raising of families. To me that is a sad result of the decline of religious influence where the state now feels it is necessary to intervene to fill the void. Behaviours are legislated by endless laws in order to control the behaviour of people, laws that we in Africa were not subjected to, in at least the part of Africa I know. Parenting was left to Parents and not to the State. Of course abuse of children is another matter that would be subject to prosecution as any violent act would be. In Africa, India and perhaps some other parts of third world countries it's true to say that every older person whether known or not is addressed as 'uncle' or 'auntie' as a sign of respect and if a child did not acknowledge the elderly or if misbehaved they would often be reprimanded and were viewed as unmannerly and rude and sometimes their behaviour would be reported to their parents who would carry out the discipline as they saw fit.

As of late I am of the opinion, from my observations during my visits, that folks at home enjoy more freedom of interaction and expression than we do in the western world including here in the United Kingdom. I just feel like we are being slowly throttled and I am disturbed about future expectations. I live a Christian life together with my family abiding by the laws of the land so am not really exposed to the unwholesome activities one views on television such as the spillover violence from pubs and the evident disrespect often directed at our police forces who endeavour to maintain law and order.

The world has certainly changed in more ways than one. We have become so technically advanced and yet so degenerated morally as far as I can see. The sense of 'Living in the age of entitlement' partly due to affluence I guess is everywhere as so aptly explained in the book "The Narcissism Epidemic." My generation was certainly not an age of entitlement but the opposite. It was an age of hard work and self-determination, an age of, if one didn't work one wouldn't eat. As the good book says in 2 Thessalonians 3: 10 "If anyone does not want to work, neither let him/her eat." It is one of the Christian tenets to work hard and live an honest life. I have always fended for myself with that view in mind that if one does not work one dies, as social services back then were inadequate. I was never 'mollycoddled' or 'pampered' as the expression goes. We were brought up with moral rules, strict guidelines accompanied by timely discipline. This same aspect is also re-laid amongst the older generation in England. So, what has been the overall result, have I been somewhat influenced by my new cultural surroundings? Have I become a better person? Yes, I have, as I believe I have taken on board and have adapted whilst retaining the good aspects of both my African heritage and my new British culture. I have become milder and approachable, I think. Although I may not appear to be so on the outside, I am less abrupt, still direct though, but with more consideration of the feelings of others, I have become a better Christian I would like to think as a result of not only the positive aspects of our cultures but mainly by the application of the Bible's principles in my life. Retirement has certainly freed me from many negative influences and challenges from unwholesome human behaviours. As a general rule of thumb I conclude that the basic cultural difference between the white British populace and us foreigners, whether African, Jamaican, Polish, Filipino or other is that generally English people come across as a reserved and cautious people who warm up to you when they get to know you whilst we come across loud, boisterous and in your face.

Now with regards to work ethics, it's true to say that all of us spend a great deal of our lives at our places of work. It is around this work environment that we have our experiences of the general ethics and attitudes in society, good and bad. Mine has been no different. My work office was an open plan office adjacent to the Works as our role was twofold; we were the guiding hub between Design and shop floor manufacturing personnel. The office seated some twenty to twenty five Manufacturing engineers, all white English folks. I stood out like a sore thumb I thought, so, each morning, it was my custom to say a greeting to all my colleagues as I walked to my desk. Some would say a greeting back, others not. I tried to give all the benefit of the doubt, thinking, ok! Perhaps they didn't hear me or were just deep in thought of other matters of concern, an early morning disagreement at home perhaps or whatever. Eventually I came to realise that this was a cultural norm with some, a kind of standoffishness, an act of caution rather than malice. An "I don't know you yet" scenario, "but perhaps I will warm up to you at a later time when I get to know you better" and yes it did take a while for my work colleagues to 'warm up' to me. I drew the conclusion that in British culture people only really warm up to you once they get to know you whereas peoples of Africa and perhaps other cultures too take you at face value, judged innocent until proven guilty scenario. So, my colleagues got used to my custom and reciprocated likewise in time. I eventually developed some close friendships with some of my colleagues throughout my seventeen years right until my retirement in 2018.

With regards to my general work environment, I lay low for at least the first six months, observing the work culture and methodologies. My boss would ask "Francis, any input to our discussions?" Whenever we had project meetings my reply would be "not yet, but in time." That time did come, and I became rather vocal, driven by my sheer passion for the job. The projects were interesting and challenging and the company provided many training courses such as health and safety, heavy lifting, paint technology, various computer skill programs such as excel, word, Power-point and 3D Cad systems including degree courses for those that qualified. There were plenty of opportunities for young people within the business. I was really grateful for having been given an opportunity to improve my skills set as I had only acquired basic computer training when I left Zimbabwe in 1997. I had just a basic working knowledge of M S Word and Excel. All my engineering knowledge up to that point was manual based, AutoCad as an example was just introduced in some companies around 1995. Furthermore, I had not been exposed to the internet until 2001. So, basically this was a new environment for me and a challenging one at that as most of my fellow engineers were graduate level and highly proficient with computers. I felt like a dinosaur and wondered what my work colleagues would think. One thing that I discovered though and that my Boss had come to appreciate was my multi-skilled qualifications. I soon realised that these were proving to be my trump card and more relevant to my role rather than my computer skills. I was given the necessary computer training in time which enhanced my skills. I had come to discover that the skills environment in England was very specialist based rather than multifaceted; perhaps this was intentional so as to expand the employment market and job creation. Sometimes the understanding of these basic skill sets was confused from what I could tell, for example a fabricator / Boilermaker was understood to be the same as or in some cases a lower skill set than a Welder. In Southern Africa a Fabricator / Boilermaker was and probably still is viewed as a higher skill set due to the overall technical aspects such as the application of mathematical concepts like trigonometry and geometry in particular, knowledge of pattern development for various shaped components, and having a working knowledge of forming machine tools necessary to work the metal to required shapes over and above and including welding technology skills. To me this was a great misunderstanding that had to be addressed as these highly skilled tradesmen, who very often could do both, had been undermined for many years in the company and so I resolved to bridge the gap and create a better appreciation and understanding for the skill sets. It took me some years to do so together with my welding engineer colleague, through training presentations, to educate my fellow Design Engineers and Senior Engineers to understand that these two technical trade skills, although closely related, were quite different skill sets. One day in 2017 one of the senior Engineers told me that he had come to that realisation after 28 years, through my training presentations. I was flabbergasted but pleased at the same time that my training program had achieved the right outcome and resulted in these men receiving the respect that was well deserved and well overdue. Welding was and still is a very specialist field, different in its own right, vital on Fabricated, welded and precision machined components of extremely high value throughout the world. I overcame my first hurdle and within a short period of time I proved to be the most multi-skilled Manufacturing Engineer in the business having acquired the ability to manage projects from cradle to grave as it were, from design models to producing cost estimates, manufacturing processes, producing CAD working drawings including jigs and fixture designs using 3D Cad programs such as Solid Edge and Inventor. My role also included an element of project engineering as I had to deal with material suppliers who manufactured the component materials in kit form for final assembly in our workshops. It is this aspect that has somewhat undermined the Fabrication skill set, as technology has moved on to enable the creation of piece parts and material forms by outside subcontract companies. This reduction in the fabricator's role, at shop floor level, has made this skill set to appear limited as having been reduced to a mere assembly role. Unions too have gotten involved in curbing the crossing over of skill sets so as to permit additional job creation opportunities. So, the Fabrication skill base has been somewhat fragmented and broken up into its subcomponent parts which have been taken up by subcontract facilities that now provide a service for the mechanical profiling, forming, and shaping of materials. In addition, the advancement and progression of the fabrication and welding industry has allowed the creation of the Manufacturing Engineering Job role which was originally a shop floor fabricators role. All the above, in my view, has resulted in the undermining of this trade skill but on the positive side it is this shift that has resulted in my employment as a Manufacturing Engineer, a profession that was non-existent in my part of Africa during my early days right up to my move to the UK. Manufacturing Engineering is certainly a daunting task with no room for error, a role that demands more practical know-how than just a college qualification. I was in awe at the technical advancement in England as my role included the creation of step by step written manufacturing processes and 3D isometric and detailed drawings / diagrams to enable a fully documented manufacturing history of components. Manufacturing technology had certainly moved on from my early days as a Fabricator when the process began with a drafted drawing pack handed to me, left alone with the task to produce the finished product. Those were the days from 1973 to 1985. Time had moved on. I had now received training in 3D C.A.D. modelling and my cad skills were eventually recognised throughout the business, I was pleased to have achieved what I had, and having developed the multifaceted manufacturing base skills in Africa, a fact that had surprised some of my co-workers in England. Even my last Engineering / production Manager once assumed, during a 'round table discussion,' that I was not aware of a welding process called 'back gouging', a mechanical process for removing weld defects. The question was not about me having to advise him of my knowledge of this process, but rather it was based on an assumption of my lack of knowledge. I concluded, wrongly or rightly so, that his comment was prejudicial, and a direct personal challenge based simply because I come from a Third world country. I had to make a stand and informed him that we were not miles behind in terms of manufacturing technologies and that this process was standard to enable weld defect repairs. I further gave him the example of the three headed photo electric eye gas burner type plate profiler we were using back in the early 70's which was an advanced technology to his surprise. The following morning, he approached me at my desk to apologise for his uncalled-for remark which was obviously based on his ignorance of technology in Africa. He quietly said to me "Francis I came to apologise for yesterday's remark, I was out of order" I accepted his apology and admired his display of humility. In fact, we developed a very good working relationship following that incident and a friendship right up to this day. Many seemed not to be aware that Rhodesia was a British Colony and hence benefited from the transfer of technical knowledge, so they thought that I had acquired my skills in England but only the people that interviewed me understood from the information detailed in my CV, some six pages of working history. It seemed to me that there was a lot of ignorance about the real Africa amongst much of the populace in the United Kingdom due I guess to the education curriculum and the general media which always portrayed the negative images of the continent. It was just absurd that some folks I conversed with during our early years in England actually thought we still live in mud huts and have lions roaming about. How often I had to provide photographic evidence of our life in Africa. Therefore, the view that my engineering base was from Africa seemed surprising to some. I informed my colleagues that Zimbabwean Tradesmen were highly skilled and very often sought after in South Africa and as far afield as Australia and New Zealand. It seemed too that our work ethic was different, the apartheid system created in us firstly a drive for betterment through education and sheer hard work, a sense of proving to the world that we were just as capable as white folks. The shop floor environment was one of contests and time-frames, the Works managers and Foremen were viewed with fear and with much respect, they were 'slave' drivers in my opinion. It was a case of less talk and getting on with the job. It was only years later after the country's independence in 1980 that the government, through the Ministry of Labour, introduced the system of Workers Councils in order to enable workers rights and better worker / management relations that created a better more professional working environment. In England, workers rights had long been established so the shop floor workforce came across as more relaxed I feel. The influx of Polish tradesmen proved this work ethic divide to be true because they too came across as highly skilled self-motivated multifaceted workers. It seemed to me that the relaxed work ethic in England, well, at least at my place of employment resulted in less productivity, which I proved to be generally 20% slower than the workforce I managed in Zimbabwe. Whether this fact was only apparent in this company I was not certain at first until I had it confirmed by family members and friends, who worked in different fields in and around London, Manchester, and Southampton. They too felt that general productivity seemed lower than what they were accustomed to.

In terms of project Engineering the first real project that put me on the map was the manufacture and installation at, Airbus Bristol, of the undercarriage test rig for the Airbus A380 super jumbo sometime in 2007. This was a cradle to grave project from the customers basic cad models through to the finished installed product. This project including many others was my baby literally from the cradle of compiling the cost estimate, producing the manufacturing processes, the cad shop floor drawings, bought out requisitions for Buyers orders, liaising with material suppliers, overseeing the shop floor supervision and finally oversight of the site installation at Filton Bristol Airbus base. My boss at the time saw fit to reward me for that achievement as I became the highest paid Manufacturing Engineer in the company. My line manager had tried to get me promoted to Fabrication Manager prior to this time but to no avail. It seemed that our overall Engineering Manager was of a different view for whatever reason. Perhaps he felt that there was no need as I was managing my projects well enough anyway or perhaps my personality was the problem and would have caused more upset in the workforce due to clash of culture. I was not really concerned about that though because I was satisfied with my remuneration package. At The end of the day it's what one takes home that matters rather than a title.

One of my greatest engineering achievements was a Project for a large engineering business based in the United States. Due to Non Disclosure Agreements I cannot divulge details of the project nor name the company nor its employees hence can only use vague language and terms as the prime reason is to reveal the challenges and prejudices I was subjected to. I was the Lead Manufacturing Engineer for that project developing and carrying out the required manufacturing processes similar in nature to the Airbus Project. However, this one demanded the design of manufacturing Bespoke Fixtures including a specially designed 500 Tonne Modular Press for the manipulation of the main component piece which weighed some twenty tonnes. This was a massive challenge that I had never done before which required all my engineering know-how and intuition. I carried out all the concept designs and worked hand and glove with a subcontract company to design and manufacture this bespoke hydraulic press. The components for this project were large scale precision machined fabricated and welded pieces and designed to very tight tolerances which we achieved to the delight of our customer. This press was a one-off in England produced solely for the project and at this point in writing is still in use.

I relate my experience dear Reader not out of some self-praise braggadocio mode but to convey to you my feeling of the injustice due to the lack of recognition for my history of achievement in the seventeen years of my employment in this company. I sincerely believe that if I was white, English and young, things would have been different. I was just the odd man out. I believe it was a case of prejudice based on many factors such as race, colour and place of origin. Perhaps my people skills were not what they were looking for. I was too direct, too confrontational, too bossy even but then again people management courses were available and readily provided across the business. I could have been offered that as others had been if it was deemed necessary. Nevertheless, despite the negatives I came through it all. I guess my strong personality and principles saw me through to the end to the respect of many of my work colleagues right as far as Director Level. I will now describe some of the few incidents that became a challenge for me and how I faced them.

One of the early incidents occurred when I bought my second vehicle in the UK a black 5 series BMW, around 2003 and one of my work colleagues labelled me a 'Drug dealer'. Of course we laughed about it but the question in my mind was if I was one of his white colleagues would he have said the same thing? Was this a racist comment, perhaps not, but just a joke? A second incident took place one morning as I drove into work. I noticed that there was a different security guard on that day. Most employees usually drove via the rear entrance gate which would open once one presented a badge fob which would activate it electronically. There were other vehicles in front of me as usual which he let through without question. These were my white colleagues. However when my turn came, he endeavoured to stop me to which I asked him for his reason which was rather dubious. So I ignored him and drove on at which moment he banged the rooftop of my car in an angry gesture to stop me. I felt that he had no legitimate reason to stop me other than racial bias, so I reported him to my Engineering Manager who promptly had his security company transfer him to a different site. This brings to mind another incident but this time it was at the French border port of Le Havre. My wife and I used to visit France regularly each year as we had a little cottage in the village of Gilliers in Brittany, we were developing it into a holiday home. On our return trips we would purchase loads of wine for the family and friends as wine was cheap in France. It was on one of these trips when I was stopped. My vehicle was thoroughly searched just before we were about to board our ferry back to England. My wife said to me as we approached, "I bet they are going to stop you, a black man driving a black 'bema'! (BMW)" and yes, she was correct, and they did. I was asked whether I had any weapons to which I responded "well, you are welcome to check for yourself" It just seemed like we were always the odd ones, the only people of colour on this route during these occasions. I paid attention to that out of interest, as we were like a fish out of water. So, I guess the Border Policeman was intrigued rather than racially motivated. I'll leave you to draw your own conclusion on that one dear reader. I have now digressed and will re-focus on incidents at my place of employment.

As far as I know, most companies in the UK have an appraisal system for their employees which is a management tool that gauges the performance of each worker on a score system. This was no different at my place of employment. Generally, I was scored very favourably on my technical skills, but a ball of contention was the rather low, in my view, score against the 'Leadership' aspect. Basically, the appraisal system worked this way: the employee scored themselves against each role scenario such as technical skills, attitude, teamwork and leadership etc and the line manager would include his / her assessment and provide a score in the adjacent column of the spreadsheet. Finally, the agreed format would be signed and dated by both parties and submitted to HR. My strong disagreement and ball of contention was with regards to the leadership score I was always given which was low in comparison to my honest self-appraisal. I would provide my line manager with my proven record in Zimbabwe, Africa, of having successfully managed a workforce of some two hundred shop floor personnel on one of the largest heavy haulage superlink trailer production line projects ever undertaken in Zimbabwe in 1995/6. It was a project to manufacture 200 sets of super-link semi-trailers at a production rate of one set comprising a tri axle front trailer and a rear tandem axle every two days. Was this not proof of not only my technical skills but also my leadership and management skills I would ask? Was my role in my home country irrelevant I would ask? That question was always ignored and never answered. Perhaps it was because they did not have an understanding of the work environment I grew up in which was at odds with the work culture in England. Did I feel discriminated against? Of Course I did. Was it racial or some other like "nothing good comes out of Africa" bias, I do not know and just couldn't understand the motive and the silence behind it. It would have been better and acceptable on my part to have been told of their reasons. Then again could it have been a case of not wanting to offend me.

I was also bypassed for a Team Leader role in favour of a younger colleague. To be honest this Team leader role was not my thing, not my genre. Thus when my Engineering / Production Manager called me to his office and told me about his decision I was upset to learn that his decision was based solely on the fact that he wanted a younger person. It was not about my technical abilities or lack of communication abilities: it was about age. To me this was an example of blatant age discrimination. If he had offered me the position, I would have declined it as it wasn't my genre. Furthermore I decided to take the matter further with HR as a formal grievance to be addressed. A grievance not because I wanted the position but because it was unjust based solely on age discrimination which was and still is illegal and contrary to company policy. I wanted to prevent any such future discrimination occurring against others. My position was that no one should be discriminated against due to their age, race, sexual orientation, or disability so I had all the legal grounds and backing for my formal complaint. I let it ride for a while until my line manager appealed to me indirectly to withdraw the complaint as the lesson had been learned. My Engineering / Production Manager had not fully considered the impact of his decision and seemed to have been disturbed by my challenge. I did eventually, for the sake of maintaining peace, withdraw the complaint. Some years later I did eventually get a promotion in 2010 to Senior Manufacturing Engineer after successfully manufacturing a prototype component for a customer in the United States. This was a key future project of great financial value to the business.

Discrimination is very subtle in England. It comes in many different forms: racial, ethnic, national, one's appearance, where you live, sometimes it's about class distinctions. Sometimes you have to question yourself, "what did he mean by that, what was that gesture all about or that look?" I would try to give my colleagues the benefit of the doubt by not always ascribing their actions to racial bias which was not an easy thing to do having being 'pre-programmed' it seems by the Apartheid system to think that way. One incident in mind was when I was working closely with a colleague to provide cost estimates on different projects, he from a mechanical background and I from a Fabrication and Welding bias. Then one morning he started to make 'monkey sounds' as I walked in. I wondered whether that was directed at me, but I wasn't sure so I chose to ignore him though I must admit that I was taken aback as I didn't expect it from him. However, another work colleague noticed his behaviour and approached me on the quiet and said to me "Francis, report him as that kind of behaviour is not acceptable." I was not long in my employment at that time, so I thanked my colleague but chose to leave it at that and not make an issue of it. I think my Estimator Colleague realised his error or perhaps he was reprimanded by his fellow white Britains as he never repeated that act ever again. We were actually the same age and later developed a good working relationship. We travelled together on some projects as far as Scotland and Spain. Everywhere we visited, I was the odd man out. Back at my employment environment, it seemed like I just didn't fit in. I was just too different, my accent, my mannerisms, my attitude, my principles so much so that recognition across the business was not forthcoming without a struggle despite my performance. A fight I did carry out as far as HR and senior management. Was I expected just to sit back and accept the status quo as it was nearly impossible to change people's mindset? That is what my dear wife would say. I couldn't just leave it, this was not Rhodesia. England is not apartheid there are laws against any form of discrimination, so I felt justified to raise this issue. I am glad to say that recognition did eventually come after raising my grievance with HR which referred me to the Production Director. He subsequently invited me to a private audience with him where I related, in detail, my grievance regarding the lack of recognition by the company for my technical role in securing the multi-million pound project. He was dumb founded for choice of expression as he had not been told any inkling of my involvement. I was then eventually awarded a certificate of performance sometime after; during one of the company's yearly get togethers. This was a small token of recognition for having engineered the project in question. This was no small project; it was worth millions of pounds to the business. In addition to that I received by way of an email from the Project Manager a statement of recognition of my expertise, a statement made by the Expeditor / the on the ground representative of the customer based in the USA. The question was raised by senior personnel to the effect "what analytical model we, (as the company) used to concept such a slick fixture (meaning the 500 tonne Modular press a one off bespoke design that enabled the company to meet the required dimensional tolerances of which failure would have jeopardised the entire contract. The answer I learned did not come from my employer but was addressed by the very customer's own representative who said "he is called Francis." When I received this email I was lost for words and wondered why it was that my employer had failed to respond. Why did it take the customer's representative / Expeditor to respond on my behalf? I have no answer to that. In addition to this, I have reflected on my paper award, the certificate of recognition, in comparison to my previous monetary rewards for successful projects in my past life in Zimbabwe and have truly found it inadequate, a little insulting in fact baring in mind we are talking about a multi million pound project. I was not even considered for a successful innovation scheme monetary award. Would you have been satisfied, dear Reader, with such a 'schoolboy brownie points' piece of paper?

On a separate occasion, during the presentation of 'my' bespoke Press by my Engineering Manager to senior management in Britain, a gentleman whom I did not recognise at the time walked up to me in my quiet 'background' corner and extended his hand in a handshake and quietly said "thank you for getting us out of trouble." That individual as I learned later was the Head of Engineering who was based elsewhere. That was a really welcomed sense of recognition by such a senior member of the company. I had not envisaged it, it came as a pleasant surprise. My struggles did not end there though. There were other incidents where I would be excluded from delivering my own presentations on this project. I was never introduced even to the American customers Expediter who was closely involved in the Project and was monitoring its progress. Till this day I do not know of any reason why this was the case. Was I that irrelevant in the eyes of my management team, after all, I was the lead Engineer of the Project. I had developed the production flow chart, carried out the Fabrication and Robotic Welding and Machining fixture concept designs, controlled the manufacturing process together with the overall oversight of the dimensional laser inspections. I am pleased to confirm at this point that I did eventually meet up with the Expeditor during the inspection and trials of the Modular Press where I introduced myself and explained my role in the project. We developed a good working relationship from that day onwards and thereafter and hence he was able to come forward to my defence to acknowledge my role to his employers. Eventually I did become part and parcel of the presentations to the different bodies who had mutual interests in the project.

Another case in point that I raised with HR just prior to my retirement was the issue of apprenticeships for ethnic minorities. This happened during one of our annual company across the board meetings in 2016. I had witnessed the implementation of the company's positive policies in terms of recognition and equal opportunities for women and people of LGBTQ+ background but what disturbed me was the fact that there seemed to be an unawareness of advancement of people of colour, ethnic minorities. I was not sure whether this was deliberate or just an unintentional oversight by HR, but it took me almost sixteen years to bring it to light. I am glad to say that the first non-white apprentices from ethnic minorities were included in the apprenticeship intake of 2017/18. The company had followed through on my concerns. Finally, I was promised promotion to another Senior Post just prior to my retirement but declined as I had decided to retire when my time came. I was satisfied with the legacy I would leave. I had fought the fine fight. I had experienced the pinnacle of ultimate engineering, travelled abroad for different projects and visited a number of companies in Spain, including going on occasional visits to our head office to enable transfer of knowledge and other project related meetings. I had the opportunity to visit suppliers within the UK and our final customer across the 'pond' in the United States. I was always the odd man out though, the only person of colour from our delegation. This was a legacy acknowledged by the shop floor staff and across the board. I recall one day just prior to retirement saying to the Quality Manager of the U.S. based customer, a Black American, that I was like Obama, the first and last person of colour in that position to which we both laughed. It was the joke of the day. I was actually responding to his comment that he had noticed that there were "no brothers around" meaning black colleagues, only white men. He too had noticed the racial divide, so he kind of understood my position. This consciousness of ethnicity is a direct result of the apartheid era; it never leaves you. I mean 'us' the generation that was subjected to it. It is a thorn in the flesh that will go down with us to the grave, a real sad state of affairs. Gladly the younger generation appears to have overcome this to some extent judging by their interactions amongst themselves. I have especially noticed this throughout the years in England and most recently when I was employed as a part-time Invigilator at my grandchildren's school in Bristol where I observed first-hand the social interaction amongst the kids of different ethnic backgrounds. It was an interaction that was wonderful to see, a colour-blind interaction.

My time soon arrived to retire. I was a little taken aback on my final day as I expected a formal 'Leaving' interview which would express gratitude for my service. This was not forthcoming from HR as I had expected. I handed in my badge, and signed the leaving form at HR and left. I could have been the janitor as no one noticed, maybe I just expected too much. I must conclude this part by expressing my special thanks to my colleagues in the Production department who gave me a wonderful leaving presentation attended by some 100 plus personnel including some senior managers. My line manager had given his speech acknowledging my role in the company during my seventeen years of service. He concluded with an unexpected remark when he said "maybe we should have promoted him." I was startled at that comment but let it pass and did not question what was insinuated. I shall leave you to draw your own conclusion on this one dear reader. My turn came as I was given the platform to address the staff, to say something. This was a common practice in the Business when someone retired, however some would just accept their gift, give a short speech and leave. I was the opposite. I took the opportunity to reveal to my colleagues who I really was with the hope that my life's experience would encourage the spirit of 'Ubuntu' an ancient African word meaning 'humanity to others' in the work environment. My speech followed a rather very emotional pattern for me as it traced my life's journey in engineering describing my progression and struggles with the apartheid system. To many of them this came as a surprise and an eye opener as none were aware of this history. I delivered my speech with passion and emotion, through many tears both mine and that of some of my colleagues. They finally came to know who I really was, not just someone at the other end of a computer screen without a history, someone they only knew from a technical point of view until this day. I am still in contact with some of these colleagues who have acknowledged that I left a lasting positive legacy. I had gone through the whole circle forced in some ways to face adversity and discrimination head on and came through it unscathed.

The religious environment in England was another cultural shock for me. Zimbabwe was and still is a predominantly Christian country. Maybe less so in practice now due to the change in the perspective of the younger generation. A change influenced by many outside forces such as social media, peer pressure, westernisation and the like. I believe that the overall peaceful nature of Zimbabwean people is due mainly to our Christian heritage and the high percentage of religiousness prevalent in the country, the built-in natural fear of God. Sad to say that the England that I came to was by far removed from Christian practice on the ground. The paradox was profound.

Many folks would insist on church weddings as an example although they would not be practising Christians. Christmas together with Easter has become highly commercialised and celebrated by the majority not for its 'Christian,' in reality pagan combination origins, but for the sake of family time. It has become more of a family celebration rather than a celebration of Jesus' presumed 'birth' day which of course is historically incorrect anyway. I wondered why they didn't change it to Family Day, after all that is what it has become in my eyes. British society is one of the most secularised in the world so it's not a surprise anymore to discover that although 48% of the country claim to be Christian only 6% describe themselves as practising. My door-to-door ministry as one of Jehovah's Witnesses has proved that breakdown to be a fact. People claim more to be either atheist, agnostic, or are just plain indifferent. I have encountered many people who feel this way. Christianity is certainly on a massive decline whilst the Islamic faith is fairly visible on the ground particularly in Birmingham and certain parts of London. My discussions with some Muslims prompted me to investigate Islam, its origins and practices. I followed through to read the entire Koran including historical information and watched documentaries on their history so as to enable me to have an informed understanding of their faith in comparison with my Christian faith. I believe that the more you understand someone else's beliefs the better the dialogue. How I wish people would do that rather than pass judgments on what they do not know nor understand. Being informed about others beliefs and understanding the reasons behind attitudes is a positive thing as it destroys prejudice. Prejudice is very often a result of ignorance. I have much respect for Muslims for their devotion which is very similar in a way to ours. I have had a number of encounters by way of religious dialogue with them and have discovered that they too have much respect for my faith as we seem to have some common moral convictions in some respects. The apathy in general in England certainly has its challenges. We are all human after all. Certainly no one welcomes rejection nor a rude encounter but I keep my head high because their rejection is not of me as an individual, but it is a rejection of the message of hope that I bring. So, I plod on looking for those who wish to engage in respectful dialogue and those that are interested in the Bible's message. I must say though that of late, the situation is slowly changing as many are disturbed by the events transpiring around them and in the media. The moral breakdown, the uncertainty of life, war, climate change, increasing crime rates has made some more willing to talk as they search for answers to the catastrophes befalling us. The future of religion in England and perhaps the United Kingdom as a whole is bleak in my view and is heading to some confrontation in the near future. The signs are all there but for the majority, due to their irreligiousness, are ignored and as most are oblivious of them, taking no note. Only the future will tell. I remain sceptical but vigilant to events around me and so are my family as they too have the same awareness.

I will now discuss my adaptation to the change in culture in England. This has not been easy for me for a number of reasons, and I am sure that I am not alone in this. My mother being a Black indigenous Zimbabwean brought us up in accordance with her Black African culture. I emphasise this because it may not have been the way for other folks such as in the Coloured and White communities in general who were influenced by their own family histories. I was the first born of my siblings and being a boy, I was to be the later Bread winner and was expected to carry out the family's responsibilities after my father's death. We boys were not taught to cook, not even to make a cup of tea (I probably would have burnt the water I often joke) nor do the dishes or the internal house chores. Our tasks were external like going shopping at the grocery store, bringing water by wheelbarrow from the communal borehole, in 200 litre drums, ploughing, sowing seed and harvesting the sugar cane and maize as a family. It also included milking the cows that my parents had for a short time, bearing in mind that we also had a gardener and a domestic worker. Sometimes my mother employed two of them when there was a need. She was meticulous in her housekeeping. Our house was always immaculate. The floors were a mirror finish and maintained. She often did the floors herself whenever she was dissatisfied with the girls, the domestic workers I mean. So, when I got married this was the way we lived and it was a common aspect of Zimbabwean culture. The husband worked and was viewed as the breadwinner. He provided materially for the family whilst the wife stayed at home and took care of the home and upbringing of the children. She was the motherly figure who loved her children and respected her husband. This was the environment I grew up in. It was the same pattern of living that I observed with my grandparents, my own parents, and the families around me, so, for me, this was the ideal family structure to be adhered to for the upbringing of children in a safe and loving environment. So, when we got married this is exactly what my wife and I decided to do. I was the breadwinner and I provided well for my family as I have already described in my previous chapters. Our life was comfortable, boiling the kettle for a cup of tea was not my thing. That's just how comfortable my life was. It never ever occurred to me to do such a thing. Well, dear reader, moving to England changed all that. So, did I adapt? Yes indeed.

Adaptation came with a price tag as both my wife and I had to make many adjustments. We had to work long hours for the upkeep of our family. My children lost to some degree the close bond with their mother that they had experienced previously in Zimbabwe. For example, she was not there to see them off to school nor was she there when they returned from school each day. That role unfortunately due to circumstances was transferred to our eldest daughter at the onset of arriving in England. So how did I adapt? Basically, my wife and I had to share the chores. There were no maids now nor any gardeners like 'back home' we had to do everything ourselves. The cooking, the cleaning, the garden, the interior decorating, taking care of the kids, all this whilst going to our places of employment. This was a painful shock to the system and there was no choice in the matter. As time went on things became a little easier as both my wife and I were fortunate to find decent employment with good salaries and time frames, so we were able to be with our children at the end of each day and every day. My wife adjusted her working hours and often changed jobs in order to be available for our children. I soon learned to cook a meal for my family and boiling the water for a cup of tea became second nature. My wife and I were housekeepers and interior decorators. England too adapted to the cultural influences just as we did. There are many aspects in British society that prove this to be true. For example, when we first moved to England in 1997 one had to occasionally complete legal ethnic identity forms. This included applications to open a bank account, registering for national Insurance and others. These forms did not have our ethnicity, so we always filled in the word 'other' mixed race to the question ethnicity / race. Of course, in time this form was later changed to include such additional categories, so even the Government adapted in this small way. The other aspect I noticed as the years went on is that television personalities such as news readers and that of other programs which were predominantly white British became more mixed to become all inclusive. Today Black faces and that of mixed-race people are evident in mainstream media. So, as the country evolved and adapted to cultural influences, such as the 'Black Lives Matter' movement in such a positive and profound way, I too had to adapt in kind. My wife always jokingly says I am no longer the chief of the village nor am I 'King George' but ordinary me: a changed man indeed! The end result has been a positive one as the more we did things together the closer we have become in our relationship so much so that we have become inseparable to this day.

So, dear reader, you now might be wondering what is my overall impression of England now that I have lived here for some 27 years to date? My response is: I have come to love this land of many contrasts and have adapted to its positive customs. I have been astounded by its variety of peoples from all sorts of lands and backgrounds, with their endless array of beliefs and customs from Goths to Pagans, White Witches, Christians, Jews, Muslims, Sikhs, Agnostics, Atheists and many others. I have even come to tolerate its unpredictable weather too. It's a land of equal opportunity no matter what one's background or gender. A land of many paths and destinies for those that embrace it. A land of football, sports, theatre, music concerts and festivals like the five day yearly festival at Glastonbury, not many miles from where we live, that commands an attendance of some 200,000 people from all over the globe. It's like a repeat of the old

Woodstock Festival of the seventies, an occasion of wild abandonment. It's a land of Carnivals too, held in most cities each year, where music is the thing blaring from a parade / procession of attractive hand made colourful costumes and performing stages / displays. The largest being the Notting Hill Caribbean Carnival that has taken place in London since 1966 which celebrates Caribbean culture and commands some 2 to 3 million attendees. It is basically a mobile street party, comprising music, scantily clad dancers and food, one of the largest in the world where everything goes, even drink and drugs, a free for all occasion, policed by some 9000 policemen. We attended it once in 1998, soon after we arrived in England, out of curiosity, and were frightened to death of losing our children in the immense crowd. It's a land also of stately homes, castles and Pagan sites like Stonehenge. A land of The Arts too, including the great Masters of the bygone years. A land of Museums with a display of its rich history. A land of immense beauty. Whenever I visit the Art Galleries, particularly the National Gallery in London, I am in awe to see close-up the great artworks of the Masters of the past; up close. Very often my wife's patience would run out and she would break the spell and drag me away back to this life. Finally, it's a place where we feel safe where everything works, where order exists, a land of ease where its people are foremost and cared-for in every way.

RETIREMENT

I retired at the end of November 2018 out of a personal choice. I say personal choice because in England one does not have to automatically retire when one's time is due. Many choose to stay on out of necessity whilst others plod on as the saying goes because they are still in reasonably good health and perhaps feel that they have to keep themselves busy as the 'devil may just find work for idle minds'. Some choose to go part time and so compromise in a way to keep the wife happy to avoid being 'swept out of the house' as the joke goes. You may chuckle at this dear reader but it's absolutely true as I have been told these things by some of my own work colleagues who retired before me but chose to work part time. I chose to differ in this respect and so retired when my time was due for a number of reasons as I shall now explain.

My first and most important reason was for my spirituality and secondly for my health. I had had a great job and was well remunerated, advancement was on the table. I was to be promoted to a more senior role as part of the company's restructuring program. I had built up a good positive reputation which came with great respect from my work colleagues, so employment wise I was at the pinnacle of success but I chose to end my career there at that point. My spiritual life has always been important to me and my family. We lived the 'Way' as the Bible says. Ours was not a case of attending a church service once or twice a week portraying a pious attitude then reverting back to one's chaotic unbridled life in between. Ours was and still is a way of life. We live our Christianity every day. None of us can claim perfection though in this regard as we stumble many times but we get up and I am no different. My stumbling block was work related, particularly in my last employment where I remained for seventeen years from January of 2002 to end November 2018. This was my Goliath, my love, my passion, my anxiety, my stress and my sense of accomplishment. It was a whole mixed bag. You see my job slowly but surely began to affect my spirituality and my relationship with my Creator as time went on. I was stagnant spiritually speaking just going through the motions at times. The projects were challenging. I struggled with borderline conflict with conscience with regards to some of the projects I worked on. Most were technically stressful and to add to all this, interactions with fellow work colleagues proved challenging. At times there were conflicts driven by ego, jealousy, backbiting, prejudice and the like. All the negative human traits which I had to contend with. I would be forced to make a stand at times and to face these challenges head on which I did for many years as I have already discussed. It is these challenges that were affecting my spirituality. I was becoming someone else at work, struggling with inner anger at times; brought on by the way I was treated but at the same time had to be normal at home. Hence at the end I chose to make the final break for my own sanity. As a consequence of all this I was not making any progress within my religious circles and my church environment. I loved the door-to-door ministry though and still do, because of its one-to-one aspect. It's a privilege to engage with the public, with people of all sorts and backgrounds, with the hope of assisting them to find God and answers to the world's troubles and sometimes these include dealing with their own conflicts. It is a wonderful way to help people deal with these issues and to see their joy when they discover the simple truths of the scriptures. This form of ministry together with my weekly church attendance kind of kept me sane and gave me the strength to face each working week renewed as it were. The majority of my work colleagues were very supportive and showed me great respect due to my achievements and my role as Senior Manufacturing Engineer. It was the few odd incidents that were the real thorns in my flesh in the same way as one literal thorn that can cause one much pain and irritation, stumbling blocks to my Christian personality that I had to get rid of. At the end of it all I had to make a choice and I chose to follow the words of Jesus Christ my Lord who said "also If your right hand makes you stumble, cut it off and throw it away from you" and so I chose to do just that at the end of November 2018.

My health was deteriorating too particularly from the year 2015. I was on blood pressure medication due to the constant work pressure coupled with feelings of anxiety, and then one day, out of the blue, I had the fright of my life. We were at a restaurant with family visitors on a weekend in 2016. After a meal and some drinks I went to use the toilet to pass water when suddenly instead of urine, blood was discharged. Fortunately I was the only attendee in the toilet at that moment so I quietly finished, washed my hands and joined the family as we walked home. I said nothing until my wife and I were alone. She immediately advised me to contact the doctor which I promptly did and within the following period of two weeks I was in the operating theatre for removal of a 3 cm diameter tumour in my bladder. A tumour that had erupted discharging a large volume of blood flow. The diagnosis after a biopsy was the dreaded letter 'C' malignant cancer of the Bladder. My good fortune is that it was contained within the bladder and had no metastasis beyond the bladder wall. I was given two options, chemotherapy or surgical removal at the root. I chose the latter. My wife had done her homework and researched the options and their aftermath and so she advised me to accept the second option which I did. I too had contemplated the options and in discussion with the consultant I explained my reasoning for my choice in terms of similarities in engineering procedures carried out on defective welds. I explained to the consultant that as an engineer I was very familiar with defective weld repair procedures which include a process called back gouging which removes the defect by mechanical means followed by magnetic particle or dye penetrant inspection to ensure the defect was removed in its entirety prior to re-welding and re inspection which included ultrasonics. This methodology ensured soundness of the welded joint. So to me, the surgical procedure was a similar process and the right choice for me and the fact that the cancer was of lower grade and still within the confines of the bladder. The Doctor and nurse were rather astounded by my knowledge of ultrasonic inspection and understanding of the surgical procedure they were about to carry out on me so they accepted my decision. The procedure was a success although I experienced some pain and discomfort for a number of weeks. As of this writing in 2024 I am cancer free having had a number of procedures as and when necessary during the previous years. I am grateful to our National Health Service in the United Kingdom. A service that I can proudly say is second to none in the world. Whether I will remain cancer free is anybody's guess as time and unforeseen occurrences befall us all. Relapses and recurrence happen; especially for this type of cancer, but for the time being I praise God for the current state of affairs as I continue to be monitored by the Health service. I chose not to divulge my experience and condition to my family in Zimbabwe nor to other family members in England and elsewhere so as not to cause alarm and undue concern for me until now. I feel that now is the right time to inform all that know me. My view is, the procedure is a minor one and can be successfully carried out indefinitely. In the meantime I live a healthy life. I have arrived at the ripe age of seventy, three score and ten years, as of this writing under God's undeserved kindness and my wife's constant supervision and advice. She has proved to be my support throughout.

We now live, since 2016, in a small seaside town called Weston super mare in the South west of England in a comfortable dwelling close to all amenities. A location that affords us constant exercise as we walk most days along the beach front promenade. I am of the opinion that my changed and relaxed lifestyle together with a healthy diet, moderate habits, fresh air and daily walks have contributed to my overall reasonably good health as of this writing. I am now more involved in my church activities and ministry without hindrance and have since qualified to be appointed once again as a Deacon / Ministerial Servant. My sanity has been restored. I am no longer under any medication nor am I anxious as I used to be due to work pressure. My only anxieties now are those common to all of us: concerns over the cost of living, family, friends and world events. However as a Christian I understand all these issues, their reasons and what the future holds in accordance with the bible's message that we preach: a message of hope for all. Other than that my wife and I have part time jobs just to fill the void in between and once again I have resumed my passion for painting, my gift of art, portrait painting in particular which I now do as and when commissioned. I last did a pastel portrait of our, then, two children in 1985 and next picked up a brush in 2008 with a portrait of our late son Benjamin from a photograph taken when he was around 12 months old. I decided to do another painting of Benjamin, but this time from a photograph taken literally a month prior to his death. I began this portrait in 2017 but kept returning to it as I was not entirely satisfied but eventually finished it to my wife's satisfaction in 2022. Never did we contemplate how this painting would affect us, oils on a canvas 60 x 75 cm tall. It took me around 50 hours to paint the initial first pass portrait and during that time, in fact, towards the completion of it, I noticed a change in my wifes demeanour. She was sad for a time and I didn't know why. At first I thought I had upset her in some way but she later revealed that the more she watched me paint she felt like she was witnessing our son's revival, his coming alive as it were, from a pencil sketch to completion. To once again see his beautiful sheepish smile and glitter in his eyes. It brought back all the emotions of the day the tragedy happened, back in 1985. It made me reflect on the fact that although we cope with tragedies, life goes on. The memories are for a lifetime tucked away in our subconscious until something triggers them, and the same emotions resurface. The portrait hangs in our lounge and now and again I stop by to contemplate and reminisce on the Bible's promise of the resurrection with the conviction that we will see him again. I am living a contented, calm, and quiet life now together with my beloved wife a 'stone's throw,' half an hour away, from my children and grandchildren. What more could I ask for.

REMINISCING - LIFE'S SUCCESSES AND REGRETS

My life, when I look back now, has been one of adventure, of happiness, sadness, adversity, discrimination, ambition together with strife, success, failures, and many regrets. It has been a real mixed bag of experience inclusive of the whole spectrum of our humanity. There are things though, that if I could go back in time, put the brakes on as it were and engage reverse gear and reverse back into my past, I would have done differently. My retirement has allowed me to reminisce, to have my quiet moments whilst my beautiful wife is asleep, to reflect, to step back in time, to screen my life like a movie and to watch it close-up but this time without popcorn, just me in my mind's movie theatre. My successes, failures and regrets played out before me.

Firstly, I would like to deal with my successes as I see them in hindsight: the positive aspects of my life, following that, my regrets. Beginning with my childhood I believe my personality, whether home grown, inherent or developed has proved to have some bearing on who I am, was and later became. I was always strong willed, free spirited. I did what I wanted to do, not what someone else wanted me to do. Peer pressure was not something I experienced as I was always one who expressed my mind neither did I experience any form of bullying neither in primary school nor during my high school education. I don't know whether this is because of the relaxed lifestyle and cultural influences of that time period or whether this was just my experience. I have come to see the effects of negative peer pressure amongst, in particular, young people of today. I feel very sad for them, especially those with 'weak' personalities, the timid and the shy. I felt very strongly about this and hence taught my sons never to allow anyone to bully them but to always stand up for what is right; to be themselves no matter what. Success does not come on a plate. It is earned, as many would agree and involves hard work and self-discipline. Mine was no different. I was self-driven and ambitious with a sense of pride. My secular development was the typical example of a success story of sheer hard work driven by ambition to be on top of my game. My apartheid experience with its deprivations was the flame in my psyche and that of others, my fellow countryman, a flame that energised me to be the best possible in comparison to my white counterparts. I always viewed myself as an equal and not a lesser being as the system wanted us to believe and accept. Sadly many people of colour just seemed to accept the status quo as lesser ones and often cowered before their white bosses or sold each other off as a means to gain some sort of favour in accordance with their mindset. I am of the view that perhaps this was the thing, the difference, my white bosses saw in me, coupled with my intelligence and technical abilities that eventually resulted in my promotions and my climb up the secular ladder. I was the pioneer in the workspace as I have already detailed. I broke barriers; engaged with white folks in high levels of society in the business environment on an equal footing and gained their respect. That to me is a success story when you consider the politics of apartheid with its segregation laws, its class distinctions, and the emotional impact it has had on those subjected to it. The only way I can explain this scenario to you dear reader is by way of an analogy, one that I used to explain the emotional impact to one of my work colleagues in England who had asked me the question out of curiosity. I explained to him that, in my humble view, apartheid had and has the same effect as a child that is subjected to abuse and bullying all his/her life. It causes feelings of anger, inferiority complexes, a chip on the shoulder as some would say, deep resentment for some, mistrust of white people and also creates a strong desire to be recognised, to be acknowledged, to be judged fairly. In my case it has developed in me a strong sense of justice. I am appalled at the injustices I have come to see occurring in our world so much so that my wife has often said I should have become a politician. At the same time she has very often reiterated "Francis, you cannot change the world!" Of course I agree. The world is bigger than little me. Finally, I conclude that my secular success, with all its pressures, has been a life's journey that unfortunately my family had to put up with.

That's my next story, my family. For many, success comes at a price and very often the family is sacrificed for it and sadly many families result in breakups and divorce. Mine is still intact though battered and bruised in some respects. My wife and I recently celebrated our forty-fifth wedding anniversary celebrating the fact that we have been together in totality for some forty-nine years to date as of this writing in 2024. That is a lifetime, and we are still very much in love. She has been my backbone, my life, my partner, my direction, my confidant, and my best friend. We have been together on a long journey at times with itchy feet as the word goes, more hers than mine. We have enjoyed our experiences of adventure having moved house approximately twenty-five times in our lives to date including that of four countries. The moves were for various reasons. At times we just wanted a change of scenery. A kind of feel-what the white folks had the privilege to enjoy. Some of these previously 'whites only' areas we lived in were, four up market City centre Flats, Paddonhurst, Tegela, Romney Park, Parklands, Hillcrest, and on our return from Botswana, North End and finally Riverside. At other times it was due to the growing family, and still other times it was just sheer necessity such as change of employment.

Our adventurous spirit continued when we moved to England as we started off in London then Wolverhampton, followed by Birmingham, Bristol and finally our retirement home in the seaside town of Weston Super Mare. We even went as far as purchasing a 'holiday home' in a village setting called Couroussaine just outside Guilliers, a little village town in Brittany, France. This was in 2005 during the time when Britain was still part of the European Union when we enjoyed freedom of movement including indefinite residence in Europe. Many Brits purchased holiday homes during this time before the all-time property market crash of 2008. Ours was just a modified Barn of some fifty-two square metres of ground area in the middle of the village. It had been partially completed with just a roof, loft bedroom and ground floor concreted room without any ablution facilities. It was just a structure situated in and inclusive of approximately three quarters of an acre of agricultural land. We had our friends who had relocated to this part of France from Southampton in England who had informed us of this opportunity. It proved to be a long-term project until we sold out in December 2019 partly due to the political climate of Brexit. We had developed it into a comfortable cottage with full ablutions, running water, including the latest technology in septic tank construction, solar power energy with gas fridge and cooker. The lounge and kitchen diner were tiled and the loft bedroom complete with bathroom and toilet with laminate flooring finish. It was comfortable and we holidayed about twice a year at first. Our children accompanied us at the early stages. It was an adventure for them: the ferry ride across the English Channel from Portsmouth to the French port of le Havre followed by a four-hour drive. Of Course, the excitement soon lost its lustre for them however my wife and I journeyed on to complete the project sometime in 2017. Besides the aforementioned in 2007/8 we invested in three 'Buy to Let' properties, one in Birmingham and two in Wales literally just months before the property market crash of 2008. The timing was unfortunate but we thought perhaps the markets would recover by the time we qualified for our state pensions. We knew that we would not receive full state pensions which required 30/35 full years of national insurance contributions, after all we had only immigrated in 1997. Our pension receipt would be calculated pro-rata, so our thinking was to invest in properties in order to top up, as it were, our pension pot. Great idea you would have thought but unfortunately things did not turn out as intended. The areas that we chose to invest in were unfortunately not prime market areas. These were mainly ex council properties and would be rented by predominantly DSS (Department of Social Services) Tenants. Some were trustworthy but others not so much. We suffered financial setbacks due to not only bad tenants, but also vandalism and unforeseen maintenance costs. The result was that over the years our income from them fluctuated from profit to losses. My wife and I eventually, in 2022/23, decided to sell up and count our losses. We sold up at the same overall value as purchased so we just about broke even.

At the end of the day it brought peace of mind. Our children encouraged us to get rid of them although we still had some 10 years left for the mortgage redemption. The nagging thoughts in my head was to delay and go full term with the hope that the market would eventually recover substantially to provide us with the pension pot we desired. However I changed my mind on second thoughts and went along with the rest of the family; and I am glad I did. Today we are debt free and stress free as a result. In addition to this we had also invested in an Off-Plan property, a one bedroom apartment in Bodrum, Turkey in early 2008. This was to be an attractive tourist Golf course development comprising one and two bedroom fully furnished self contained apartments together with a communal swimming pool. It was an exciting development that would be managed by the construction company (Koroglu Construction). The plan was to own it for some five years then sell it on. We had made a huge down payment of some £17000, which equated to 40% of the full purchase price. The rest of the funds would be by mortgage, that was the plan. We were going places we thought. The property would be rented out accordingly, to mainly European tourists and we could also use it as a holiday home from time to time for ourselves, our children and friends. The development began according to plan and was programmed to be completed in two phases with our apartment being in phase two of the development. Unfortunately once again things did not go that way. The whole thing came to a sudden grinding halt. The construction company went into liquidation, sold out and disappeared with all our invested funds. I am not sure to this day whether they were in financial trouble from day one or whether the whole thing collapsed because of the Bank failures and stock market crash in 2008. Our endeavour to sue the company as creditors fell on deaf ears. Our solicitor advised us to count our losses and run, "This is Turkey" he said, "don't waste your money". He knew better as he was Turkish although he achieved his qualifications in England. I still have all the paperwork and site plan together with the glossy schematic diagram and CAD generated pictures of the development. It was to be named "The Village" It was ideally situated just near Milas airport some 36 kilometres outside the beautiful city of Bodrum in Turkey. Some years ago I looked it up on Google Earth and one could see the evidence that construction had begun. I have lost hope and have not checked it out ever since. We did at one point think of visiting Bodrum again just to drive past to view what was actually there but my wife convinced me not to bother as it would be just too stressful. I think back to the sales pitch which was done by a middle-man company called Prime overseas property. They were property investment specialists in emerging markets based in Manchester England. Everything was very well presented and professional. Many of us were convinced that this would be an attractive investment in time. The company provided a free all inclusive visit / holiday to view the off plan sample property on site. We were excited to fly to Bodrum to enjoy the sightseeing. Our Guide took us around the city every day for a week fully paid for and including free meals of our choice. It was a treat of a lifetime. We were accommodated in a 4/5 star hotel close to the seafront. The development was to be completed, as I said, in two phases; first phase February 2010 with the second phase eighteen months later. Phase one would comprise 29 units . ie. 2 shops, 2 offices and 25 dwellings , swimming pool, reception management office and gymnasium. Phase two would have some 15 units, another swimming pool and the golf course would be just across the main motorway. The site was well thought out, close to the airport. Our dream soon ended as already described. We got up, dusted our feet and clothes as it were and moved on with our lives. This was another lesson learned from an adverse event, true, but nevertheless a lesson learned.

Somehow our children coped with all the moving and adjusting, they had to; as there was no other choice as everything we did was for the betterment of the family as a whole unit. Each of us carried our own load of trauma. They are the most resilient children I know. All four of them remain in stable family relationships, successful at that, happily married and close by. We have a special bond: we are united in worship together in the same Faith having the same spiritual outlook. If that is not success, then I do not know what is. I feel as the apostle John wrote in his third letter and the fourth verse (3 John: 4) *"No greater joy do I have than this: that I should hear that my children go on walking in the truth"* the Faith. My joy has been filled to the brim. I never took lightly the marriage vow "for better or for worse" that many take with a pinch of salt as the expression goes. To me marriage is an everlasting covenant, the family is God ordained " what God has yoked together let no man put apart" and here we are fulfilling that vow and still together. My conversion and subsequent change of heart brought about by the power of God's word, has made me who I am today and has to a large degree kept my family together. The principles I learned regarding family life, its God ordained structure set me on the right path. To be honest I don't think that my wife and I would be still together if that was not the case. I was too ambitious, too headstrong and too self-confident. It was a case of 'my way or the highway'. I was the typical 'Old African' cultural mindset: the head of the family with the wife in total subjection. I was like Abraham I guess who when facing a family issue only acted after God's intervention for him to listen to his wife. The almighty too intervened in my life and changed my mindset and saved me from myself. In the words of Psalm 27 :13 *"Where would I be if I did not have faith That I would see Jehovah's (God's) goodness in the land of the living?"* Yes I have many regrets, many wrongs and many sins that I have committed some of which I have chosen to share with you dear reader and with my immediate family in particular to show that life is what you make of it and that we should not sit back and allow it to shape us as if we have no choice in the matter. There is no such thing as fate either; in my view. There are unforeseen situations that occur, yes, being in the wrong place at the wrong time for example, but we have two roads before us in life. One wide but easy going sometimes full of strife and self-inflicted wounds and the other narrow, difficult, full of trials and upsets but with a peaceful outcome, success and a long life: the choice is ours to make.

Regrets and mistakes are painful and always there to haunt us. We tuck them away in our subconscious, but at the end they resurface, come to the fore every now and again causing us much guilt, reminding us of who we once were and where we went wrong. In my case I have had the interventions that enabled me to see my errors and to make the necessary corrections and adjustments in my personality and conduct. To be a better Father, husband, and friend. So, what are some of my regrets: I think for one that I was too self-absorbed in my early days with too many responsibilities on my shoulders. I struggled to achieve a good balance between what I had to do and the emotional needs of my family. When I was on my own and single that was not an issue as I had no one to answer to for my actions. I lived my life within the boundaries of the law and respected authority: my parents' authority and that of my teachers and employers. I regret the rebellious attitude I manifested at times, the grief I caused my parents and later my girlfriend. When she came along, I just didn't know how to strike a balance with the fact that I now had someone in my life, another person to share my experience and my life. I loved her so much and cared about her but at times I think I was overbearing because of my strong nature. God gave me two ears and one mouth: to listen more, to pay more attention to be more considerate to others. I regret that I did not do that very well at the beginning. She was so innocent, so beautiful, so reserved that some thought that I was not worthy of her love, as I was this 'seemingly battle-hardened' street wise rogue, the bad boy. Deep in my heart, I felt different: this was the woman that I would spend my life with. I regret the pain that I caused her at times through my misbehaviour, my overindulgence and my wanting the best of both worlds. God intervened in my life and brought order into it which I have already described; however, I still struggle to maintain a good healthy balance at times between my job, hobbies, church life and family. It's my nature that needs constant attention.

I had turned my life around when we got married. We were now a threefold cord with God Almighty in the centre. My job was stable, we had a lovely home and finally we were ready to raise a family. The kids came, one after the other, all five of them. I was making great progress in my secular life and within our church and ministry. Mine was like the perfect family on the outside but inside I struggled to maintain a balance between all these aspects. My job was challenging. I used to have to bring work home. I sometimes just could not get away in time to meet my wife and kids who would so often be waiting for me at the corner of Meikles department store in the centre of Bulawayo every Friday. We would arrange a time to meet but I would always be late, and not by just a few minutes, to the frustration of my wife. I never realised the impact this would have on her and I am reminded of the hurt I caused her right down to this day which I regret so deeply and feel like I should have made greater effort. The pressure of family life grew as the children got older and as a Christian father, I had the responsibility to bring them up in accordance with God's instructions; to inculcate the love of God in their little hearts. We had all the tools to do that and I sincerely believe that both my wife and I worked very hard to achieve that. My regret is that I was too distant at times. I was like in zombie mode doing what I had to do, dragging myself to the park or to the swimming pool to entertain my children, to keep company with my family. Yes, I provided well for my family. I gave them the best life possible; they were never in want of anything but all that came at a price. I think I went overboard with discipline too as I wanted my children to be on their best behaviour at all times and to grow up to be responsible God-fearing adults. We have spoken about this openly now that we are old, and I have come to accept my wife's comment that I had neglected them to some degree. Yes, I could have done better, yes, I could have expressed my love for her and my children in a better way, that is my greatest regret. As I have already described in my previous chapters our life was filled with adventure and misfortune which brought great strain on me as the breadwinner and provider and sadly I had less of me left to give to my family because of too much conflict within. Another thing that contributed to my seeming distant nature at times was my upbringing. The word love was never mentioned when we were kids, it was unheard of. Our parents never once told us that they loved us. The same applies with my wife's experience. Yes they provided for us, cared for us, cuddled us and healed us when we were injured, disciplined us when necessary but never told us that they loved us. We knew, though, that they did by their actions, the way they treated us and the way they cared for us. I think this basic cultural norm was experienced by many, so we were no different to other families. The difference I guess is how we have come to correct this ingrained scenario. To make amends to pluck up the courage to say those words to one another and to our children in their older years and to ask for forgiveness for our wrongs. It's taken a lifelong journey to come to that point. Today I no longer struggle to utter the words "I love you" to my wife and children but it's been a long hard journey. Social media has made it so much easier as we communicate with emojis on our regular Family Group Chat. I look back now in my old age, and I think what was it that influenced a change of heart and that enabled me to courageously turn around to my wife's satisfaction and confirmation that I am now a different person, loving, patient and mellow. I have concluded that the positive influences were my religion, my love of God, the counsel and spiritual guidance we have received throughout the years, the application of God's word in our lives, first and foremost and secondly the positive aspects of British culture. In my cultural upbringing it was the case of 'children should be seen and not heard'. It was also a generation thing too. There was this divide between children and adults but what I observed in England was the opposite. The new generation Parents and their children interact openly. The words darling and love are very open expressions in British culture. It's true that at times I have witnessed the negative inappropriate language applied to young children by their parents as they would vent out their frustrations but this was infrequently and certainly not the practice of the majority. Discipline too is practised differently. Mainly legislated parenting methodologies taught at state level, so much so that to some extent children have become untouchable knowing their 'rights'. The 'naughty step or corner' is an expression we have all come to know about where children are allowed to exhaust their tantrums in a quiet corner. Physical chastisement, when necessary, is not often applied as I have previously stated. The result in my view is that there seems to now be a country wide loss of respect for adults and authority. Probably a direct result of the mollycoddling effect influenced by the views of child psychologists and paediatricians such as the famous American paediatrician Doctor Benjamin McLane

Spock. Nevertheless, to many, his influence has been a positive one in some respects. I indeed have now adapted the good aspects of the culture and my regret is I never knew different. It's taken a lifetime to address. I am content now as my family is united and happy and in a good place with all the support and friendships that we enjoy from within our unique spiritual brotherhood.

CONCLUSION

In December of 2018 my sister Gwen organised the Cohen family reunion. A special event of togetherness to celebrate our small beginnings all the way from my father's origins in Lithuania. Origins and ethnicity which have now been, at last, proved by my DNA profile included in this writing. Being mainly of Ashkenazi Jewish descent was not surprising but my mothers genetic pool was an unexpected big surprise: Nigerian and Kenyan although she is Matabele!!. I have endeavoured to research this seeming anomaly and the conclusion I draw including many others is that Black genetics are very complex. One thing that is true, though, is that our Black origins come from Noah's son Ham and grandson Cush who migrated to Africa spreading his genes westwards, eastwards and southwards as far as the Zulus and Ndebeles and other tribes in southern Africa etc. I digress now into Black History which is a fascinating subject for another day, a subject I recommend though for all to investigate to understand the extent of the intermingling of the races throughout history that we are basically one race, the human race in accordance with the Bible's account in Genesis Chapter 10. That history sadly includes man's subjugation, "man's inhumanity to man" and racial prejudice in the modern era mainly directed towards people of colour.

Our family celebration was to be a joyous occasion to meet up with family members we never knew, the whole extended family which had now been scattered as far afield as South Africa, England, Canada, Portugal and New Zealand. I was surprised to learn that Gwen had listed one hundred and twenty members of which some sixty attended. I guess these numbers were of the ones she knew about and that there were others unknown to us perhaps dwelling elsewhere. That event was a revelation. We discovered the various roads that life had taken us. We learned of each other's successes and misfortunes. I looked back at what we, as the Cohen brood, have accomplished from the humble beginnings of my father and throughout all our struggles and am proud to reveal the following list of accomplishments. These include various technical trade skills, professional qualifications and Businesses in such fields as hairdressing, Boilermaking, Mechanical and electric fitting, Baker and event Planning, Catering, Graphic Designing, Marketing, Advertising, PHD and Doctorate in Fine arts, Architectural Interior designing, Engineering, Quality Assurance Business certification, Construction Contracts Management, Projects and Logistics Management, Finance, Accounting qualifications, Degrees in Applied Statistics and operation Research, in Commerce and Marketing management, Radiography, Bachelor of Science Degrees in Optometry - includes one nephew who became the first coloured to achieve this in Zimbabwe to this day, Nurses, and finally we include a Pilot and an Advocate with a law degree in our midst. This list may not be exhaustive but it proves what determination and single mindedness can achieve despite adversity and setbacks in life.

After hearing of all these accomplishments of our wide family, never did I contemplate that I would lose my two closest and last of my brothers, Billy and George a few years later. Billy sadly suddenly passed away in February of 2020 after a short unexpected illness, septicaemia and undiagnosed stage four colon cancer. My brother George followed in December 2022 from aggressive stage four Prostate Cancer. I was devastated. Tragedy had struck me with another blow. At this point in time, I console myself by imagining that they are still alive, the fact that I live in England kind of lends itself to that pretence.

My life has certainly been a long road of unexpected events, a road that meanders through challenging terrain in twists and turns, dips and rises towards an unknown destination. I am reminded at this point of the words of the prophet Moses in Psalm 90 verse 10 which read *the span of our life is 70 years, or 80 if one is especially strong. But they are filled with trouble and sorrow; they quickly pass by and away we fly."* (NWT) I have reached that span of 70 years at this time of writing and I look back at just how quickly time has passed by whether I will be included amongst those who are especially strong to live past the

80 years, only time will tell. I never contemplated reaching this age as my life was too erratic in the early days. I think of my childhood where it all began. The carefree innocent little boy playing in the dust without any goals nor any consideration of what the future might hold. I don't believe I was ever asked the question "what do you want to be when you grow up?" My parents probably just stumbled through life without any goals either. True to say that my father's father wanted him to be a Rabbi. A goal he rejected but did he have one of his own I wonder. As for mother: I think she was a blank page that just lived her life based on her observation of her parents and grandparents' lives influenced by cultural norms. Just as the writer Moses said that life is filled with trouble and sorrow, adversity in many forms for most of us. It is also about the choices we make and how we navigate through the challenges life throws at us. I have come to appreciate the truth of Moses' words when I look back on my life; just how quickly life passes us by. I've also come to learn that bad situations and experiences come to an end too at some point although at the time of such experiences we never see the light at the end of the dark tunnel. Nevertheless the light does eventually come through, albeit slow at first but it inevitably shines through and that patience is truly a virtue. I have also come to learn that a simple unburdened life is the prerequisite to a long life. If one is to live a simple life, we must involve ourselves only with the things needed to maintain a reasonable livelihood. That may be easier said than done particularly in today's world which seems more complex than ever with so many distractions, options, and roads of opportunity. I have come to realise that many young people today are more focused, because their parents are more educated and understand the available options in life and so the majority are able to provide the direction needed for their children's future. The school system is also better geared to provide such direction to children that may not have such guidance from their home environment. Many of us never had such guidance, such opportunities. Our schooling only provided the basic education that was necessary to give us a fighting chance in life. From where I sit, most of us were left to our own devices, to choose

our own roadmap. A roadmap full of strife and uncertainty: one that can only be navigated successfully by determination, self-belief and hard work. I have come to also accept that at the end of it all, no matter what we have accomplished, the Biblical adage is proved true "......That *"there is great gain in godly devotion along with contentment. For we have brought nothing into this world, and neither can we carry anything out. So having food and clothing, we will be content with these things"* (1 Timothy 6: 6-8) NWT. So, at this moment in time I await the inevitable, the fulfilment of the prophet Moses words "away we fly." I await that time, but meanwhile I am content, retired and happy with my beautiful wife at my side and all my children and grandchildren close by living stable uncomplicated lives with God Almighty at the centre of us all.

It is my hope, dear reader, that my story has encouraged you and given you a new hope that no matter what life throws at you, you too can come off victorious. In my case, I am reminded of the words of the Lord Jesus when he said *"I have said these things to you so that by means of me you may have peace. In the world you will have tribulation, but take courage! I have conquered the world"* (John 16:33 - NWT)

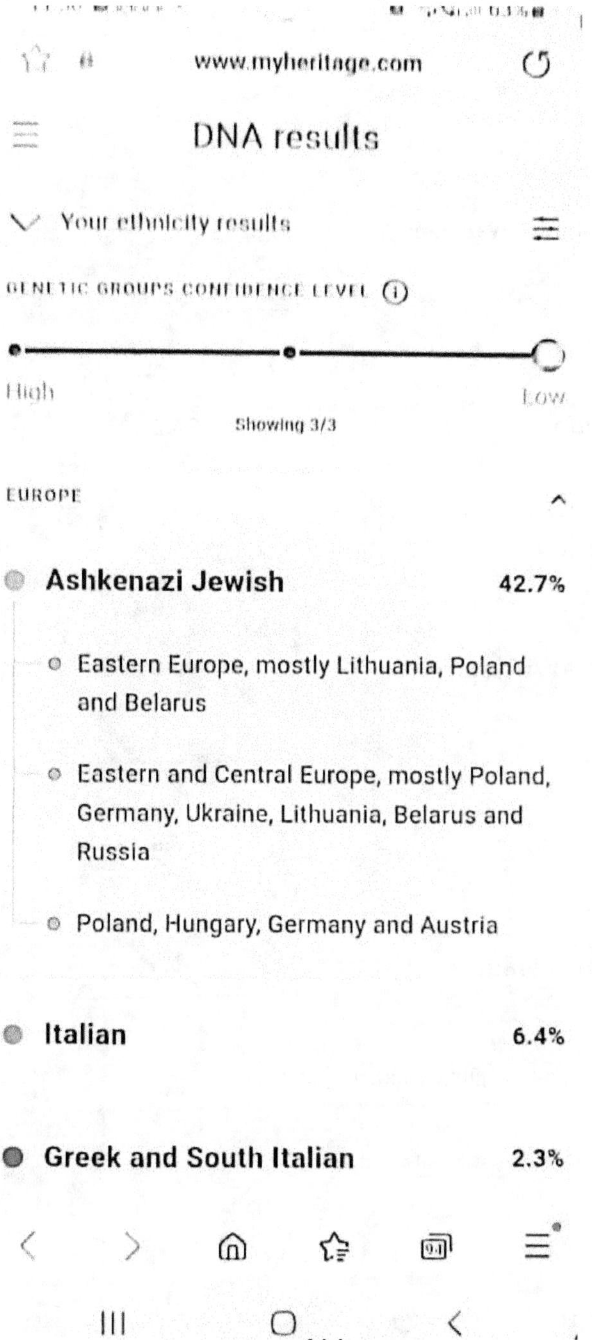

www.myheritage.com

DNA results

Your ethnicity results

GENETIC GROUPS CONFIDENCE LEVEL

High   Low

Showing 3/3

EUROPE

Ashkenazi Jewish   42.7%

Eastern Europe, mostly Lithuania, Poland and Belarus

Eastern and Central Europe, mostly Poland, Germany, Ukraine, Lithuania, Belarus and Russia

Poland, Hungary, Germany and Austria

Italian   6.4%

Greek and South Italian   2.3%

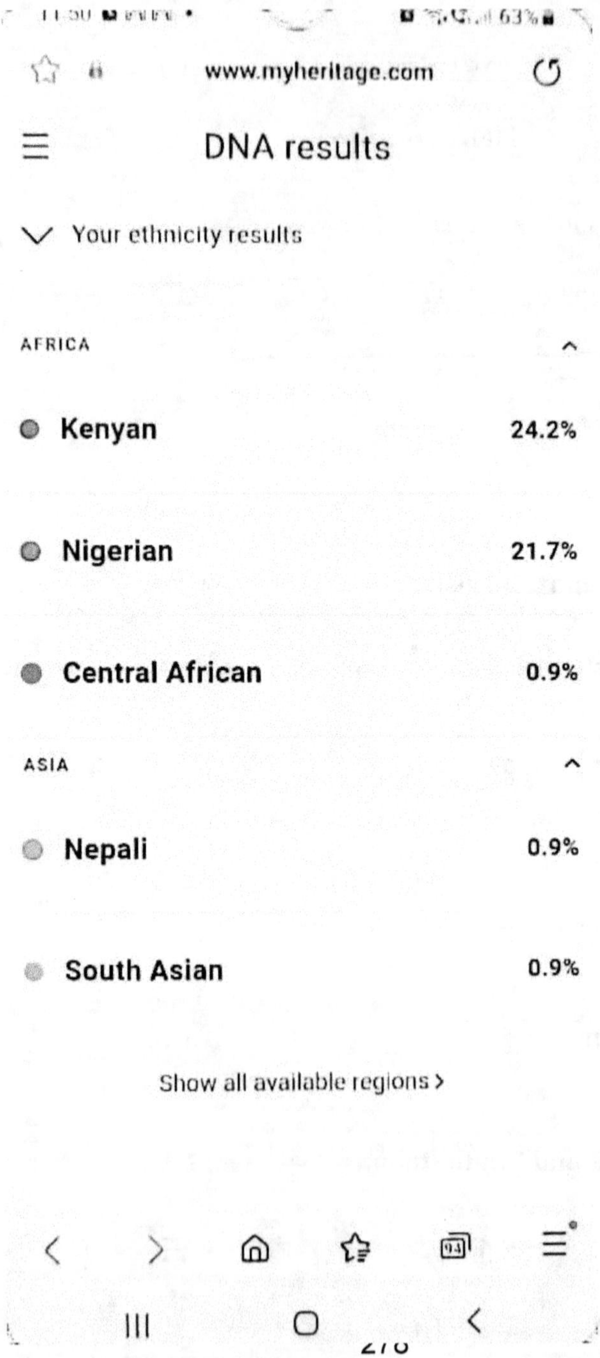

DNA results

☰

∨ Your ethnicity results

AFRICA ⌃

● **Kenyan**   **24.2%**

● **Nigerian**   **21.7%**

● **Central African**   **0.9%**

ASIA ⌃

● **Nepali**   **0.9%**

● **South Asian**   **0.9%**

Show all available regions >

www.ingramcontent.com/pod-product-compliance
Lightning Source LLC
Chambersburg PA
CBHW051550030726
47592CB00001B/226